THEORIES OF
INTERGROUP
RELATIONS

THEORIES OF
INTERGROUP
RELATIONS
International Social Psychological Perspectives

Donald M. Taylor and
Fathali M. Moghaddam

PRAEGER

New York
Westport, Connecticut
London

Figure 3.3 in Chapter 3, is reprinted by permission of John Wiley & Sons, Ltd., from "The Effect of Situational Meaning on the Behavior of Subjects in the Prisoner's Dilemma Game," by J.R. Eiser and K.K. Bhavnani, in *The European Journal of Social Psychology*, 1974, *4*, 93–97.

Table 6.1 and selected quotes in Chapter 6, are from F. Crosby and M. Bernstein, "Relative Deprivation: Testing the Models" paper presented at the meeting of The American Psychological Association, Toronto, 1978. Reprinted by permission of the authors.

Selected quotes in Chapter 7, are reprinted with permission of AMS Press, Inc., from V. Pareto, *The Mind and Society* (1935).

In Chapter 7, "The Great Day," from *The Collected Poems of W.B. Yeats*, edited by A.N. Jeffares, is reprinted with permission of A.P. Watt Ltd. on behalf of Michael B. Yeats and Macmillan London Ltd.; and with permission of Macmillan Publishing Company, NYC.

Library of Congress Cataloging-in-Publication Data

Taylor, Donald M.
   Theories of intergroup relations.
   Includes index.
   1. Intergroup relations.   2. Social psychology.
I. Moghaddam, Fathali M.   II. Title.
HM291.T36 1987   302.3   87-2524
ISBN 0-275-92348-7 (alk. paper)
ISBN 0-275-92639-7 (pbk. : alk. paper)

Library of Congress Catalog Card Number: 87-2524
ISBN: 0-275-92348-7
ISBN: 0-275-92639-7 (pbk.)

First published in 1987

Praeger Publishers, 521 Fifth Avenue, New York, NY 10175
A division of Greenwood Press, Inc.

Printed in the United States of America

The paper used in this book complies with the Permanent Paper Standard issued by the National Information Standards Organization (Z39.48-1984).

10 9 8 7 6 5 4 3 2 1

Contents

Preface

Coauthoring a book that is coherent in style and content represents an exciting challenge. To produce such a book when the overriding aims, themes, and specific content must reflect the views of two authors who have had dramatically different life experiences is an even greater challenge. Either the task of writing is divided, with the risk that the book appears disjointed, or you try to make the book truly a collaborative effort. This is what we set out to do, but because of our very different backgrounds we would not have been surprised if chaos had followed. To our delight, we found almost complete unanimity on important issues. This has given us cause to reflect, and we now realize that while our life experiences seem very different on the surface, they are overshadowed by a much deeper set of shared experiences.

One of us was raised as a "majority" group member in a developed world society, but in a province that has experienced deep cultural and linguistic tension; the other knew firsthand about life in a Third World society. One pursued his interest in intergroup relations in a North American academic context; the other followed precisely the same interest in a European context. The one based in North America has spent considerable time researching and teaching in Europe and in the Third World; the one from the Third World now holds an academic position in North America, after studying intergroup relations in Europe. Both have lived in societies experiencing fundamental conflicts between groups: one in a national context where the separation of regions has been an important issue; the other, in a society experiencing violent revolution.

Thus, the consistencies in the perspective emerging from this volume perhaps arise in part out of these shared life experiences, despite very disparate backgrounds.

Many of the ideas expressed in this volume have evolved over a long time period and have been shaped through the influence of numerous individuals working on both sides of the Atlantic. The authors have had close links with researchers at Bristol University since the 1970s, and are indebted, intellectually and otherwise, to Rupert Brown, Howard Giles, Henri Tajfel, and John Turner. We are profoundly grateful for the opportunity we have had to share our ideas with a number of colleagues and former students, especially Jeannette Bellerose, Mick Billig, Richard Bourhis, Faye Crosby, Lise Dubé, Bob Gardner, Richard Lalonde, Wallace Lambert, David McKirnan, Phillip

Smith, Peter Stringer, Patricia Walker, Gillian Watson, and Durhan Wong-Rieger.

We would like to thank Sheila Morrin for the secretarial help she provided during the many revisions that brought the present volume to its final shape.

Finally, we appreciate the support for this project given by George Zimmar from the very beginning.

1 The Social Psychology of Intergroup Relations

Race riots, religious intolerance, rivalry between the sexes, language groups in confrontation, radical forces clashing with the establishment, the constant threat of terrorism, bitter labor disputes, the arms race between the superpowers and the threat of nuclear war—these are some of the issues that immediately spring to mind when considering the social psychology of intergroup relations. The crucial role that these pervasive issues, along with a variety of more local social conflicts, play in our lives is leading the topic of intergroup relations to assume greater importance in social psychology. Unfortunately, to date there is little or no scholarly work that systematically reviews social psychological theories of intergroup relations.

The present volume is designed as a first step toward filling this gap. Specifically, our aim is to outline a number of major theories, comment upon their key features, describe the research strategy used to test the major hypotheses of each theory, and highlight common themes and important differences. In addition, our aim is to present a broad international array of theoretical orientations, with a particular concern for presenting a balance between North American and European perspectives. We are optimistic about the role social psychology can and will play in our understanding of intergroup relations. It is our hope that this volume can help to set the stage for a more concerted effort in the field.

Until recently, intergroup relations has not been given as much attention as it deserves in mainstream social psychology, and there are very few books that deal systematically with this topic from a social psychological perspective. The volumes by Billig (1976), LeVine and Campbell (1972), and Kidder and Stewart (1975) come closest, but do not represent up-to-date attempts to review systematically social psychological theories of intergroup relations. In addition, there are very few edited books on the social psychology of intergroup relations (Austin & Worchell 1979; Gardner & Kalin 1981; Turner & Giles 1981). These do not, nor was it their aim to, review major theoretical approaches to intergroup relations.

The reason for such a paucity of material on the social psychology of intergroup relations requires some explanation. In order to address this state of affairs, and more broadly appreciate the context of the present volume, in this first chapter we review some of the key concepts in the title of this work: "social psychology," "intergroup relations," "theories," and "international perspectives." Having established the context, we alert the reader to certain recurring themes that emerge in one form or another in each of the chapters. Finally, we present a concrete description of the specific chapters and their organization.

SOCIAL PSYCHOLOGY AND INTERGROUP RELATIONS

Social psychology is the study of individual behavior in social contexts. Although the unit of analysis in social psychology is the individual, the context of such behavior can involve, either implicitly or explicitly, both other individuals and social groups. The unique perspective of social psychology in the intergroup context is that the perceptions, motivations, feelings, and overt actions of individuals are studied to identify how they influence, and are affected by, relations between groups.

Within the context of psychology, social psychology is that subdiscipline whose major aim is to bridge the gap between the social and the psychological forces in human behavior. Central to this aim would be the topic of intergroup relations, yet, for some reason, it is not. Most major reviewers of intergroup relations have emphasized the neglect of this topic in social psychology (for instance, Austin & Worchel 1979; Billig 1976). Austin and Worchel (1979) have noted that ". . . writings on groups in social psychology are typically one-sided. Texts appear to concentrate uniformly on intragroup processes to the exclusion of intergroup behavior" (p. v.). There are currently dozens of introductory texts in social psychology that attempt to cover, in cafeteria fashion, the major topics in the field. An examination of the table of contents of any of these texts will suffice to reinforce the point that intergroup relations is not a central theme. Nor are theories of intergroup relations reviewed in books on theories of social psychology (for example, Shaw & Costanzo 1982). Exploring the titles of articles in key social psychological journals leads to the same conclusion: intergroup relations is not a central topic.

Moreover, on those few occasions where groups are mentioned, the meaning, from an intergroup relations perspective, can be misleading. The focus has been almost exclusively on small, closed groups rather than societally based groups that are open and have changing membership (see Lawler, 1985). Thus, the concern is with small work groups or therapeutic groups rather than societally based groups such as social classes, ethnic groups, labor movements, or protest groups. The aspects of small-group life studied tend to concern group productivity, leadership, social influence, and decision making. For example, chapters 29–31 of *The Handbook of Social Psychology* (Lindzey & Aronson 1968) reflect this concern (see Collins & Raven 1968; Gibb 1968; Kelley & Thibaut 1968). Finally, the concept of prejudice may surface, suggesting intergroup relations along racial lines (for example, see Harding, Proshansky, Kutwer, and Chein 1968). But even here discussion focuses on the individual shortcomings of persons who display inordinate amounts of prejudice, rather than the dynamics of group conflict. The concern is more on what makes a particular individual a bigot or red-neck, as opposed to why an entire society shares prejudicial attitudes.

There is no simple explanation for the underdeveloped state of theory and research on the social psychology of intergroup relations; however, we can at least speculate on some of the possible "whys." Steiner (1974) offers one possible explanation. In his view, research topics in a particular discipline are a reflection of the broader concerns of society. Since most social psychological theory and research originates in the United States, an examination of the concerns of that society ought to give us insights into what scientific issues would be salient. Steiner notes that during the 1950s and early 1960s, broadly based intergroup conflicts were not an issue in the United States; hence, there was little scientific interest in the topic. He predicts that the rising social concern for group conflict of the late 1960s and 1970s will be reflected in a renewal of interest in the topic. Whether this is so remains to be seen, since, according to Steiner, scientific research usually lags ten years behind an initial societal interest in an issue.

A number of writers have taken this "response to societal concerns" explanation one step further, suggesting that it is the "pervasive individualistic ideology" which is characteristic of North American society that allows us to understand why so little attention is paid to group issues (Billig 1976; Moscovici 1972; Tajfel 1972b; Taylor & Brown 1979). They argue that it is the North American belief in the sanctity and importance of the individual—what Sampson (1977) has labeled "self-contained individualism"—that has led to this neglect. The implications of this interpretation are far-reaching. The "response to societal concerns" explanation paves the way for a renewed interest in groups, but the "pervasive individual ideology" explanation leaves little room for the possibility that intergroup processes will become a central concern, at least in North American social psychology.

There is a third possible reason for neglect of intergroup relations as a topic, one that affects not only social psychology but all of the social sciences. Coser (1956) notes that at one of the first meetings of the American Sociological Society, held in 1907, the major topic was social conflict. By 1930 social conflict was still a central issue at the annual meetings. By 1950, however, Bernard (1950) was prompted to ask, "Where is the modern sociology of conflict?" A partial answer may be found through an examination of the position of the social scientist in society and how that role has changed. Initially the social scientist was an advocate of change; his or her theory and research were not dependent upon funding from the establishment, be it government or industry. The social scientist was a champion of social reform, change, and the associated conflict.

As soon as funding for universities and research emanated from the establishment, interest in social conflict gave way to a focus on social management. Perhaps, then, to a certain extent the piper is calling the tune and intergroup conflict, because it can be a threatening topic from the point of view of the established order, has become less central. The accuracy of this analysis requires validation, of course, but it must be raised here as one possible explanation for the current status of research into intergroup relations.

Whatever the reasons, social psychology has not kept pace with sociology and political science when it comes to making a concentrated and coordinated research effort to understand relations between societal groups. The result is that the research in social psychology has not been integrated, and the disparate direct and indirect strands of thought have not been systematized so as to provide a solid base from which to build. In this volume we attempt such an undertaking, and the reader will be as surprised as we were at the richness of information that social psychology has to offer when the strands are woven together. Thus, the importance of this volume is underscored by the neglect of intergroup relations as a topic of study in social psychology, and by the richness of the potential contribution of social psychology to understanding individual behavior in an intergroup setting.

A DEFINITION OF INTERGROUP RELATIONS

We have an intuitive grasp of what the topic of intergroup relations entails. Not surprisingly, however, the lack of attention to the field of intergroup relations is matched by an almost total neglect of the task of defining key concepts. At this stage, then, we can offer only preliminary definitions of the terms "relations" and "group," but ones that we hope can orient the reader to the scope of the present volume.

To begin with, we have chosen the title "intergroup relations" rather than "intergroup behavior" or "intergroup conflict." Our reasoning is that the latter two labels are too restricting. "Behavior" denotes the concrete, observable component of intergroup relations but does not include important cognitive processes, such as categorization, stereotyping, attributions, and attitudes, which, although not directly observable, play an important role in understanding relations between groups. To our knowledge, the only authors even to consider the ambiguity in terms such as "intergroup behavior" and "intergroup relations" are Sherif and Sherif (1969). Part of their analysis is consistent with our own. They define intergroup behavior as "the actions of individuals belonging to one group when they interact, collectively or individually, with another group or its members in terms of their group membership" (p. 223). Sherif and Sherif (1969) view the term "intergroup relations" as broader in scope, defining it as ". . . functional relations between two or more groups and their respective members" (p. 223). By functional relations they mean that ". . . the actions by one group and its members have an impact on another group and its members, regardless of whether the two groups are actually engaged in direct give-and-take at the time" (p. 223).

Similarly, we find the term "conflict" to be restricting, but in a different way. Throughout this volume the primary focus will be on conflict between groups. However, while it is conflict that primarily sustains a commitment on the part of social scientists to investigate intergroup and group processes, relations between groups need not always be conflictual. By choosing the term "relations," for the present volume, perhaps we are revealing our optimism, in the sense that at some stage in the future it may be realistic to address the potentially multifaceted nature of relations between groups. In any case, we have chosen the label that seems to offer the fewest predetermined restrictions.

Defining what human interaction qualifies as "intergroup" is more challenging. Once again, our approach is to provide a definition with the fewest possible restrictions. By "intergroup relations" we mean *any aspect of human interaction that involves individuals perceiving themselves as members of a social category, or being perceived by others as belonging to a social category.* A number of points need to be raised about this very broad definition.

First, our definition involves no limitations in terms of the size or type of social category involved. It is true that most often the focus is on large social categories such as race, social class, sex, religion, language, and ethnic background. However, it is our contention that any valid principles about intergroup relations apply to all social categories, regardless of type and size.

Second, our definition does not contain many of the qualifications found in most definitions. For example, we do not insist that in addition to the perception of identity with a social category, there must be shared motivation, goals, or social structure before we define a number of individuals as a group (see Shaw 1976 for a review). Nor do we require, as do Tajfel and Turner (1979), that individuals share an emotional involvement with the social category or share an evaluation of it before they can be considered part of a group. While all or some of these characteristics may be important, it is nevertheless possible for an individual to be influenced by the mere fact that he or she is identified with a particular social category. Just ask any member of a visible minority group how often he or she has received treatment obviously directed at his or her group identity rather than his or her role position or individual personal characteristics.

Third, we do not require that there be cohesion within a social category, especially as cohesion has been defined traditionally. Group cohesion is usually defined as the sum of the strength of mutual positive attitudes among individual members of a group (Lott & Lott 1965). We do not consider mutual liking among individuals to be essential for intergroup relations, especially in the context of broad social categories. A person may identify strongly with a group even if he or she does not personally like some or many of its members. Indeed, a person may not even know many of the members of large social categories. Similarly, a person may like several persons as separate individuals, but there may be no sense in which they constitute a category or group.

Finally, our definition does not suggest that only interactions involving large numbers of people qualify as intergroup. For, ultimately, whether an interaction has intergroup implications is psychologically defined (see Turner & Brown 1981). Take the example of two lovers having dinner by candlelight in a quaint restaurant. By any definition this would be described as an interpersonal interaction in which the focus is on the unique personal characteristics of the particular man and woman. But what if the man makes an inadvertent chauvinistic statement? The woman may feel the need to respond as a representative of all women, and may even express certain opinions that she herself does not endorse but states because she feels the obligation to represent the majority of women at that moment. The man may become defensive and feel the need to defend himself as a man, and if the debate escalates, those in the restaurant may well be treated to a public spectacle. The point here is that just because an interaction involves only two persons it is not necessarily interpersonal. The psychological meaning of the interaction is what determines whether the relationship is intergroup.

Conversely, the interaction of large numbers of people representing two groups does not necessarily define the behavior as intergroup. A collection of men and women at a social gathering, each making overtures to the other, may be defined by the participants as a series of very interpersonal interactions.

A second example may be useful to indicate even more clearly that the number of people in an interaction is not necessarily a valid criterion for qualifying an interaction as intergroup. Imagine an encounter involving a Hispanic student who speaks in Spanish to an Anglo student he meets on campus. The interaction would appear on the surface to be an encounter between two individuals that is awkward because neither speaks the other's language. However, the Spanish-speaking student may well be making a collective political statement by his refusal to use English. The Anglo student may well be aware that the Hispanic student can speak English—after all, he is studying at an institution where the language of instruction is English. So both parties may recognize that the individual encounter really involves a minority group statement of public defiance designed to assert pride in group identity and to signal a desire for change in the power relationship between the groups.

Our definition is naturally psychological in its emphasis. The essence is the meaning attached to behavior, not the more concrete observable features of it. In the present context, then, a jealous lover who murders his rival is not engaged in intergroup relations. However, a person who commits murder on behalf of a political group, selecting as the victim some person who is symbolic of the establishment, is very definitely engaging in intergroup relations. Ambiguity arises when the jealous lover happens to be white and his rival black. The meaning for the perpetrator and the victim may have nothing to do with race, but the minute people in the community, reading newspaper accounts of the incident, focus on the racial overtones, intergroup relations are involved.

In summary, for the present volume our concern is with understanding human behavior when it is affected by the perception that category membership is involved. It is hoped that by defining intergroup relations in the broadest terms, we have not made the field even more ambiguous, but have provided a framework for appreciating just how much of human behavior is influenced by the processes of intergroup relations.

WHAT CONSTITUTES A THEORY OF INTERGROUP RELATIONS

The purpose of this volume is to review major theoretical orientations to intergroup relations. The need for such a review stems from the current state of social psychology as a discipline, and specifically from the psychology of intergroup relations. Walster, Walster, and Berscheid (1978) state the problem succinctly: "Currently, social psychology comprises a myriad of elegant little 'mini-theories'. . . . What we now need is a general theory that integrates the limited mini-theories" (p. 1).

Our belief is that in order for theory and research in intergroup relations to be truly integrated, and our knowledge to become cumulative, it is essential that we review in one volume those theories which qualify as major theoretical orientations. "Major," for the present purposes, refers to those theories which claim to deal with the fundamental issues associated with intergroup relations: how intergroup conflicts arise, what course they take, and how they become resolved. Thus, our focus is on those theories which are broad in scope, theories with enough range that they have the potential to provide some direction for research in the entire field of intergroup relations. Inclusion of a theory is not on the basis of how "good" it is in terms of criteria that are discussed and debated in the philosophy of science (see Kaplan 1964; Shaw & Costanzo 1982). Rather, the focus is on theories offering a set of interrelated propositions that deal with a wide range of issues central to intergroup relations.

Fortunately, there are a sufficient number of major theoretical orientations to warrant a careful analysis, but it is not uncommon for researchers working in the context of one orientation to be unfamiliar with the others. The theories represented in the present volume include realistic conflict theory, social identity theory, equity theory, relative deprivation theory, elite theory, and a five-stage model of intergroup relations.

Each of these theories is broad in scope and attempts to address the pervasive issues in intergroup relations: how do conflicts arise? what course do they take? how are they resolved? However, not all of the theories address the issue of intergroup relations directly. For example, equity theory and relative deprivation theory are more often applied to interpersonal than intergroup relations. Nevertheless, extrapolations are constantly made to relations between social groups, and the obvious relevance of these theories to intergroup relations demand that they be included.

Notably absent as central considerations are certain key social psychological concepts that are normally associated with intergroup relations. These include stereotypes, attributions, and attitudes, to name three of the more important. In our view these do not constitute major theoretical orientations to intergroup relations. Rather, they are important but specific processes, and so are incorporated into many of the major theories. Thus, they emerge in many of the chapters but do not by themselves constitute a central concern.

THE NEED FOR AN INTERNATIONAL PERSPECTIVE

We have already noted that social scientists studying intergroup relations from one theoretical orientation often are unaware of alternative perspectives. One of the factors contributing to this isolationism is that several of the theories are rooted in North American social psychology, while other influential theories are European-based. The "isolationism" of U.S. psychology has been noted by a number of researchers (such as Berlyne 1968; Brandt 1970; Sexton & Misiak 1984). This isolationist orientation has tended to create a "monocultural" science of psychology in the United States (see Kennedy et al. 1984). In the field of intergroup relations, there is a tendency for U.S. researchers to neglect work conducted outside North America. A work on social conflict by Pruitt and Rubin (1986), two influential U.S. psychologists, contains minimal references to major European researchers working in the same field. For example, the only work by Tajfel referred to by Pruitt and Rubin is a 1970 article published in *Scientific American*. This gulf between U.S. and European research underscores the importance of our attempts to achieve a more international perspective.

The need for an international perspective is even more critical in light of our earlier discussion of how "self-contained individualism," as a North American value system, may well have had a profound effect on the limited interest in the social psychology of intergroup relations and the directions it has taken. The European-based theories described in this volume—social identity theory and elite theory—are far less individualistic in their approach and provide an important contrast with the North American-based theories. By bringing both perspectives together in one volume, we hope to provide at least the beginning of a more international and integrated approach to the study of intergroup relations.

EMERGING THEMES

An overall assessment of the current status of theory and research in intergroup relations can best be attempted after dealing systematically with each of the theories. However, certain themes are so striking that it may be useful to alert the reader to them at the outset.

The first overriding feature to be noted is the reductionist nature of many current theories of intergroup relations. This was hinted at in our earlier discussion of social psychology and has begun to be recognized in the context of intergroup relations (see, for example, Billig 1976; Sampson 1981; Tajfel 1972b, 1979; Taylor & Brown 1979). At the level of theory and research, the emphasis has been on intra- or interindividual, not intergroup, processes. The result is that individualistically based findings are extrapolated to the group level. While there may be certain valid parallels, it is equally clear that in many instances individual and group processes differ. More important, by not addressing issues in a group context, a number of potentially valuable questions and hypotheses are not even considered.

While the dominant theoretical orientation in intergroup research has involved working from intra- and interpersonal processes to intergroup processes, and from microsocial to macrosocial issues, a few theories have adopted the opposite approach. These theories are characterized by a concern for long-term social changes and large, open groups rather than short-term changes and small, closed groups. They take broad social structural issues as their point of departure, then make assumptions about the role of psychological processes in determining structural changes. In short, their theorizing starts at the macro level and moves to the micro level rather than starting with intra- and interpersonal processes at the micro level and then extrapolating to intergroup processes at the macro level.

A second significant theme is the extent to which the nature of the groups that the theories deal with are open or closed. There is in the field of small-group research a tradition of dealing with closed groups (Ziller 1965), in which group members are not provided with an "exit" option (Hirschman 1970, 1974). This tradition has been influential in intergroup relations as well. The assumption that a group has fixed membership, that existing members cannot leave the group and new members cannot be recruited, partly explains why social psychologists have not emphasized the issue of identification with the group; the extent and form that group identity takes is of relatively little significance in groups of fixed membership. However, once we include in our theoretical model groups that have a changing membership, then the issue of identification takes on central importance.

A third persistent dilemma is the relationship of cognitive and emotional states to behavior. One has only to examine the attitude literature to recognize that this is a pervasive issue for much of social psychology (see Wicker 1969). Negative attitudes toward a person or group do not necessarily mean there will be discriminatory behavior. A person prejudiced against visible minorities may nevertheless serve them in restaurants, respond politely to their questions, or offer jobs to those who are qualified. This same relationship lies at the core of understanding intergroup relations. Many theories in the area of intergroup relations attempt to predict when people will have strong negative feelings. A fundamental recurring problem is understanding when the negative feelings experienced by group members will lead to collective action, individual action, or apparent acceptance of an undesirable situation.

A forth significant theme concerns the treatment of individual group members by a theory of intergroup relations. That is, are the individual members of a group distinguished on the basis of some characteristic, such as ability, or are they treated as a homogeneous unit? This is particularly important with respect to groups that are "open" and permit social mobility. Will all the members of a group have the same capacity or motivation for attemping upward social mobility, or will only certain individuals attempt this move?

A fifth theme concerns the extent to which a theory focuses on advantaged or disadvantaged groups, or, more generally, how a theory deals with the notion of power (Ng 1980, 1982). In most intergroup situations there is a disparity of power between social groups; groups seldom enjoy equal power and status. There seems to be a tendency for theories of intergroup relations not to give equal attention to the perspectives of both advantaged and disadvantaged groups. While some theories adopt the perspective of the advantaged group, others tend to view the situation more from the perspective of the disadvantaged group.

A final theme concerns the relationship among the theories. We will have much to say about this later, but for the moment it is important to point out the extent to which the theories are more complementary than conflictual in terms of the hypotheses they generate. The various theories appear to address issues in parallel rather than making differential predictions about intergroup behavior. We hope that one of the consequences of bringing the theories together in a single volume will be a more discriminating approach to the whole field, with real attempts to understand and predict collective behavior.

ORGANIZATION OF CHAPTERS

Having defined the context and scope of the present volume, it remains to describe the content of the specific chapters more precisely. The theories to be presented in the chapters that follow may not always address the question of relations between groups exclusively or directly, but all do have major insights to offer. What the theories have in common is a concern for the burning issues associated with relations between groups: what are the conditions associated with feelings of collective discontent? what are the social psychological processes that explain the current discontent of blacks in South Africa that was not so apparent a decade ago? why are women in Western societies expressing collective discontent while those in more traditional and stratified societies seem less vocal? why do unions seem militant and the unemployed relatively tranquil? This issue of collective discontent is, of course, only one dimension of relations between groups, but it is the issue of greatest concern to lay people and scientists like.

Beyond this commonality, differences in emphasis will occur. Some theories are especially concerned with how conflicts can be resolved, others focus on how feelings of discontent become translated into action, some focus on relations between groups of equal power, and others are more concerned with unequal power situations. Any complete theory must, of course, ultimately deal with all these major issues, and our assessment of the scope of any theory must take this into account.

We begin in Chapter 2 with a review of Freud's contribution to the field of intergroup relations. Despite the breadth of his theorizing, his insights in many ways do not qualify as an integrated theory of intergroup relations. However, the scope and depth of his impact provide an important context for reviewing the major theoretical orientations. In chapters 3 through 8 we review six major theories: realistic conflict theory, social identity theory, equity theory, relative deprivation theory, elite theory, and a five-stage model of intergroup relations. In Chapter 9, three important social psychological concepts are discussed: stereotypes, causal attributions, and attitudes. These are often linked to intergroup relations, but do not by themselves constitute a major theoretical orientation to intergroup relations. Their influence on many of the major theories, however, requires that their role be discussed in some detail. Finally, in Chapter 10 an attempt is made to consolidate the recurring themes and to speculate about what direction theory and research might take in the near future.

Each major theory is described in a separate chapter, and an attempt is made to maintain a consistent organizational structure within the chapters. However, maintaining consistency of structure is made difficult by a number of factors. First, the theories grow out of very different psychological and social traditions. Hence, definitions and fundamental assumptions differ widely among the theories, as do the approaches to methodology. Second, certain theories address questions of intergroup relations directly, whereas others are more concerned with individuals and impact on our topic only by extension. Finally, certain theories began with a series of propositions that stimulated experimental research designed to test the propositions, whereas in other cases the research preceded—indeed, was the inspiration for—the theory.

However, despite these sometimes profound differences among the theories, a standard format is maintained for all the chapters dealing with major theories. We begin each chapter with a thumbnail sketch of each theory in terms of the scope of the issues addressed by the theory, the fundamental orienting assumptions the theory makes about human behavior, and the specific propositions the theory offers for explaining intergroup relations.

Following the thumbnail sketch, an introduction section places the theory in context by discussing its historical underpinnings. In the third section of each chapter, the fundamental propositions of the theory are presented and, where appropriate, prototypical experiments to test the theory are described. The final section involves a critical review of the theory and focuses on its strengths and weaknesses. A conclusion statement rounds off each chapter.

SUGGESTED READINGS

Austin, W. G., and S. Worchel (eds.). 1979. *The Social Psychology of Intergroup Relations.* Monterey, Cal.: Brooks/Cole.

Billig, M. G. 1976. *Social Psychology and Intergroup Relations.* London: Academic Press.

Kidder, L. H., and V. M. Stewart. 1975. *The Psychology of Intergroup Relations: Conflict and Consciousness.* New York: John Wiley.

LeVine, R. A., and D. T. Campbell. 1972. *Ethnocentrism: Theories of Conflict, Ethnic Attitudes and Group Behavior.* New York: John Wiley.

Turner, J. C., and H. Giles (eds.). 1981. *Intergroup Behaviour.* Oxford: Basil Blackwell.

2 The Freudian Legacy in Intergroup Research

Scope: Freud offers insights into how aggression toward out-groups develops. His explanation has to do mainly with the dynamics of relations between members of the in-group and, especially, their relationship to the group leader.

Assumptions: Freud focuses on the irrational side of human behavior. He assumes that intergroup conflict arises out of irrational feelings and the emotional needs of group members, rather than out of any conflicts of material interests that might exist between groups.

Propositions: Freud begins with the basic proposition that the emotional tie between two people involves feelings of both love and aversion. When a group is formed, love relations bind group members together through their bonds to the group leader. However, although the corresponding feelings of hostility are no longer present in the in-group, according to Freud's "hydraulic" model they do not disappear altogether. Such feelings of hostility are displaced onto out-groups. The more dissimilar the out-group, the more likely it is to be the target of aggression. Thus, Freud proposes that intergroup hostility is one inevitable consequence of strong in-group ties.

This chapter is devoted to Freud's influence on both theory and research in the psychology of intergroup relations. His analysis of group processes, insightful as it is, does not constitute a major orientation to intergroup relations. Unlike the major orientations to intergroup relations that will be presented in the following chapters, Freud's model does not deal with relations between groups. Rather, Freud adopted a reductionist approach, in that he looked within groups to explain relations between groups, and he extrapolated from the level of intra- and interpersonal processes to that of intergroup processes. His analysis was, first and foremost, a psychological theory. Moreover, his model represents an extreme "irrationalist" view of intergroup behavior. Thus, this chapter is presented in recognition of Freud's insights and general influence on our thinking about the psychology of intergroup relations, but is not in the same format as the chapters on the major theories of intergroup relations.

Although writing in the tradition of grand theories attempting to explain all behavior at the levels of the individual, the group, and society, Freud generated concepts and hypotheses that have been influential in the much narrower traditions of logico-positivistic scientific research. His fundamental influence on scientific research concerning intergroup relations is reflected in such major pioneering studies as *Frustration and Aggression* (Dollard, Doob, Miller, Mowrer and Sears, 1939) and *The Authoritarian Personality* (Adorno, Frenkel-Brunswik, Levinson and Sanford, 1950). Many of the most important concepts used in research bearing upon intergroup relations are influenced by Freud. Examples of such concepts are displacement, interference, catharsis, and goal-directed behavior.

The fundamental influence of Freud on the broad area of studies related to intergroup relations can be partly explained by the fact that he wrote directly about the destructive, aggressive tendencies in human behavior (for example, see Freud 1933). His ideas seem to have direct relevance for war and peace, an issue that confronts everyone living in the atomic age. A concern with war and peace also underlies a great deal of more recent intergroup research. However, the experimental methods used by the majority of more recent researchers, such as Deutsch (1973), are very different from those employed by Freud.

Freud's ideas of group processes were most clearly elaborated in *Group Psychology and the Analysis of the Ego* (1921). In this work, Freud is concerned primarily with the properties of the in-group and the relationship between group members and their leader. Although he did not write directly about intergroup processes, the assumption is made in his writings that intergroup behavior can be adequately explained in terms of his model of group processes.

Freud stresses the irrational side of human behavior, focusing upon motivations and forces within the individual that are to some degree subconscious and beyond the reach of rational analysis by the individual. Thus, Freud's analysis can be said to present an "irrationalist" model of human behavior.

Freud tended to venerate the individual and to be suspicious of the group. In this respect, he can be seen as part of a tradition, particularly strong in the latter part of the 19th and early 20th centuries, that views the collective in a negative light. For example, Sighele (1981) wrote about what he termed the "criminal crowd." Le Bon (1897) and McDougall (1920), both of whom are quoted extensively by Freud throughout his writings on group processes, were also very much part of this "anti-collective" tradition. McDougall argued that in the group context, the minds of lower intelligence bring those of higher intelligence down to their level. He assumed that the group leads to a lower sense of responsibility for each individual member.

This "anti-collective" theme is also evident in certain areas of more recent social research, such as that concerned with the "risky shift." For example, the apparent tendency for people to take riskier decisions when acting as a group member than when acting as an isolated individual has been interpreted as an example of deindividualization, involving a tendency for the group to release the individual from a sense of responsibility (see Pruitt 1971). The implicit implication is that collective action involves higher risk and is based upon a less responsible attitude.

FREUD'S MODEL OF GROUP AND INTERGROUP PROCESSES: THREE GUIDING QUESTIONS

Freud's analyses of group processes were guided by three questions: "What . . . is a 'group'? How does it acquire the capacity for exercising such a decisive influence over the mental life of the individual? And what is the nature of the mental change which it forces upon the individual?" (Freud 1921, p. 72). The assumptions and biases implicit in these questions had a fundamental influence on Freud's interpretations of group processes. The first point to be made about these questions is that they present the individual as the target of change, in a sense as a victim. The potential influence of the minority party is neglected, and all the focus is placed on majority influence. Second, the nature of this influence is presented as fundamental, the group being assumed to have a decisive effect on the individual. These biases are also inherent in much of the more recent research in minority-majority relations (Moscovici, Mugny and Van Avermaet, 1984; Papastamou 1983).

In setting out to analyze how Freud proceeded to answer these three questions, it is useful to keep in mind a bias he showed for seeing humankind as a "horde animal" rather than a "herd animal" (Freud 1921, p. 121). He dismissed the idea of a herd instinct or gregariousness, partly because it does not allow for a model of group processes that incorporates the role of the leader. Freud saw the role of the leader as being of central importance, if not the most important factor influencing the behavior of individual group members.

What Is a Group?

In outlining what Freud understood to be a group, it is useful to begin by elaborating upon the key role of the leader in his group psychology. Freud limited his analysis to groups with leaders and did not attempt to extend his model to interpret behavior in leaderless groups. He has been criticized on this point (for instance, see Billig 1976, p. 24), and there are two reasons why such criticisms are to some extent valid. First, there are cultures in which the concept of the group leader, as it is known in most modern societies, does not exist (see Middleton & Tait 1958). Although fairly exceptional and very limited in numbers, these examples are conceptually very important because they help to focus attention on the potential for the development of leaderless groups. The second shortcoming of Freud's exclusive focus on groups with leaders is that if one is interested in the poor, blacks, or women, for example, these groups do not always have widely endorsed leaders. However, from a Freudian perspective this criticism might be countered by claiming that only in conditions where such groups as the blacks do have widely endorsed leaders can they achieve the cohesion and direction necessary for effective group action.

The importance given by Freud to the role of the leader was linked to his views about the social psychological evolution of human societies. He viewed the group as a revival of the primal horde, that is, a collection of individuals ruled despotically by a powerful male. From the beginning, the psychology of the leader was different from that of the followers, particularly in terms of needs and motivations. While the members of a group need to feel that they are equally loved by a leader, the leader need love no one else. This distinction is potentially very important, since it prepares the ground for a structural model of group processes, incorporating subgroups consisting of leaders, who have more power, and followers, who have less power.

Beyond the stress that Freud placed on the role of the leader, through identification, in the formation of a group, his writings entail a number of assumptions about the characteristics of a group. These tend invariably to be negative and in accord with Le Bon's views. Freud saw the group as tending toward extreme behavior; as respecting force and seeing kindness as weakness; of demanding strength and violence of its heroes; as being conservative, traditional, and mistrustful of innovations; of tolerating and being able to abide by contradictory ideas; and of preferring illusions to reality. However, Freud also believed that a group is capable of high intellectual performance, provided it is organized in the correct manner.

From the Freudian perspective, however, the poor, blacks, and women would remain sociological rather than psychological groups until they evolved clearly recognizable leaders through which to identify with the group. That is, for example, a number of individuals might meet the criteria for inclusion in the social category "poor" (such as low income level, low education level), but this does not mean that they necessarily feel that "the poor" is a distinct group or that they are members of this group. However, if a widely endorsed leader of "the poor" were to emerge, psychological identification with such a group would be more likely, through the links that identification with the leader would bring about between individuals who are potential group members.

The link between the leader and his or her followers is best explained through the concept of identification which has a central role in all of Freudian psychology. Freud sees identification as the earliest form of an emotional tie with an object, which is usually another person. "Identification" refers to a process by which an individual, having developed an emotional tie, behaves as if he or she were the person with whom the tie exists. This behavior may be wholly or partially unconscious. For example, a little boy will show identification with his father. He tries to copy his father's behavior and desires to be like him. At about the same stage of development, the boy develops a sexual object-cathexis toward his mother. These two feelings eventually merge and the Oedipus complex develops. The outcome is that the little boy's identification with his father takes the form of desiring to replace his father in relation to his mother.

In the group context, Freud sees identification as forming the essential link between the leader and followers. Identification can arise through the perception of a common quality shared with some other person; the more important the common quality, the more important the tie. A number of individuals have this shared common quality when they introject the same leader within their egos. Thus, Freud defines a primary group as ". . . a number of individuals who have put one and the same object in place of their ego ideal and have subsequently identified themselves with one another in their ego" (Freud 1921, p. 116).

As an example of how identification can lead to stronger ties between a number of individuals, Freud describes the situation of a "troop" of females or "groupies" who crowd around a singer after his performance. These females could become jealous of one another and try to get near the "loved one" ahead of the others. But since their large numbers do not allow this, they act as a unit and collectively pay homage to the hero. In short, they identify with one another by means of a similar love for the same object. Subsequent research suggests that identification may be such a fundamental process that it can even evolve in relation to an oppressor.

An extreme example of identification with the oppressor is presented in Bettelheim's (1943) research on Jews in Nazi concentration camps. Year after year of harsh physical conditions and mental torture led some prisoners to surrender mentally. Their efforts to please the guards eventually led them to imitate their oppressors. For example, prisoners showed anti-Semitism (taking on the attitudes of the guards) and wore bits of clothing belonging to guards (symbolic power). It could be argued that the tendency for black children to identify with the white out-group is a less extreme example of the same process (Milner 1975).

In summary, Freud believed groups with leaders to be the only groups worthy of study. He considered such groups to be composed of individuals who are similar in the sense that they have identified with one another by introjecting the same leader within their egos. Thus, the criterion of similarity plays a key part in Freud's concept of a group. Also, in elaborating the characteristics of a group, he stresses the evolutionary relationship between leaders and followers, and the different psychologies of these two categories of people.

How a Group Influences the Mental Life of the Individual

In explaining how an individual who is part of a group differs from an isolated individual, Freud begins by assuming that subconscious forces become more effective in the behavior of the individual in the group context. The apparently new characteristics that individuals display in the group context are the "manifestations" of the unconscious. In Freud's view, this helps to explain the regression to more primitive states experienced by individuals after they become group members, since all that is "evil" in the human mind is contained in the unconscious "as a predisposition" (1921, p. 74). As evidence that group members revert to primitive states, Freud makes repeated use of descriptions by Le Bon and others depicting human groups as being easily swayed, contradictory, illogical, of low intellectual capacity, and ruled by emotions.

However, the evocation of unconscious forces would not in itself be sufficient to explain the similar and sometimes uniform behavior of group members. Thus, Freud proceeds to elaborate a model of how group members are directed, through suggestion, by the group leader. Just as an analyst can influence a patient through suggestion, so the leader can be viewed as the source for suggestion in a group. Freud went on to draw comparisons between the relationship involving the hypnotist and a patient in psychoanalysis, and the leader and group members. But his model of relations within a group also assumed strong links among the group members themselves, a relationship that can be usefully explained by introducing the concept of libido.

Freud makes the fundamental assumption that love relationships constitute the most important factor binding group members together (1921, p. 91). "Libido" refers to the energy of those instincts which have to do with all that may be comprised under the word "love." Freud does not separate love that involves sexual union from other kinds of love, such as love for one's parents or for one's country. All these tendencies are seen as an expression of the same instinctual emotions.

The idea of libidinal ties among group members, and between the leader and his followers, is elaborated by Freud in his analysis of two important groups: the Catholic Church and the army. The most important feature of such groups is the "illusion" that holds them together: "In a Church . . . as well as in an army, however different the two may be in other respects, the same illusion holds good of there being a head—in the Catholic Church Christ, in an army its commander-in-chief—who loves all the individuals in the group with an equal love. Everything depends upon this illusion . . ." (Freud 1921, pp. 93–94). Freud compares the ties that bind group members to each other and to their leader, and the ties that bind the members of a family to each other and to the father.

Christ is described by Freud as being for the group of believers ". . . their substitute father" (1921, p. 94). The Catholic Church is like a family, with all its members being brothers. All believers share brotherly love, and are bound to each other and to their leader, Christ, through this love.

Thus, in such groups as the Catholic Church and the army, each individual is tied by libidinal ties to the leader (Christ, the commander-in-chief) and to the other members of the group. By examining these ties, we can appreciate and explain the lack of freedom experienced by individual group members. These two-way libidinal ties initiate and strengthen feelings of belonging, dependence, and responsibility, which in turn lead to greater conformity and a tendency to obey the leader.

However, the loss of the leader can lead to the disappearance of mental ties between group members. This is because the establishment of bonds among followers is brought about by the establishment of bonds between leader and followers. When the follower-leader bond is eliminated, follower-follower bonds also disappear. It is in such conditions that group panics occur. Freud argues that group panic does not arise from a perception of danger, but is a result of the disappearance of mutual ties between the leader and followers, and consequently among group members (1921, p. 97).

However, in Freud's individual psychology, libidinal ties involve feelings of hostility as well as of love. That is, each intimate emotional relationship between two people that is stable for some time, such as a marriage or friendship, involves a mixture of aversion and love. The concept of psychological ambivalence was central to all of Freud's thinking. For example, its influence can be seen in his analysis of the fusion of love and hate in *The Ego and the Id* (1923), and of the polarity of love and hate in *Beyond the Pleasure Principle* (1920). In *Civilization and Its Discontents,* Freud asserts that love and hate seldom, perhaps never, appear in isolation from each other (1930, p. 119). Freud extended the important concept of psychological ambivalence to the group level and argued that the same ambivalent feelings, involving love and hate, characterize relationships between group members, and particularly between leaders and their followers.

The key difference between psychological ambivalence at the level of the individual and of the group is in terms of the strategies adopted to cope with such mixed feelings. At the individual level, feelings of aversion and hostility tend to be repressed, while at the group level they tend to be redirected toward the out-group. It is in this connection that we can best interpret Freud's claim that it is always possible ". . . to bind together a considerable number of people in love so long as there are other people left over to receive the manifestations of their aggressiveness" (Freud 1930, p. 114). An important assumption entailed in this view is that love and hate are proportionally linked. Freud first developed this idea at the individual level but later extended it to explain intergroup behavior.

When a group is formed, feelings of intolerance and hostility disappear within the group, so that only the "love-related" aspects of libidinal ties tend to remain to influence relations between group members. As long as these libidinal ties remain, feelings of aversion between individuals do not emerge within the group. However, such hostile feelings are redirected toward out-groups. This is an instance of the important process of displacement, of which "displaced aggression" is an often cited case.

We can clarify the meaning of "displaced aggression" at the intergroup level by considering the example of the Catholic Church. Its members are bound together by libidinal ties, but "nonbelievers" stand outside this tie. Even a religion that claims to be a religion of love finds it necessary to be hard and unloving toward those who do not belong to the family of believers: ". . . indeed every religion is in this same way a religion of love for all those whom it embraces; while cruelty and intolerance towards those who do not belong to it are natural to every religion" (Freud 1921, p. 98). The explanation for such cruelty and hostility toward outsiders is that all the aggressiveness of the believers, the in-group, is displaced outside the group toward nonbelievers, the out-group.

The displacement of hostile feelings onto out-groups is necessary for in-group cohesion to be maintained. Since each emotional tie between two individuals involves feelings of both love and aversion, feelings of aversion as a result of emotional ties among followers, and between followers and the leader, are assumed to arise. However, if hostile feelings are allowed to grow within the group, the opportunity for developing group cohesion and productivity will be decreased. Consequently, it is important that hostile feelings are redirected outside the group. The selection of particular out-groups as targets of displaced hostility also serves to create a "common threat," and this in turn serves to further strengthen in-group ties.

The decline in religious persecution experienced in modern societies should not, according to Freud, be interpreted as a sign that we have become more tolerant toward nonbelievers. Rather, this greater tolerance is an outcome of weakened religious feelings and the subsequent weakening of libidinal ties that depend upon them. Thus, Freud saw the hostility shown toward out-groups as changing in direct relation to the strength of the libidinal ties within the in-group: the stronger the in-group libidinal ties, the greater the hostility toward out-groups.

In summary, the capacity of a group to exercise a decisive influence over the individual can be explained by referring to "subconscious forces" and "suggestion." That is, subconscious forces become more effective in the group context. Also, the individual becomes more susceptible to suggestion after becoming a group member. However, suggestion is not exercised by the group, but by the group leader. The power of the group leader is acquired through the two-way libidinal ties that bind each group member to the leader and to the other members. Such libidinal ties involve feelings of both hostility and love. Hostile feelings do not emerge within the in-group, but are displaced onto target out-groups. While the group leader has a major influence in directing displaced aggression, the out-groups onto whom this aggression is more likely to be directed are those perceived as being more unlike the in-group. Thus, in Freud's group psychology the criterion of similarity plays a key role in the selection of target outgroups onto whom aggression is displaced, as it does in the development of libidinal ties between group members and the actual formation of an in-group.

The Nature of the Mental Change a Group Forces on an Individual

Three central assumptions underlie Freud's views about the changes that a person undergoes by joining a group. First, it is assumed that a person necessarily undergoes major psychological changes by becoming a group member. Second, it is assumed that such changes generally involve a loss for the individual, particularly in terms of intellectual abilities. Third, the assumption is made that by organizing their group in the necessary way, individual group members can regain what they lost by joining the group. Thus, the more highly evolved and organized groups are assumed to be more similar to individuals in terms of psychological characteristics.

There is a set of consequences of the individual's joining a group to which Freud returns again and again in his writings: ". . . the dwindling of the conscious individual personality, the focusing of thoughts and feelings into a common direction, the predominance of the affective side of the mind and of unconscious psychical states, the tendency to the immediate carrying out of intentions as they emerge . . ." (1921, p. 122). Among these many changes that arise as a result of the individual's joining a group, the two most important are that the individual becomes more susceptible to outside influence and that he or she experiences a loss of intellectual abilities (Freud 1921, p. 88). However, the individual in a group also has a greater sense of certainty and purpose, and a feeling of power.

Freud argued that what the individual loses by joining a group can be regained if the group achieves the necessary level of organization. In this context, increased organization means greater permanence and continuity in the group, stronger shared goals and value systems guiding the behavior of group members, the presence of ideas guiding the actions of group members, greater specialization and division of labor, and more intense in-group cohesion and rivalry with out-groups. Most important, increased organization means having the ability to act at a higher intellectual level. Groups that are more highly evolved are also more organized, and thus have more of the characteristics of the isolated individual. This is an important point that allows us to better interpret what Freud means when he states that he is concerned only with groups that have leaders and have not been able to organize themselves to such a degree that they take on the characteristics of an individual (1921, p. 116). Such groups as the Catholic Church and the army are still "primitive," according to Freud, in the sense that they have not been able to achieve sufficient organization to acquire the psychological characteristics of an individual.

Apart from organization, another means through which a group can achieve a better performance is suggestion. Le Bon argued that while the intellectual capacity of a group is always below that of an individual, its ethical standards can rise above those of an individual. For Freud, the key element in the potential for high achievement by a group was the group leader and his influence through suggestion. Freud's major criticism of Le Bon's "brilliantly executed" account of the group mind was what he saw as insufficient appreciation of the functions of the group leader. To explain the changes that Freud believed individuals undergo by joining a group, it is useful to return to the role of the group leader.

According to Freud's model of group processes, probably the most important difference between an isolated individual and a group member is that the latter comes under the influence of a group leader. Freud saw the ties between leaders and followers as having a long history in human evolution, and of forming the basis for the two different psychologies of leaders and followers. Central to this view was the model he had of the family and the development of parent-child relationships, focusing particularly upon the father. This is clearly reflected by the terminology Freud used to discuss the psychologies of leaders and followers:

> from the first there were two kinds of psychologies, that of the individual members of the group and that of the father, chief, or

leader. The members of the group were subject to ties just as we see them today, but the father of the primal horde was free. His intellectual acts were strong and independent even in isolation, and his will needed no reinforcement from others. Consistency leads us to assume that his ego had few libidinal ties; he loved no one but himself, or other people only in so far as they served his needs. . . . Even today the members of a group stand in need of the illusion that they are equally and justly loved by their leader; but the leader himself need love no one else, he may be of a masterful nature, absolutely narcissistic, self-confident and independent. (1921, pp. 123–24)

To conclude, Freud argued that by joining a group, a person acquires characteristics that are fundamentally different from those of an isolated individual. Such changes tend to involve a loss for the individual in terms of intellectual capacities, but a gain in terms of feelings of power and security. However, through organization, group members can regain the characteristics they possessed as individuals, although major groups such as the church and the army have not yet evolved to such a level. Most important, individuals who are group members differ from isolated individuals in that they are influenced by group leaders, and their freedom is severely restricted by the two-way libidinal ties binding them to the leader and to each other.

THE IMPLICATIONS OF FREUD'S MODEL

Freud's model of group psychology entails at least four major implications for the field of intergroup relations. All of them have to some extent been realized in social research, although in some cases it is difficult to ascertain the extent to which Freud has directly influenced the lines of research adopted by later, more experimentally oriented researchers. These four implications concern (1) the assumed basis for intergroup hostility, (2) the model of intergroup relations adopted, (3) the out-group selected as the target of aggression, (4) subgroups that should be the focus of study within each group.

Freud did not view intergroup conflicts as arising out of conflicts of material interests. At the start of World War I he wrote that nations in conflict put forward their interests in order to justify "satisfying their passions" (1915, p. 288). He explained out-group hostility in terms of psychological ambivalence and displaced aggression. Out-group hostility was seen by Freud as a necessary condition for harmony within the in-group, since if hostile feelings are not displaced onto an out-group, they could turn inward and destroy the in-group.

Second, Freud offered a purely psychological model of intergroup conflicts, as opposed to viewing real conflicts of interests as being the basis of such conflicts. Moreover, his model of intergroup relations is reductionist, in the sense that it tries to extend intra- and interpersonal processes to the intergroup arena. Freud used the same "hydraulic" model that he elaborates at the individual level to interpret intergroup behavior.

Freud's model of intergroup relations is "hydraulic" in the sense that he assumed that the aggressive energies motivating behavior in the group context do not dissipate if they cannot attain their original goal, but surface in the form of displaced aggression toward out-groups. This idea was later taken up by Dollard et al. in their formulation of frustration and aggression theory (1939).

However, Freud proposed that the choice of an out-group toward whom aggression is directed is not random. Rather, the criterion of similarity is assumed to play a central part in this choice. In *Group Psychology,* Freud asserts that the greater the difference between two groups, the greater will be the hostility between them; this explains the strength of such hostilities ". . . as the Gallic people feel for the German, the Aryan feel for the Semite, and the white races for the coloured" (1921, p. 101). More recent research tends to confirm the importance that the criterion of similarity plays in determining intergroup harmony and conflict (see Brown 1984).

A fourth important implication of Freud's group psychology for intergroup relations is in terms of the different social strata within each group upon which we should focus in order to better understand intergroup processes. Freud stressed that there are two kinds of psychology, the psychology of the leaders and that of the followers. He generally viewed the followers in negative terms. For example, in *The Future of an Illusion* he postulates a greater degree of ethnocentrism among the masses and refers to them as "lazy and unintelligent" (1927, p. 7). In contrast, Freud regarded leaders as having greater personal abilities, charisma and strength.

Most important, Freud's analyses lead us to focus upon leaders and to explore intergroup relations primarily by examining the behavior of leaders. Power is monopolized by this minority, who can influence the numerical majority to adopt particular attitudes toward different out-groups. Thus, Freud's model of group processes is in this sense also sociological, since it deals with the power differences between two categories of people: leaders and followers. The different psychologies of these minority and majority groups are viewed as being directly linked to their power differences, and this seems to prepare the way for a structural model of group and perhaps intergroup processes.

FREUD'S INFLUENCE ON INTERGROUP
THEORY AND RESEARCH

Freudian concepts have had a fundamental influence on both theory and research in intergroup relations. As illustrative examples, we shall discuss this influence as it is reflected in two major pioneering studies, *Frustration and Aggression* (Dollard et al. 1939) and *The Authoritarian Personality* (Adorno et al. 1950). These pioneering studies have influenced the way social scientists, particularly psychologists, sociologists, and political scientists, view intergroup conflict. Moreover, they have demonstrated that although Freud's general model of group processes is probably too diffuse to serve as the basis for a social psychology of intergroup relations, certain of his insights can be experimentally tested and used to explain intergroup conflict.

The research traditions established by *Frustration and Aggression* and *The Authoritarian Personality* continued the Freudian bias of reductionism in dealing with intergroup relations. That is, like Freud's model of group processes, they are basically concerned with intra- and interpersonal processes, but they extrapolate from this level to that of intergroup processes. Thus, for example, Dollard et al. (1939) assumed that processes linking frustration and aggression are the same at the interindividual and intergroup levels. This assumption led them to elaborate frustration-aggression theory at the individual level, and then to proceed on that basis to discuss intergroup attitudes and prejudice.

Freud influenced frustration-aggression theory in at least four major ways. First, the fundamental proposition that ". . . aggression is always a consequence of frustration" (Dollard et al. 1939, p. 1) is derived from Freud. In making this assertion, Dollard et al. also conceived of an intervening variable between the frustrating stimulus and the aggressive response. Frustration is viewed as an outcome of a blocking or a prevention of a goal response. A frustrating stimulus produces in the person an instigation to aggress. However, a number of factors can make it difficult or impossible for a person to attack the frustrator, such as the frustrating agent being too powerful. In such circumstances, it is predicted that aggression will be displaced onto an alternative target, a scapegoat. A classic contemporary example of this would be an unemployed man coming home after another fruitless day of searching for a job, and picking on his wife, since the society that will not give him a job seems too powerful to fight. This notion of displaced aggression reflects the second major way in which the frustration-aggression hypothesis has been directly influenced by Freud.

Third, Dollard et al. were influenced by Freud with respect to the characteristics that they believed the scapegoat would have. Following Freud, they identified similarity as the key criterion according to which out-group targets for aggression would be selected: "For the outgroup to be a good scapegoat it must be so far removed from the ingroup by differences in custom or feature that it will not be included effectively within the scope of ingroup taboos on aggression" (Dollard et al. 1939, p. 89). Thus, like Freud, Dollard et al. assert that the more similar the out-group, the less likely it is to be selected as the target of aggression.

The fourth and major way in which frustration-aggression theory has been influenced by Freud is in terms of the hydraulic model assumed by Dollard et al. Following Freud's general model, they assume that the energy motivating human behavior will not "fade away" if it cannot reach its original goal. Rather, this energy will be redirected along alternative channels. Intergroup hostility can arise from this process in the following manner. Frustration leads to an instigation to aggress. However, if the frustrating stimulus cannot be attacked, perhaps because it is too powerful, then the instigation to aggress will not dissipate but will be displaced onto another, possibly weaker, out-group. The occurrence of aggression has a cathartic effect, in that the likelihood of further aggression without fresh instigation decreases. Thus, the instigation to aggress can be decreased only through the expression of aggression.

The influence of Freud is also clearly reflected in more recent applications of frustration-aggression theory to intergroup relations (Berkowitz 1962; Gurr 1970; Horowitz 1973). In particular, the concept of displaced aggression has had an important influence on the way intergroup conflicts have been analyzed. For example, Gurr (1970) has undertaken an extensive interpretation of why rebellions and revolutions occur by relying in fundamental ways on frustration-aggression theory. Central to his thesis on social violence is the notion of displaced aggression. However, the general tendency has been for research on frustration-aggression theory to focus upon behavior at the individual level, the results of these studies being extrapolated to the intergroup level (see Billig 1976, p. 123).

The Authoritarian Personality, introduced by Adorno et al. (1950), also reflects Freud's influence on the ways in which intergroup behavior has been construed and researched. The events of World War II and the threat of fascism led Adorno et al. to research the "potentially fascistic" individual, ". . . one whose structure is such as to render him particularly susceptible to anti-democratic propaganda" (1950, p. 1). The authors were explicit about the direction their political biases gave the study, as well as about their debt to Freud: "For theory as to the structure of personality we have leaned most heavily upon Freud . . ." (Adorno et al. 1950, p. 5). Although Adorno et al. viewed intergroup attitudes as being determined primarily by personality (intraindividual) variables, their ultimate concern was with the large-scale implications of the potentially fascist personality. As the reader is repeatedly reminded in *The Authoritarian Personality*, the main concern of Adorno et al. was the threat to democratic society posed by the potentially fascist personality types.

Following Freud, Adorno et al. presented an irrationalist account of human behavior. This is clearly reflected in the factors they introduced to account for the potential threat of fascism. They argued that fascism necessarily favors the minority and cannot prove that it will serve the best interests of the majority: "It must therefore make its major appeal, not to rational self-interest, but to emotional needs—often to the most primitive and irrational wishes and fears"

(Adorno et al. 1950, p. 10). Thus, it is not material benefits and logical arguments that lead a person to support fascism, but primitive and irrational wishes and fears inside the potentially fascistic personality.

Typical authoritarians were presented by Adorno et al. as having suppressed their hostilities toward their parents, projecting this aggression onto "scapegoat outgroups," such as the Jews and blacks. Thus, following Freudian traditions, they placed particular emphasis on the respondents' childhood experiences and relationships with parents. In the case of male participants, the study focused particularly on the respondent's relationship with his father and his history of rebellion against the father, on the assumption that ". . . the pattern developed in relation to the father tends to be transferred to other authorities and thus becomes crucial in forming social and political beliefs in men" (Adorno et al. 1950, p. 315).

In the case of the authoritarian personality type, the repression of aggressive tendencies against parents is seen as part of a general tendency to repress "unacceptable" tendencies and impulses in the self, such as ". . . fear, weakness, passivity, sex impulses . . ." (Adorno et al. 1950, p. 474). This repression leads to the growth of an irrational "shield" of the beliefs that protect the authoritarian personality type from the "unacceptable" aspects of reality. Through the mechanism of projection, much of what cannot be accepted as part of one's own ego is externalized, with the result that ". . . it is not oneself but others that are seen as hostile and threatening" (Adorno et al. 1950, p. 474).

Although the implications of both *Frustration and Aggression* (Dollard et al. 1939) and *The Authoritarian Personality* (Adorno et al. 1950) for intergroup behavior have been criticized (see Billig 1976; Brown 1984), they have nevertheless had a fundamental influence on social science models of intergroup relations. Indirectly, this impact has maintained the influence of Freud's group psychology.

CRITICAL REVIEW OF THE FREUDIAN LEGACY

Freud did not carry out empirical studies on intergroup relations, but relied mainly on the writings of Gustave Le Bon for his raw data. The anti-collective sentiments of Le Bon's writings are reflected in Freud's work—for example, by the veneration of the individual and a mistrust of the group. These biases can be usefully viewed in the context of the general social and political upheavals experienced by Western societies in the late 19th and early 20th centuries. These upheavals involved a transformation of social traditions, a general move toward democratization, and an apparent weakening of control by the elite in the political and economic spheres. To some, such apparent changes brought the threat of rule by the mob, a breakdown of law and order, and an increased possibility of chaos and war.

Freud continues to have a fundamental influence on our views about behavior in the intergroup context, although his model does not constitute a major orientation to intergroup relations. The Freudian legacy is directly reflected by such powerful and highly influential concepts as displaced aggression. This is an example of Freud's ideas that have become influential in the mass media. For example, terrorism has often been interpreted in the media as an example of displaced aggression. From this perspective, a minority group (terrorists) that is too weak to show aggression toward the real object of its hostility (a government) is forced to displace its aggression onto scapegoats (very often the innocent public). The implications are that as terrorists gain access to more powerful weapons, they will probably select more important scapegoats onto whom they can displace their aggression. Of course, such purely psychological interpretations of terrorism do not deal with the political factors leading to minority group rebellion or the processes of marginalization experienced by political minorities.

However, the reductionism of Freud's model, as well as its extreme irrationalism and its focus on the in-group rather than on relations between groups, means that it does not constitute a major orientation to intergroup relations. Freud attempted to explain relations between groups by analyzing within-group dynamics, and by extrapolating from the levels of intra- and interpersonal behavior to that of intergroup behavior. Also, he relied entirely on irrational factors to explain such phenomena as war between nations.

An aspect of Freud's model that is promising but has not been followed up in intergroup research is his distinction between the psychology of followers and that of leaders. His different treatment of these two categories could provide a point of departure for a structural model of group and intergroup processes. Also, his emphasis upon the role of leaders in intergroup relations seems to be in harmony with our everyday views about many types of intergroup situations, including that involving superpower confrontations. The concentration of power in the hands of a top elite, personified by men such as Reagan and Gorbachev, and the confrontation of these leaders in superpower summits would seem to endorse at least some of Freud's emphasis on the role of leaders in intergroup relations.

CONCLUSION

Freud's model of group processes has a number of important implications for intergroup relations, the most critical being that hostility toward outgroups is one inevitable outcome of in-group cohesion. While this is in some ways a pessimistic conclusion, more optimistic possibilities arise when we consider the potentials presented by displacement. Feelings of hostility need not be displaced onto out-groups, but can be channeled along more constructive paths, such as competitive sports. Thus, according to Freud's model, the most promising way to achieve intergroup cooperation lies in creating constructive paths along which displaced aggression can be channeled, rather than changing the material conditions in which social groups exist.

SUGGESTED READINGS

Adorno, T. W., E. Frenkel-Brunswik, D. J. Levinson, and R. W. Sanford 1950. *The Authoritarian Personality.* New York: Harper & Row.

Billig, M. 1976. *Social Psychology and Intergroup Relations.* London: Academic Press.

Dollard, J., L. Doob, N. Miller, O. Mowrer, and R. Sears. 1939. *Frustration and Aggression.* New Haven: Yale University Press.

Freud, S. 1921. *Group Psychology and the Analysis of the Ego.* Vol. 18 of J. Strachey (ed. and trans.), *Standard Edition of Complete Psychological Works.* London: Hogarth Press.

———. 1930. *Civilization and Its Discontents.* Vol. 21 of J. Strachey (ed. and trans.), *Standard Edition of Complete Psychological Works.* London: Hogarth Press.

3   Realistic Conflict Theory

Scope: Realistic conflict theory addresses the three major issues in intergroup relations: how conflicts arise, the course they take, and their resolution. Emphasis is placed on relations between groups of equal power and on how conflicts between such groups can be resolved.

Assumptions: Realistic conflict theory is based on a rational view of humankind. Conflicts between groups are assumed to arise from competition for scarce resources.

Propositions: In the process of working toward shared goals, group members develop a sense of group identity. Conflict between groups arises when there is competition for scarce resources. The resources may be concrete, such as geographical territory, or abstract, such as power or status. Intergroup cooperation emerges when there are superordinate goals: a situation where groups can achieve a mutually desired goal only by combining their resources.

Realistic conflict theory (RCT) is essentially an economic theory of intergroup behavior that is based upon three central assumptions about human behavior. First, it is assumed that people are selfish and will try to maximize their own rewards. Second, conflict is assumed to be the outcome of incompatible group interests. Third, it is assumed, sometimes explicitly, that the social psychological aspects of intergroup behavior are not determinants of—but, rather, are mainly determined by—the compatibility or incompatibility of group interests. For example, the negative attitudes, stereotypes, and attributions that members of one group have regarding members of an out-group are assumed to stem from the incompatible interests of the two groups involved.

The psychologist as peacemaker is the major underlying theme of social psychological research guided by RCT. The possibility of a world nuclear war has been the principal reason for psychologists such as Deutsch adopting the role of peacemaker: "I started my graduate study not long after Hiroshima and Nagasaki and my work in social psychology has been shadowed by the atomic cloud ever since" (Deutsch 1969a, p. 1076). The ultimate aim of research guided by RCT has been to develop strategies for achieving cooperation and peace between the superpowers of East and West. Thus, in RCT there is an emphasis on relations between groups of equal strength and power, and a special interest in conflict resolution.

The work of social psychologists guided by RCT is in an important sense devoid of social psychology. Once it is assumed that real conflicts of interests are the cause of intergroup hostility, and intergroup behavior is mainly determined by the compatibility or incompatibility of group goals, then social psychological phenomena assume the role of dependent variables in the intergroup setting. For example, Sherif states that "The bounds for the attitudes of members in different groups towards one another are set by the nature of the functional relations between groups" (1966, p. 63). He proceeds to describe in more detail what these functional relations are:

> Groups may be competing to attain some goal or vital prize, in which the success of one group necessarily means the failure of the other. One group may have claims on another group to manage, control, or exploit them, to take over their actual or assumed rights and possessions. On the other hand, groups may have complementary goals, so that each may attain its goal without hindrance from the others or even with their helping hand. (1966, p. 63)

The intellectual roots of this functional approach can be traced directly to the sociologist William Sumner. In his articulation of the concept of ethnocentrism, Sumner wrote:

> The insiders in a we-group are in a relation of peace, order, law, government, and industry, to each other. Their relation to all outsiders, or others-groups, is one of war and plunder. . . . Sentiments are produced to correspond. Loyalty to the group, sacrifice for it, hatred and contempt for outsiders, brotherhood within, warlikeness without—all grow together, common products of the same situation. (1906, p. 12)

Thus, according to this functionalist tradition, which Sherif followed, it is competition between groups for scarce resources that leads to perceptual and attitudinal biases against the out-group.

The social psychological aspects of Sherif's research on intergroup behavior concern the development of intergroup processes within the bounds of certain functional relations between groups. This point is further clarified below when we describe his research on intergroup behavior. With reference to the field of intergroup research, Sherif has been described as ". . . the most important social psychologist in the history of the field" (Triandis 1979, p. 321), and his experiments on intergroup behavior have become classics. Therefore we describe his work in some detail.

Probably the most important factor influencing Sherif's research on intergroup behavior is that it was carried out between 1949 and 1953, at the height of the "cold war" and with the memories of the atrocities of World War II still very fresh. Two major concerns of applied psychologists after the war were (1) to understand how seemingly normal people could carry out the mass murders that characterized the war, and (2) to try to prevent the outbreak of World War III. The first concern led to studies such as *The Authoritarian Personality* (Adorno et al. 1950), which attempted to explain negative behavior toward out-groups in terms of intraindividual personality variables. The second concern led to studies such as Sherif's intergroup experiments, which attempted to map the processes of intergroup behavior and to identify strategies for transforming hostile intergroup relations into cooperative ones.

Following our discussion of Sherif's experiments, we focus on gaming research, particularly the work of Morton Deutsch. Gaming research has not been included under RCT by reviewers such as LeVine and Campbell (see LeVine & Campbell 1972, pp. 29–42). However, it is our contention that most gaming research shares the theoretical and normative underpinnings of RCT. They both adopt the assumption that conflict is bad as their point of departure. Second, in the typical gaming experiment it is assumed that subjects try to maximize their own profits; thus a selfish model of humankind is adopted. Third, conflict is assumed to arise when subjects try to maximize their own rewards at the expense of others—that is, real conflicts of interests cause conflicts. Fourth, the competing nature of interests is assumed, sometimes explicitly, to be the most important factor determining such social psychological phenomena as attitudes of the parties involved. However, certain scientists in gaming research, such as Deutsch, have explicitly placed greater emphasis on the perceptions and interpretations of the conflicting parties than have the strict functionalists, such as Sherif. Thus Deutsch states that the objective state of affairs does not "rigidly determine" the presence or absence of conflict (1969a, p. 9), and that the "processes of misperception and biased perception" are among those which can lead to conflict escalation (1973, p. 352).

The strengths and weaknesses of RCT will be discussed in our critical review of the theory. Psychologists guided by RCT have tended to view the resolution of conflict as the most important applied task facing researchers. Deutsch and other would-be "peacemakers" represent the liberal conscience of North America, the "doves" who have urged successive U.S. administrations to settle disagreements with the USSR through negotiations and closer cooperation on joint projects, which they believe could in turn lead to greater superpower interdependence and mutual trust. In outlining the course of "constructive" and "destructive" conflicts (1973, pp. 351–400), Deutsch clearly is extrapolating from his gaming research to the international scene (see also Deutsch 1985).

THE PIONEERING WORK OF MUZAFER SHERIF

The details of Sherif's research have been described in a number of publications (Sherif 1951; Sherif, Harvey, White, Hood & Sherif, 1961; Sherif & Sherif 1953; Sherif, White & Harvey, 1955), but the volume in which the research is most clearly described in its larger social context is *Group Conflict and Cooperation* (Sherif 1966).

Sherif states that "The appropriate frame of reference for staging intergroup behavior is the functional relations between two or more groups, which may be negative or positive" (1966, p. 12). It is particularly important to note how these functional relations are operationalized in the experimental context, with reference to Sherif's definitions of the terms "group" and "intergroup behavior." In Sherif's experiments, "functional relations" are equivalent to complementary-noncomplementary group interests. He defines a group as ". . . a social unit that consists of a number of individuals (1) who, at a given time, have role and status relations with one another, stabilized in some degree and (2) who possess a set of values or norms regulating the attitude and behavior of individual members, at least in matters of consequence to them" (1966, p. 12), and intergroup behavior as ". . . relations between two or more groups and their respective members. Whenever individuals belonging to one group interact, collectively or individually, with another group or its members *in terms of their group identification,* we have an instance of intergroup behavior" (1966, p. 12). An important implication of this latter definition is that intergroup behavior need not necessarily involve the physical presence and interaction of entire groups, but can simply mean individuals from two different groups interacting in terms of their respective group identities.

In Sherif's experiments, a group of boys were given tasks to carry out and were placed in a competitive position vis-à-vis another group of boys who had also been given tasks. While taking part in competitions that placed one group against the other, group members showed positive in-group bias and out-group hostility, and generally acted in terms of their group identity—thus meeting Sherif's criterion for intergroup behavior. Throughout the processes of group formation and intergroup behavior, the material conditions of the experimental context—the tasks and resources given to groups, and particularly the complementary or noncomplementary nature of tasks—were the independent variables, while social psychological phenomena, such as intergroup attitudes and group identification, were the dependent variables.

Sherif and his associates carried out three major experiments on intergroup behavior. All of them were conducted in summer camps, and the participants in all three were boys eleven or twelve years old. Only boys who did not have personal ties with each other prior to the experiment, were healthy and well-adjusted, and were from white, middle-class, Protestant families were included. This selection procedure was designed to decrease the chances of personal acquaintance, abnormal personality tendencies, and pronounced differences in background and physical appearance influencing the results.

The research context was naturalistic, in the sense that the boys believed they were in a normal summer camp situation; they engaged in the kinds of activities boys usually do in such camps. All research staff played the role of camp officials, organizing and officiating events while also acting as participant observers. The groups that Sherif studied had a history from group formation to intergroup conflict, cooperation, and group dissolution; and the time scale of the history was naturalistic, in the sense that the process of group formation and dissolution in such camps is normally completed in a few weeks. There were four experimental stages: (1) spontaneous interpersonal friendship choices, (2) group formation, (3) intergroup conflict, and (4) intergroup cooperation/reduction of intergroup conflict (see figure 3.1).

Spontaneous Interpersonal Friendship Choices

The first two experiments carried out by Sherif and his associates began with this stage, which served the function of eliminating personal attraction as an

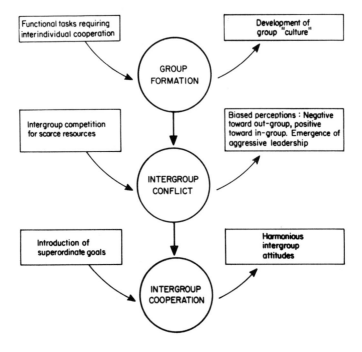

**Figure 3.1   Schematic Representation of Realistic Conflict
Theory**

explanatory factor. During this stage, the boys were housed together, and
were free to interact and work with whom they preferred. After relationships
had stabilized to some extent, assessments were made of interpersonal attraction among the boys. Next, the boys were divided between two cabins, with
about two-thirds of any boy's best friends being placed in the other cabin. By
separating the boys from most of those they were spontaneously attracted to,
Sherif diminished the possibility that the research results could be explained in
terms of interpersonal attraction.

After the formation of the two groups, the boys interacted and carried out
tasks almost exclusively with in-group members. The patterns of interpersonal
attractions among them changed, so that best friends were now chosen more
from the in-groups. Sherif concluded that ". . . friendship choices shift steadily
from strictly interpersonal attractions toward ingroup exclusiveness, as a part
of group formation and functions'' (1966 p. 75).

Group Formation

Sherif's third major experiment, known as the "Robber's Cave" study because it was carried out near a famous hideaway reputed to have been used by Jesse James, started with the stage of group formation. The main purpose of this stage was to give the groups a number of tasks, such as cooking, camping, and building, that required the boys in each group to work as a team. In carrying out these group tasks, a status hierarchy and leadership structure emerged within each group, as well as a kind of group identity and subculture involving nicknames for members, group secrets, symbols, names, and preferred ways of doing things.

Intergroup Conflict

The boys did not have contact as groups prior to the stage of intergroup conflict. In the Robber's Cave study, neither group was aware of the presence of the other. As soon as the groups became aware of each other, however, their competitive spirit seemed to be stimulated. That is, the mere knowledge of the presence of an out-group seemed to be sufficient to motivate competitive feelings. It is important to note that upon learning about the presence of an out-group, the boys were extremely eager to take part in intergroup competitions, such as tug-of-war and a treasure hunt. The intergroup rivalry began in a healthy way, but quickly turned harsh and antagonistic. In the early experiments, boys turned against formerly best friends. This trend of escalating intergroup hostilities led groups to sabotage each others' work.

Sherif found that the presence of a negatively valued and "threatening" outgroup increased in-group solidarity. There was a tendency to overestimate the achievements of in-group members and to underestimate those of outgroup members. Attitudes toward the outgroup generally became negative, while those toward fellow in-group members became more positive. There was also some tendency for leadership to change, so that more "warlike" and aggressive individuals emerged as leaders.

The most interesting psychological findings of Sherif's experiments emerged during this stage, and it is worth deliberating further upon two aspects in particular. First, there was a tendency for subjects to refer to notions of justice and fairness. Second, the boys systematically perceived events in a manner that favored the in-group.

Throughout the stage of intergroup conflict, the boys in Sherif's experiments repeatedly referred to notions of justice. They made claims about their own group playing fair, and the other group "playing dirty" and being cheats. When their own group was caught out by a surprise attack or unexpected trick, the other group was described as using unfair, cowardly tactics;

but the other group "got what they deserved" when they were attacked without warning or when their schemes were sabotaged. Fairness and justice were notions that the boys interpreted and reinterpreted in ways that were advantageous to their in-group. This reminds one of the kinds of manipulations of the meaning of justice that some political parties embark upon, making their interpretations suit their own purposes, depending on whether they are in or out of government, or whether it is their own political record or that of opposition parties that they are talking about. The same action can be applauded as "just" or condemned as "an injustice," depending on whether it is the in-group or the out-group that is responsible for its execution (see Brewer 1979).

The biased perceptions that the boys developed are demonstrated particularly well in a game of "bean toss," in which the aim was to collect as many beans scattered on the ground as possible within a limited time. The boys worked individually, collecting beans in a sack with a restricted opening, so that it was not possible to count the number of beans collected. They then had the task of estimating the number of beans in each sack.

The contents of each sack were briefly exposed to the boys, and each collection of beans purportedly gathered by a different boy was identified solely by the group membership of the collector. In actuality, the same collection of 35 beans was shown each time, this being a number sufficiently large that it could not be counted in the time available. Each boy wrote down his estimate of the number after each exposure. The results showed a consistent tendency to overestimate the number of beans collected by the in-group and to underestimate the number collected by the out-group. This cleverly formulated experiment within an experiment clearly demonstrates the pattern of positive in-group bias that evolves in situations of intergroup conflict.

Intergroup Cooperation

It was in the Robber's Cave experiment that Sherif first operationalized the concept of superordinate goals as a means of transforming hostile intergroup relations into cooperative ones. Superordinate goals are those which have ". . . a compelling appeal for members of each group, but that neither group can achieve without participation of the other" (Sherif 1966, p. 89). A series of situations was created in which all the boys had to combine resources in order to overcome an obstacle and reach a goal that had common appeal for them. For example, in one situation the boys joined forces and successfully coped with a breakdown of the water supply, and in another they all helped start a truck that was to bring them food. Solving the breakdown of the water supply and starting the truck represented superordinate goals, in the sense that they had a strong appeal for members of both groups but neither group could achieve them without the participation of the other. In neither case did such mutual cooperation on the task lead to an immediate end to hostilities. However, the series of situations requiring interdependent action did gradually lead to more harmonious relations between the groups.

In evaluating the transformation from conflicting to harmonious intergroup relations between the third and fourth stages, it is important to keep in mind that the groups in this experiment had been brought into existence through their ascribed tasks, and made more cohesive through intergroup competition. Once the groups did not have separate tasks, and once the institutionalized competition had been removed, it seems plausible to argue that the functional reason for their existence had ceased. Furthermore, the introduction of new tasks that required the formation of a new, larger group for their attainment meant that the functional basis for the evolution of a group combining all the boys was present. It could be validly argued, therefore, that the cooperation Sherif achieved in the fourth stage was not between two different groups, but between individuals who had to act as one group in order to complete tasks that required all their combined resources.

The importance of Sherif's research is not in the new or unexpected nature of its results, but in its methodological approach, particularly in its operationalization of the concept of superordinate goals. It is not new or unexpected to find that real conflicts of interests lead to intergroup hostilities, or that groups have more harmonious relationships when they have to combine forces to achieve a commonly desired goal. But Sherif's work was innovative in reproducing, under controlled conditions, various processes of group formation, conflict, and cooperation that are normally associated with long-term social change. Also, by demonstrating how the concept of superordinate goals can be effectively operationalized and used to transform groups in conflict into groups in harmony, he fired the imaginations of researchers who came to perceive superordinate goals as a useful instrument for solving intergroup conflicts, from the level of small groups to superpowers.

APPLICATION OF THE CONCEPT OF SUPERORDINATE GOALS

Industrial Conflicts

An important domain to which the concept of superordinate goals has been extended is that of industrial conflicts. The most important examples of such an application are the works of Blake and Mouton (1962) and Blake, Shepard and Mouton (1964), who report a series of cases where they intervened in the industrial context to solve intergroup labor-management problems. Their most comprehensive work, *Managing Intergroup Conflict in Industry* (1964), is dedicated to the Sherifs, and they specifically follow the Sherifs' nonreductionist approach by assuming that the causes of intergroup conflict are to be found in the relationship between groups (1964, pp. 87–89).

How Blake and his associates applied the Sherifs' ideas in the industrial setting is usefully illustrated by the example of union-management conflict in the
Lakeside Company (1964, pp. 123-36). The main practical problem for the
researchers was how to influence the perceptions of the conflicting parties so that
they would view selected superordinate goals as "the" priority objectives, and
give less importance to differences of interest. After receiving an invitation from
management to intervene in the conflict, Blake and his associates set up training
programs to familiarize the participants with social science intergroup concepts,
theories, and experiments. At this stage, union representatives viewed the
researchers with suspicion and refused to take part in the training programs,
claiming they were "just another management manipulation" intended to
"soften us up" and "brainwash us" (1964, p. 125).

Despite this obstacle, the researchers succeeded in motivating the two groups
to negotiate and to accept the idea that each of them stood to gain more by
cooperating than by fighting. The solution of superordinate goals involved
changes in the perceptions of the participants with regard to the importance of
various goals, rather than changes in the material conditions that underlay their
conflicts of interests—assumed by Sherif to be the real cause of conflict.

International Conflict

The extension of the concept of superordinate goals to the international
scene is illustrated by the work of Frank (1967). He proposes that the superpowers should cooperate on a series of programs—for instance, in the areas of
environmental and space research—designed to achieve selected superordinate goals. Such activities would, he argues, increase mutual dependence,
understanding, and trust, thereby diminishing the risk of another world war.
It is this philosophy that underlies the work of the United Nations in its
various spheres. For example, through the U.N. Development Program and
the almost 40 U.N. executive agencies, such as the U.N. Industrial Development Organization and the International Labour Office, the superpowers
cooperate to strengthen the development efforts of Third World countries.
The institutional goals of the U.N. executive agencies, which include eradicat-
ing illiteracy and overcoming food shortages, could be regarded as superordinate goals. Moreover, there are a number of U.N. bodies, such as the U.N.
Peace Corps, and activities, such as the U.N. Conferences on Disarmament,
that more directly present the superpowers with the chance to work toward the
assumed superordinate goal of peace. On the one hand, it could be claimed
that such activities are effective, since a third world war has been avoided. On
the other hand, the criticism remains that the superpowers seem to be using
the United Nations as just another battleground where they pursue self-
serving policies and steamroll opposition motions by using their veto powers.

Desegregated Schools

Elliot Aronson and his colleagues (Aronson, Stephan, Sikes, Blaney & Snapp, 1978) have made a creative application of the concept of superordinate goals to desegregated schools in the United States. Stimulated by Sherif's pioneering work, Aronson (1984) noted that the key to the superordinate goals associated with intergroup cooperation is mutual interdependence—". . . a situation wherein individuals need one another and are needed by one another in order to accomplish their goal'' (p. 267). Aronson felt that if mutual interdependence could be introduced into a classroom environment to replace the competitive atmosphere between students, a cooperative attitude among students generally and racial groups in particular would develop. To test this notion, the "jigsaw" procedure was introduced; students worked in small groups that were required to perform a task, and each member of the group had information crucial to the group product. Thus, the conditions for mutual interdependence were created.

Repeated applications of the jigsaw procedure in classrooms produce consistent results. The children in these classrooms like each other better, they develop a more positive attitude toward school, have a higher self-esteem, and have better exam performances than those in traditional classes. Of special significance is the finding that the increase in liking among the students generally crosses racial and ethnic boundaries. The field of education thus represents another context where the concept of superordinate goals, defined here in terms of mutual interdependence, has an important role to play in fostering intergroup cooperation.

In summary, the concept of superordinate goals has had an important impact on the work of research and practicing social scientists. Given Sherif's historical influence in the field of intergroup relations, it is surprising that so little psychological research has been carried out to test the effectiveness of superordinate goals as a means of reducing intergroup conflict in different conditions. Clearly, superordinate goals can be effective in transforming conflict into cooperation, but under what conditions can this transformation be achieved more successfully? Also, are there conditions in which superordinate goals are not useful in achieving intergroup cooperation?

In this connection, an experiment by Deschamps and Brown (n.d.) produces evidence to suggest that in a condition where groups have comparable goals in achieving superordinate goals, group distinctiveness would be threatened, and this would lead to greater intergroup differentiation and hostility. Thus, this would seem to demonstrate one condition in which superordinate goals lead to increased rather than decreased intergroup conflict.

GAMING RESEARCH AND RCT

The model of humankind adopted by gaming research is that of a rational, thinking being who is motivated to maximize personal gain. Conflicts are assumed to evolve when incompatible interests are perceived by the parties involved as being more important than compatible interests. Most gaming research follows the tradition of "peace researchers," who assume that the psychologist's task must be to help avoid war, in contrast with the "war gamers" who have adopted the goal of making warfare more efficient (see Billig 1976, p. 182; Wilson 1970). Both "war gamers" and "peace researchers" assume that psychologists can help achieve more rational outcomes from intergroup interactions by identifying the pitfalls that lead to irrational decision making.

An essential underlying assumption in gaming research is that extrapolations from the results of experimental studies on interpersonal behavior are valid (see Axelrod 1984). Indeed, many important research questions being investigated through experimental gaming studies of interpersonal behavior are derived from the context of macro, intergroup, and international relations. This point is well illustrated in the writings of Deutsch (1973, 1985), a leading "peace researcher." With regard to the kinds of concerns that stimulated his initial experimental studies on bargaining, Deutsch states, "Our first bargaining study was concerned with the effect of threat (Deutsch & Krauss 1960, 1962). The study grew out of my concern with some of the psychological assumptions underlying the concept of 'stable deterrence', a notion that was quite fashionable among political scientists and economists connected with the Defence Department in the late 1950's and early 1960's" (1969a, p. 1083).

The theoretical and experimental approach adopted by gaming research is not, however, always compatible with the kinds of "international" concerns that inspired researchers such as Deutsch. This is not to say that processes leading to intergroup conflict and peace cannot be studied constructively in the experimental laboratory. It is to suggest, however, that to carry out research on interpersonal behavior and then to generalize from its results to the intergroup and international levels is very likely to be misleading.

However, an innovative approach to linking research on individual behavior in the gaming context to intergroup relations has been developed by Axelrod (1984). It focuses upon how individuals pursuing their own interests will act, and what effects this will have on the social system as a whole. In developing "cooperation theory," Axelrod has drawn heavily on concepts from the field of evolutionary biology and has adopted a classical Darwinian approach. He explicitly uses the terminology of evolutionary biology to present his theory of the evolution of cooperative behavior.

Axelrod treats cooperative behavior as an individual trait, like white skin and long legs, that can be passed on to offspring and spread among a population, or become extinct. The point of departure for cooperation theory is that for cooperative behavior to survive and spread, individuals must have a high chance of meeting again, so that they have a real stake in future interactions. This proposition is supported by findings from gaming research (Axelrod 1984). Also, cooperation cannot gain a foothold if it is carried by isolated individuals, but it can establish itself if there is a cluster of individuals who base their cooperation on reciprocity and have some interaction with each other. Once established among a social group, cooperation can thrive and protect itself from invasion by less cooperative strategies. This is because of the "survival of the fittest," and the idea that individuals who have cooperative relations with others are more likely to have offspring that survive and thereby continue the cooperative pattern of behavior.

Axelrod's (1984) analysis diminishes the role of planning in the evolution of cooperation. In fact, Chapter 5 of his book *The Evolution of Cooperation* is coauthored with Hamilton, a biologist, with the explicit purpose of demonstrating that foresight is not a necessary precondition for the evolution of cooperation. Nevertheless, while foresight is not required, it can assist the spread of cooperation, and Axelrod dedicates chapters 6 and 7 of his book to providing advice on how to improve cooperation.

Axelrod's (1984) analysis presents some interesting ideas about how a number of concepts originating in the work of Charles Darwin and other evolutionary biologists might be used to explain the evolution of cooperation among humans. However, he is generally more effective at explaining behavior at the interindividual than at the intergroup level. Throughout, he tends to jump from discussions of interindividual behavior in the gaming context, to interindividual and intergroup behavior from an evolutionary perspective, to the topic of war and peace among nations and superpowers. Moreover, these leaps are made in such a manner that underlying ideological biases are rather clumsily bared. For example, Axelrod (1984) asks, "How intensely should the United States try to punish the Soviet Union for a particular hostile act, and what pattern of behavior can the United States use to best elicit cooperative behavior from the Soviet Union?" (p. vii). This style of questioning does not leave much doubt as to who is the "peaceloving sheriff" and who is the "troublemaking villain" from Axelrod's point of view.

Just as Axelrod (1984) seems willing to disregard the ideological biases shaping his own research questions, so he seems comfortable with adopting models of cooperation and conflict that disregard ideology and power issues altogether. He lists the arms race, nuclear proliferation, crisis bargaining, and military escalation as examples of issues whose realistic understanding ". . . would have to take into account many factors not incorporated into the simple Prisoner's Dilemma formulation, such as ideology, bureaucratic politics, commitments, coalitions, mediation, and leadership" (Axelrod 1984, p. 190). Despite this awareness, Axelrod, like many other gaming theorists, moves constantly from interindividual behavior in the gaming context to discussing relations between the superpowers.

Characteristics of the Typical Gaming Experiment

A classic experiment in gaming research is the prisoner's dilemma game (PDG) (for reviews see Rapoport & Chammah 1965; Nemeth 1972). It owes its name to an imaginary situation in which two accomplices awaiting trial are faced with a grave dilemma. Each prisoner has the choice of keeping quiet or cooperating with the authorities and informing on the other. If one of them informs and the other keeps quiet, the informer is set free and the other receives a very heavy sentence. If both of them inform, they both receive a severe sentence. If they both keep quiet, however, they both receive a light sentence. The dilemma is intensified by each prisoner's having to make a choice without communicating with the other and, thus, without knowing the choice of the other, so that the choice of strategy always has a hazardous and uncertain outcome. Each prisoner may want to get the best possible deal for himself or herself by informing on the other and getting off free, but neither is certain that the other will not also adopt this strategy and thereby get them both a severe sentence. On the other hand, if a prisoner tries for the next best outcome and keeps quiet, in the hope that his or her accomplice will also keep quiet so they can both get off with a light sentence, his or her plan may backfire, with the accomplice informing and getting him or her a very heavy sentence.

The relationship between the two prisoners is typically represented by a "payoff matrix." However, it is useful if we discuss the terminology used in connection with these matrices before describing examples of how they are used. The reward structure for players in a game can be either zero-sum or non-zero-sum. In the zero-sum game, each player necessarily wins at the expense of the other, who suffers an equivalent loss. Thus, the joint total change in the fortunes of both players must always be zero. In the non-zero-sum game, there is no direct relationship between the fortunes of the two players; the wins or losses of each depend solely on his or her own choices. Most games are "mixed-motive" in character, in that the players involved can be motivated to be either competitive or cooperative. Also, most games have a "best rational solution," and all players who follow logical behavior patterns will arrive at the same outcome, known as the "saddle point." The rationale that such logical players follow is based on the "minimax" principle, which involves a minimization of losses and a maximization of rewards.

In the terminology of gaming research, the classic PDG is a mixed motive, non-zero-sum game with a saddle point. This is because the two players can act either competitively or cooperatively, the sum of their outcomes is not necessarily zero, and there is a "best rational answer"; that is, there exists a strategy for jointly minimizing losses and maximizing rewards, and this is achieved by both players' adopting a cooperative strategy.

Although the general concern of investigators using the PDG has been to identify conditions that lead to mutually cooperative or competitive strategies in interpersonal bargaining, the one dimension this paradigm has generally not included is any kind of bargaining or joint decision making. In the typical experiment, two persons work individually to select one of two strategies, "cooperation" or "competition," that combine to determine the outcome of the game. This outcome consists of rewards that individuals receive, and success is determined by the level of rewards received. Such rewards are usually points, with each point representing a certain amount of money. The main research interest is the repeated plays of PDG by the same individuals, on the assumption that these repeated plays will tell us something about the development of negotiation behavior. In particular, interest is focused on whether the individuals will act according to their short-term or long-term interests.

Since the two participants in PDG are made aware that they are to take part in repeated plays, they know that any competitive move from one player could lead to retaliation by the other player on subsequent trials. Thus, it is in their long-term interests to cooperate. To see how short-term and long-term interests are operationalized, let us discuss the matrix of rewards in the typical PDG (see Figure 3.2).

In this and subsequent matrices, we follow the convention established in PDG research that the actor identified on the top of the figure has his or her payoff written first in each cell.

In order to maximize their joint profits, both persons should choose strategy C, because then they would receive 5 points each. However, by

PERSON B'S CHOICES

		C	D
		C	D
PERSON A'S CHOICES	C	+5, +5	+8, -1
	D	-1, +8	+2, +2

Figure 3.2   Matrix of Rewards in a Typical
Prisoner's Dilemma Game

opting for strategy C, each person would be leaving himself or herself open to an exploitative move by the other. For example, when person A chooses C, but person B chooses D, B receives 8 points but A receives -1 point. Returning to the fable of the two accomplices awaiting trial, this move would be equivalent to one prisoner keeping quiet and the other informing the authorities, so that the informer is set free and the other receives a very heavy sentence.

A number of variations of the basic PDG design have been formulated, such as the game of "chicken" (Rapoport & Chammah 1966). This owes its name to a game, one version of which was popularized by the cult hero James Dean, in which two daredevils drive their cars down the middle of the road straight at each other (or toward a cliff), and the first one to turn off is "chicken." If neither turns off, then both are killed. If both turn off at the same time, both share the shame. But if one turns "chicken" and swerves away, and the other drives straight on, then all the glory goes to the latter.

The strong appeal that PDG has had for researchers interested in international peace issues can be explained partly by the analogous dilemmas that seem to confront the players in the PDG context and the superpowers in the international arena. Consider the position of the superpowers, involved in the arms race and fearful of each other. Each is under pressure to increase arms expenditures, and the one that decreases expenditures on arms risks falling under the military domination of the other. Both sides seem to see only two alternatives: increasing arms expenditure or submitting to the power of the other. They seem to see and act upon only the consequences of not increasing arms expenditures.

The policy of increasing arms expenditures means losses for both of the superpowers, in the sense that neither of them can use these resources for other, more constructive international and domestic purposes. When both parties choose to increase arms expenditures, their payoff is minimal. However, if they cooperate and both decrease arms expenditures, then they are both relatively better off.

A Sample Experiment

In the typical PDG, subjects are not informed about the kinds of real-life situations that these games are supposed to represent. Would their behavior reflect the norms and values that they consider relevant to such real-life situations if the representative nature of the experimental situations was explained to them? This question has been investigated by Eiser and Bhavnani (1974). The following fairly detailed description of their experiment serves the two purposes of familiarizing us with the procedures of a typical PDG and clarifying how the manipulation of a key variable can alter the outcomes.

SUBJECT (2)

		Red	Black
		Red	**Black**
SUBJECT (I)	Red	3,3	4,0
	Black	0,4	1,1

Figure 3.3   The PDG Reward Matrix Used by Eiser and Bhavnani

Eiser and Bhavnani tested the hypothesis that it should be possible to influence subjects' behavior in the PDG by altering how they perceive the requirements of the task. This was achieved by telling subjects beforehand the general context in which their behavior would supposedly be interpreted. For example, in one condition subjects were told that "such studies have frequently been used in the past to simulate international negotiations—cooperation and conflict—such as might occur between two nation states" (Eiser & Bhavani 1974, p. 95). There were four conditions. The control condition was run according to standard PDG procedures, without any reference to a general context. Subjects in the second, third, and fourth conditions were told that their behavior was supposed to be interpreted in the context of international negotiations, or economic bargaining, or interpersonal interactions.

The 80 subjects, 40 male and 40 female, were tested in groups of even numbers. The significance of the even numbers is that each subject was separated from the others, but told that he or she had been paired with an unidentified other. The subjects then went through ten trials of the standard PDG, with the rewards allocated as shown in Figure 3.3.

Subjects indicated their strategy choices by pressing either red or black counters on the same trial; then they would both receive three points or one point each, respectively. If, however, S2 pressed red and S1 pressed black, S2 would receive no points and S1, four points.

Results showed significant differences between responses across conditions, with cooperative responses being highest in the "interpersonal interaction" and "international negotiations" conditions. There were no significant differences between the responses by sex. In the interpretation of these results, one could usefully speculate that cooperation between subjects was highest in those conditions where feelings about fair play and justice had a greater chance of being evoked, rather than in the economic bargaining or control conditions where competitive feelings were more likely to be brought to the forefront. The findings of this experiment suggest that how subjects interpret the context of the PDG can significantly influence the way they act in this experimental setting. Therefore, it is important to pay attention to Eiser and Bhavnani's suggestion that ". . . extrapolations from the results of PDG experiments to particular kinds of real-life situations must depend for their validity at least partly on whether the subjects themselves interpret that game as symbolic of the situations in question" (1974, p. 97).

Gaming Research and Power

Although gaming research has generally focused on the interactions of parties that have equal power, there are a number of important exceptions to this general trend. For example, variations of the Deutsch and Krauss "trucking game" (1960, 1962) have been used to allow for some manipulation of power as an independent variable. This game typically involves two subjects, who are required to imagine that each is in charge of a different trucking company. They will receive a fixed sum for each trip they make to carry merchandise from point A to point B, minus their operating costs. These operating costs are calculated at a fixed rate per unit time. For example, they could receive 100 points for each trip made, minus 1 point in operating costs for each second they are on the road. If they complete a trip in 30 seconds, therefore, they will receive 70 points. In addition to a long route, the players have the option of taking a short route.

It would obviously be more profitable for both players to take the short route, since the time each trip takes—and hence operating costs—would then be decreased. However, the short route has only one lane, and the players have to come to an agreement about taking turns using it. By placing a gate on this short route and giving one of the players control over it, the experimenter can make one player more powerful than the other. In such situations, the player in control of the gate bargains from a position of strength, since he or she can prevent the other player from using the short route. In this condition, the player with more power has been found to do better. However, a less obvious finding is that both players in this condition did less well than their counterparts in conditions where the players had equal power (see Deutsch 1985, pp. 124-29). One interpretation of this finding is that in situations where there is a dominant power who can use threat, both parties have to dedicate some of their resources (such as time) to dealing with destructive conflict (Deutsch 1973). As a consequence, they have less resources to invest in achieving constructive tasks—in this case transporting merchandise from point A to point B.

Negotiation and Third-Party Intervention

The gaming tradition has also influenced research in negotiation and mediation, or third-party intervention. This area of research is becoming increasingly important, particularly in the growth of an applied social psychology (see

Bercovitch 1984; Fisher 1983; Kressel & Pruitt 1985; Zartman & Berman 1982). There are at least six areas in which knowledge from mediation research has been applied: (1) industrial mediation, such as areas involving labor and management; (2) community mediation, such as areas involving racial groups; (3) family and divorce mediation; (4) public resource and environmental mediation, involving ecological issues; (5) judicial mediation; (6) mediation at the international level, involving disputes between nation-states. Although the most spectacular and perhaps most important area of mediation is at the international level (see Rubin 1981; Zartman & Touval 1985), the most empirically sound data produced by research on negotiation and mediation seem to derive from the gaming tradition. We shall briefly discuss representative examples.

An important factor in bargaining situations is the medium of communication. For example, it is more difficult to communicate subtle attitudes and moods by telephone than by meeting face-to-face. This is often recognized when we postpone discussing delicate matters until we have the opportunity to talk with the person(s) involved face-to-face. Also, the degree of formality of a context influences how free we feel to express ourselves in an unreserved manner. A series of experiments by Morley and Stephenson (1969, 1970a, 1970b) investigated the influence of the medium of communication and the formality of a situation on negotiation outcomes. In these experiments the two negotiating sides always had unequal cases, so that one side was always negotiating from a position of relative strength. A 2 x 2 experimental design was created in which the medium of communication (face-to-face vs. telephone) and degree of formality (interruption permitted in procedure vs. interruption forbidden) were manipulated. The expectation was that the face-to-face and less formal conditions, by allowing more interpersonal communicating between the parties, would tend to decrease the chances of victory for the party with the stronger case. This expectation was confirmed. That is, the more opportunity there was for the personal characteristics of the negotiators to enter the situation, the less outcomes depended upon the actual strength of the bargaining case of each side.

Consistent with this finding, Stephenson and Kniveton (1978) demonstrated that a seating position that facilitated interpersonal nonverbal communication decreased the chances of a party with the stronger case exploiting its advantage. At one level these findings might seem trivial, since surely negotiations on such important matters as arms control could not be influenced by such "unimportant" factors as the seating positions of the negotiating sides. However, we need only recall the long and heated debates that the United States and the Vietcong had about the shape of the negotiating table for the Vietnam peace settlement to remind ourselves that negotiators themselves do in fact often give high priority to such apparently trivial issues as seating arrangements.

Gaming Experiments and Intergroup Behavior

When evaluating gaming experiments, which invariably involve two-person interactions, we should keep in mind that these situations are also supposed to represent instances of intergroup and even international interactions, since both individuals and groups are assumed to behave in similar ways under similar conditions: ". . . I am asserting that nations as well as individuals acquire information, make decisions, and take actions, and that they will act in similar ways under similar conditions" (Deutsch 1969a, p. 1091). Although there has been much criticism of this kind of extrapolation from the level of interpersonal to that of intergroup processes (for instance, see Tajfel 1972b), there have been few attempts to investigate the effect of increasing the numbers of participants in the basic two-person experimental game, so that it becomes intergroup rather than interpersonal. A study that did focus on this issue was conducted by Stephenson and Botherton (1975); it involved negotiations between two mining supervisors on one side of an issue that concerned their work role and two persons on the opposing side. Whereas in the situation involving only two persons a compromise position would be reached, with each participant willing to move closer to the position of the other, interactions involving groups of two persons led to outright victory for one of the groups. Also, the nature of the debates was influenced by increased size. There was less tendency to avoid argument and conflicting views, and more effort to achieve a decisive decision on the issue.

Stephenson and Botherton's (1975) findings suggest that, under certain conditions, people tend to be more competitive in the intergroup than in the interindividual context. This finding is in agreement with those of a number of other experiments using the PDG paradigm that have been carried out to compare intergroup and intragroup game playing (for instance, Wilson & Kayatani 1968; Wilson & Wong 1968). In these experiments, two teams of two subjects each play against each other in the PDG for rewards, then the two members of each team play a similar game to settle how their winnings will be divided. Thus, each intergroup trial is followed by an intragroup trial. By comparing the responses of subjects when they play as part of a team, in an intergroup situation, with their responses when they play alone against a single other, differences between cooperative and competitive behavior in the intergroup and intragroup context are assessed. Results suggest that people are more competitive in the intergroup context.

CRITICAL REVIEW OF RCT

RCT has a number of important strengths that ensure it a central place in the field of intergroup relations. First, RCT is group-oriented and has led to research that deals with genuine group interactions and intergroup processes. The classic example of this is Sherif's (1966) experiments, whose importance is derived mainly from their truly intergroup nature. Second, RCT makes logical sense and conforms to our everyday understanding about why there might be conflict between groups. That is, it makes intuitive sense that groups with real conflicts of material interests should experience greater potential conflict than groups whose material interests do not conflict.

However, RCT and the research it has stimulated tend also to have a number of weaknesses that should be mentioned. These weaknesses concern (1) the definition of conflict; (2) the assumption that all conflict is bad; (3) the treatment of minority groups; (4) the subjects typically used in research stimulated by RCT; (5) lack of concern for open groups; (6) the neglect of power as an issue; and (7) the emphasis upon psychological solutions to problems arising out of material conflicts of interest. We shall briefly review each of these weaknesses in turn.

First, the area of conflict research is plagued with the problem of defining conflict. At one extreme, "realistic conflict" has meant competition for points between subjects who have just been introduced to each other and are taking part in brief experimental games, while at the other extreme, it has meant a life-and-death struggle between nations, with the possibility of atomic war as the outcome. Clearly, when interpretations of conflict and its mode of operationalization in research are so varied, and particularly when the consequences of conflict are so different—from losing points in a game to suffering an atomic war—extrapolations from one level of analysis to another should be undertaken with great caution.

Second, there has been a tendency in RCT to assume that all conflict is necessarily wrong and must be avoided. This generalization has been accompanied by a tendency to extrapolate from conflict at the interpersonal level to conflict at the intergroup and international levels. In the editorial in the first issue of the *Journal of Conflict Resolution,* in which much of the gaming research is published, the editors say:

> It [conflict] occurs in many different situations: among members of a family, between labour and management, between political parties, and even within a single mind, as well as among nations. Many of the patterns and processes which characterize conflict in one area also characterize it in others. . . . Price wars and domestic quarrels have much the pattern of an arms race. Frustration breeds aggression both in the individual and in the state. . . . (*Journal of Conflict Resolution,* 1957, *1*[1], p. 2)

Very little experimental research has been carried out to test the assumption that "the patterns and processes which characterize conflict in one area also characterize it in others." The meager evidence that exists (for example,

Stephenson & Botherton 1975) suggests that it is an invalid assumption, at least in certain conditions.

While the "peacekeeping" concern to which RCT has led should be applauded, the use of terms such as "war" and "peace" in connection with interpersonal behavior and groups, such as labor and management in industry, can be justly criticized. The subtitle of the *Journal of Conflict Resolution* is *A Quarterly for Research Related to War and Peace,* and the journal was launched in 1957 with the words ". . . by far the most important practical problem facing the human race today is that of international relations—more specifically, the prevention of global war" (*Journal of Conflict Resolution,* 1975, *1*[1], p. 1). In this first issue we find an article by Schelling (1957) titled "Bargaining, Communication and Limited War," and one by Douglas (1957) titled "The Peaceful Settlement of Individual and Intergroup Disputes." In both cases, the implication is that just as peace must be preferred to war at the global level, so harmony must be preferred to conflict at the interpersonal and intergroup level.

However, under certain conditions conflict can surely have constructive and positive consequences. This is particularly true from the perspective of disadvantaged groups. For example, a disadvantaged group experiencing prejudice and exploitation at the hands of an advantaged group might have no choice but to resort to conflict in order to achieve greater equality. To label such conflict "harmful" and to show a bias for peace and harmony in such a situation might be to strengthen the position of the advantaged group, and thus allow the exploitation to continue.

Since war is "wrong" and since humans are rational, thinking beings, it follows that war comes about as a result of judgmental errors. Thus Deutsch talks about the United States "blundering" into the "atrocities and stupidities of the war in Vietnam" (1969a, p. 1087), and about the vicious circle of inaccurate perceptions and misunderstandings that leads to increased destructive conflict (1973). Since human behavior is determined by the world people perceive (Deutsch 1962, p. 101), and since inaccurate perceptions lead to hostility and conflict, the psychologist, as peacemaker, has the task of helping to achieve accurate perceptions and rational thinking. Such accurate, rational thinking would lead humans to give less importance to differences of interest and goals that can be achieved independently, and more priority to superordinate goals.

It is in this connection that the normative and theoretical underpinnings linking the work of Sherif and others (such as Blake et al. 1964) and gaming research become clear. In both instances, the best solution that subjects can achieve—from the perspective of the experimenters—is to perceive that they are better off cooperating than fighting, and to work toward superordinate goals. In the typical gaming research experiment, only when both subjects act cooperatively do they achieve maximum joint rewards. Thus this fits Sherif's definition of superordinate goals. If one subject acts cooperatively and the other competitively, then the cooperative subject is "exploited" and will probably try to retaliate by a competitive move on the next trial. This vicious circle could lead to the destructive conflict Deutsch describes (1973), with negative outcomes for both parties.

A third criticism is that the truly psychological implications of RCT remain unexplored, particularly as they relate to minority groups. Given the presence of real differences of group interests, what are the factors that lead minority groups to perceive themselves as groups with distinct and different interests in some conditions, and not in others? It seems to be the case that in some situations minority groups do perceive themselves to have distinct and different interests, yet their relationship with the majority group remains one of cooperation rather than conflict—despite the absence of perceived superordinate goals. What are the psychological factors influencing this situation? In some conditions, minorities enter into conflict with majorities that are far more powerful and cannot possibly be defeated—what is their rationale and how do they perceive success? These are examples of questions that reflect the psychological implications of RCT, but remain unexplored partly because of the normative approach that makes the assumption that conflict is bad and aims to resolve conflict, while neglecting the real conflicts of interests that are its assumed cause.

While the idea that war is bad and should be avoided is endorsed by most researchers, the notion that all conflict is bad does not receive universal approval (see Plon 1974); nor should it, when we consider the often conflicting interests of minority and majority groups. The present socioeconomic structure in both East and West is such that the allocation of resources among various groups is unequal. Minority groups attempting to improve their position in terms of power, wealth, status, and the like are generally opposed by majority groups, who in turn are attempting to maintain or improve their advantaged position. In this situation, the avoidance of conflict means support for the status quo, and thus the maintenance of majority group superiority. The tendency for researchers to regard intergroup conflict as necessarily wrong and something that should be avoided has, therefore, led to support for majority group interests— although this support is not always explicit or even intended.

Social psychologists have tended to study intergroup processes, such as those concerning conformity and social influence, from the perspective of the majority. Moscovici (1976, 1981), whose research represents an important exception to this trend, clarifies this issue and points researchers in a new direction.

> The psychology of social influence has, until now, been based on a psychology of conformity . . . . It has been fashioned and considered from the point of view of the majority, authority, and social control. The time is ripe for a new orientation; an orientation towards a psychology of social influence which will also be a psychology of innovation . . . a psychology which will be thought out and fashioned from the point of view of the minority, the deviant, and of social change. (Moscovici 1976, p. 2)

However, in practice this "new orientation" has had negligible influence on research. The small upsurge of interest in minority group strategies (see Mugny 1984) that came about during the late 1960s and 1970s was probably influenced by the outcome of American involvement in Vietnam. The determined policy of North Vietnam, in its long war against the French and then the United States, and the final withdrawal of the United States from South Vietnam, dramatically illustrated what a minority could achieve in the face of a relatively powerful majority group. However, the end of the Vietnam war and the thawing of American-Soviet relations in the 1980s seem to have shifted the research spotlight once again from minority-majority behavior to relations between groups with fairly similar resources—as when Sherif carried out his classic intergroup experiments on equal-power groups at the height of the "cold war."

A fourth point is that the subjects in gaming experiments are typically undergraduate students, while the persons who participate in the vicious circle of threat and counterthreat at the international level are national leaders. Deutsch's tendency to extrapolate from the results of gaming experiments to the context of international relations can be criticized on the grounds of sampling procedures: the populations from which subjects are selected are very different from the populations to which the experimental results are applied. In order to achieve results that can be used to interpret the actions taken by key decision makers, subjects should be selected from the population of key decision makers. This criticism applies less to Sherif, who has been far more careful in interpreting and going beyond his experimental results. However, in assessing Sherif's intergroup research, we should keep in mind that he used schoolboys aged 11–12 as subjects. This population is probably exceptional in its inclinations toward intergroup competitiveness, since a major part of school and social life for this age group of boys in North America consists of teamwork and team competitions.

A fifth critical point is that Sherif's findings would probably have proved even more insightful if the groups involved had been open, rather than closed, so that they had an exit option. This would have increased the parallel with real-life situations, where one of the options open to people is to drop out and actively rebel against the system and its competitive "games." As we noted in Chapter 1, the tendency has been for researchers to neglect the exit option and to include only closed groups in their experimental studies.

A sixth criticism is that the almost exclusive concern of researchers on groups with equal power has been accompanied by a neglect of power as a subject for social psychological study (for a review of some exceptions, see Ng 1980, 1982). However, although differences of intergroup power have received negligible research attention, power differences between group members are, at least implicitly, central to the research. Much gaming research, particularly that concerned with bargaining behavior, attempts to illuminate the processes

involved when group leaders, such as heads of governments and representatives of labor and management, meet to negotiate their differences in a
realistic conflict situation. These leaders have the power to take decisions on
behalf of their group members; also, their status and influence tend to be
higher than those of other group members.

Finally, while offering a materialistic account of why conflicts arise, RCT
has led to research that offers psychological solutions for resolving conflict.
Although real conflicts of interests are assumed to be the cause of conflict, the
resolution of conflict is seen to come about best by changes in the perceptions
of the conflicting parties, so that they view superordinate goals to be their
priority. Thus, the conflicts of interests that led to the conflict in the first place
need not be removed in order for peaceful relations to be achieved, but they
must be superseded by superordinate goals.

CONCLUSION

RCT has probably influenced social psychological research on intergroup
behavior more than any other theory. This influence is constructive in that it
has led social psychologists, who tend to ignore the larger social context of the
individual's behavior, to focus attention on real conflicts of interests as "the"
source of conflict. The concern to prevent global war, which inspired much of
both fieldwork and experimental gaming research guided by RCT, is to be applauded. The resolution of international conflict is undoubtedly an important
applied task for social psychologists. But putting an end to exploitation is
arguably an even more important task, especially if we adopt the premise that
conflict arises out of real conflicts of interests. Disadvantaged, exploited
groups have real conflicts of interests with advantaged, exploiting groups, and
thus there is a great need to carry out more research from their perspectives
rather than the perspectives of the majority.

SUGGESTED READINGS

Axelrod, R. 1984. *The Evolution of Cooperation.* New York: Basic Books.
Blake, R. R., H. A. Shepard, and J. S. Mouton. 1964. *Managing Intergroup Con-
flict in Industry.* Houston: Gulf.
Deutsch, M. 1973. *The Resolution of Conflict.* New Haven: Yale University
Press.
Sherif, M. 1966. *Group Conflict and Cooperation: Their Social Psychology.* London:
Routledge & Kegan Paul.

4 Social Identity Theory

Scope: Social identity theory is concerned with all aspects of relations between groups, especially groups having unequal power. The theory attempts to predict the conditions in which people will feel motivated, individually or collectively, to maintain or change their group membership and their intergroup situation.

Assumptions: A major assumption is that individuals are motivated to maintain or achieve a positive self-identity. In the context of groups, this implies belonging to groups that enjoy high status.

Propositions: People make social comparisons between their own group and other groups in order to determine the extent to which their own group provides them with a distinct and positive social identity. Where this process leads to a negative social identity, dissatisfaction arises. However, such dissatisfaction will lead to attempts to change the intergroup situation only where cognitive alternatives are perceived; that is, where the existing intergroup situation is perceived as unstable or unjust. Where such conditions are met, group members will take individual or collective actions in order to improve their social identity.

Social identity theory, as described mainly by Tajfel and Turner (1979), attempts to explain intergroup relations from a group perspective. This characteristic sets it apart from a number of other major social psychological theories that have been applied to explain intergroup relations but were not originally developed for this purpose. As implied by the name given to the theory, "social identity," its central concept is defined as ". . . that part of an individual's self-concept which derives from his knowledge of his membership of a social group (or groups) together with the value and emotional significance attached to that membership" (Tajfel 1978a, p. 63). The theory assumes that people desire to have a positive social identity. This desire will influence individuals to make social comparisons, between their own group and other groups, in order to achieve both a favorable and a distinct position for their own group. Thus, social identity theory is first and foremost a psychological theory. That is, it attempts to explain intergroup behavior through referring to psychological processes such as social identity, social comparison, and psychological distinctiveness.

Social identity theory approaches intergroup behavior from the subjective perspective of group members, and this strictly psychological approach leads to an emphasis on how people interpret the social world. For example, social identity theory assumes a person to be part of a group when he or she identifies with that group, rather than when some "objective" criterion or criteria for group membership have been met. This approach is simple and intuitively appealing. For example, a French-speaking person might have a high level of social interaction ("objective" criterion for group membership) with Anglophones and a lower level of social interaction with his or her own group, Francophones. Such a person might, nevertheless, perceive himself or herself to be, or identify himself or herself as, a Francophone. There are many instances where the identification of an individual with a group is not necessarily predictable or explainable through referring only to "objective" criteria; rather, reference also has to be made to the subjective perceptions of the individual.

The idea that people desire to belong to groups that have distinct and positive identities also makes good sense intuitively. This central proposition from social identity theory was developed by European social psychologists, and the theory can be used to understand how social psychology in Europe developed and why it developed the way it did. Appreciating the development of social psychology in Europe is important here, for it provides insights into certain concepts that are central to social identity theory.

European social psychology has aimed to define itself as a discipline, distinct from the social psychology of North America and more reflective of European social concerns and intellectual traditions. The movement took shape in the late 1960s, and its first practical outcomes were the establishment of the European Association of Experimental Social Psychology (1969), the *European*

Journal of Social Psychology (1971), and the European Monographs in Social Psychology (1971). A key figure, and perhaps the most influential member of this movement, was Henri Tajfel, whose research team at Bristol University in England has been responsible for developing social identity theory. However, we should also record the contributions of a number of other European social psychologists to the development of social identity theory. For example, Doise (1978), from the University of Geneva, contributed in important ways to the early development of the theory. Tajfel edited a two-volume appraisal of progress in European social psychology (1984) before his death, and in this way recorded the advances made in European social psychology as a distinct discipline (for a review of the history of European social psychology, see Jaspers 1986).

Among the important European intellectual traditions that influenced the development of European social psychology and, subsequently, social identity theory, were the concern for evaluating phenomena within the wider social context in which they occur, and the tendency to view society as forces in conflict rather than in cohesion. The first of these led to the attempt to "make social psychology truly social," while the latter led to a move away from what has been described as the social psychology of the "nice person" (Moscovici 1972, p. 18), to a social psychology of competing individuals and groups struggling to enhance their own position in the context of changing social conditions.

It is not coincidental that the movement toward a European social psychology took shape in the late 1960s, at a time when radical political forces were so influential. The year 1968 has been compared with 1848, when revolutionary fervor swept through Europe and the established order in many countries was seriously challenged through ideological and violent means. When the plenary conference of the European Association of Experimental Social Psychology was held at the University of Louvain in Belgium in the spring of 1969, the concern many participants showed for seeking new paths of research and theorizing was, as Tajfel noted (1972a, p. 2), probably influenced by the recent student revolution. Just as students in many countries, particularly France, embarked upon pitched battles with an establishment they saw as corrupt and exploitative, so they challenged their teachers and demanded that science, particularly social science, be explicit in its ideology and "relevant" to the major problems of the day, such as social inequality and exploitation.

As Moscovici, another key figure in the development of European social psychology, explained:

> Our disciplines do not appear to the younger generation as disinterested and objective as we claim them to be. They have taken it upon themselves to remind us of the ideological implications of

what we do and its role in the preservation of the established order, as well as the absence of social criticism in our work. They blame us for finding refuge in methodology under the pretext that using adequate methods is equivalent to scientific investigation. We assert that our interest is in the problems of society. They answer that we calmly ignore social inequalities, political violence, wars, underdevelopment or racial conflict. As far as they are concerned, we are safely ensconced in the "establishment." (1972, p. 21)

In responding to this challenge, European social psychologists were motivated to evolve a distinct identity for themselves vis-à-vis North American social psychology, which had the image of being "Establishment"-oriented and biased toward the status quo.

The two most important features of North American social psychology against which the new European social psychology "rebelled" were the tendency to adopt reductionist explanations, and the adoption of models that describe people as rational and living in cohesion. The concern for studying phenomena within the context in which they exist and providing explanations that incorporate the qualities of both the part and the whole can be traced directly to Hegel. Although some North American researchers have been influenced by this approach (see Caplan and Nelson 1973; Ittelson 1973; Ittelson, Proshansky, Rivlin & Winkel, 1974, for example), North American social psychology has tended to be unaffected by it in practice.

European social psychologists aimed to achieve a distinctly different approach by focusing on the individual within the context of broad social change, so that the "social" aspects of social psychology would be given relatively greater importance, and both the part (individual) and the whole (society) could be incorporated into the model developed. Thus, Tajfel states: "Ideally, the central issue of social psychology should be the study of psychological processes accompanying, determining, and determined by social change" (1972a, p. 4). This incorporation of wider social processes also involved an emphasis on intergroup behavior, not through reductionist approaches that focus on intra- and interpersonal behavior, but through models that deal with intergroup processes as such. The mood of Western societies in the late 1960s and the sometimes intense intergroup clashes taking place within them is undoubtedly part of the reason for the emergence of this new approach.

The widespread radical movements of the late 1960s presented social psychologists with a view that showed humankind as being neither cohesive, peaceful, nor rational, and could not be adequately explained by the model of humankind offered by major North American social psychological theories. European social psychologists increasingly felt the need to develop concepts that more accurately reflected the discord and conflict present in society. Writing about this period, Moscovici said:

I encountered . . . difficulties with some of the maxims implicit in a good deal of current research: "we like those who support us"; "the leader is a person who understands the needs of the members of his group"; "we help those who help us"; "understanding the point of view of another person promotes cooperation." This "social psychology of the nice person" was to me then—as it still is today—offensive in many ways; it had little relevance to what I know or had experienced. Its implicit moral stand reminded me of another maxim (which is perhaps not as controversial as it appears): "it is better to be healthy and rich than to be ill and poor." I know from my own social experiences that we seek out those who differ from us and that we can identify with them; that we can love someone who is contemptuous of us; that leaders may impose themselves on others through violence and through following unremittingly their own ideas—and that often, in doing this, they are not only admired but also loved; and that, after all, is it not an opponent who often comes to know us best? (1972, pp. 18–19)

In expressing these views, Moscovici seems to have been reflecting a general concern among a group of very influential European social psychologists for a move toward a model of humankind that is more reflective of the harsher realities of life, and that is also concerned with change and conflict at the intergroup level.

In contrast with the focus on individual mobility entailed in North American social psychology, the movement toward a European social psychology has placed relatively greater emphasis on social change involving groups struggling to enhance their position vis-à-vis other groups. This change of emphasis has been made partly on ideological grounds, since it is the North American capitalist ideology that has been viewed as being, at least partly, responsible for the preoccupation of social psychology with competition and conflict at the level of the individual, and a neglect of competition and conflict at the level of groups, such as ethnic groups and social classes.

Our outline of social identity theory in this chapter begins not with the central concepts but, rather, with the experiments from which the theory grew. Tajfel's early research on the categorization of nonsocial stimuli and the work at Bristol on social categorization are described in some detail. This is followed by a discussion of four concepts that are central to social identity theory: social categorization, social identity, social comparison, and psychological group distinctiveness. We have chosen this particular sequence because this is precisely how events evolved: a striking set of findings from a series of experiments led to the formulation of a broadly based theory of intergroup relations.

The scope of social identity theory is quite extensive in comparison with other social psychological theories of intergroup behavior. The theory attempts to deal with the whole range of responses that disadvantaged group members might make in trying to improve their individual and group positions. The extensive scope of the theory becomes clear from the outline of the theory that forms the core of the next section. In order that the structure of the theory may become clearer, a flowchart of the behavior paths predicted by the theory is also presented.

Finally, examples of typical research studies that set out to test aspects of social identity theory are presented. Our aim has not been to provide an extensive review, but to outline illustrative examples. This discussion is in two main parts. In the first, experiments testing the original findings of Tajfel, Flament, Billig, and Bundy (1971) using the minimal group paradigm are reported. In the second, examples of field and experimental research testing some other predictions of social identity theory are discussed. The concluding section contains a critical evaluation of social identity theory.

AN OUTLINE OF SOCIAL IDENTITY THEORY

Tajfel's Early Work on Categorization

Much of Tajfel's early work was on the cognitive basis of categorization, using nonsocial stimuli. His most lasting contribution to social psychology may be his elaboration of certain continuities, from the nonsocial to the social setting, of a number of consequences of categorization. In explaining the nature of these continuities, it is useful first to clarify the functions of categorization, then proceed to explain in some detail an example of the experiments Tajfel carried out on the categorization of nonsocial stimuli. We conclude this section by clarifying how the experiments using nonsocial stimuli are linked to the later work on social categorization and intergroup behavior carried out by Tajfel, Turner, and others at Bristol.

The Categorization of Nonsocial Stimuli. The categorization process has the function of organizing in fundamental ways the information we acquire from the environment. People actively select information from the environment and simplify the task of processing it by ignoring certain dissimilarities and giving priority to, or exaggerating, certain similarities between objects. This process orients and assists our actions. For example, if we are camping and we need a hammer with which to knock tent pegs into the ground, we might start searching for any hard object, such as a piece of wood or a stone, to serve our purpose. During our search we may ignore many dissimilarities that objects may have, such as what they are made of or their shape, and concentrate on those qualities which would make them equivalent to one another for the purpose of hammering a tent peg. That is, there are certain features that objects should have in order to fit into our category of "objects that can serve the purposes of a hammer." By ignoring those characteristics that are irrelevant to it, we are speeding up our search enormously. This process leads to our simplifying the environment, a simplification that is essential if we are to be able to process effectively, and act upon, the potentially endless amount of information available to us. While there are contradictory accounts of how information is processed (compare Bruner, Goodman, and Austin 1956 with Neisser 1967, for example), the highly important role that categorization plays in this process is generally agreed upon.

Through a series of experiments (Tajfel 1957, 1959; Tajfel & Wilkes 1963), Tajfel developed the idea that the categorization of nonsocial stimuli leads to perceived uniformity within individual categories and distinctiveness between them. In one experiment (Tajfel & Wilkes 1963), the stimuli used were a series of eight lines that differed in length by a constant ratio. Subjects were asked to estimate the length of each line in turn. There were three experimental conditions. For subjects in condition 1, the four shorter lines were labeled A, and the four longer lines were labeled B. For subjects in condition 2, the lines were randomly assigned to A and B. In condition 3, the lines were presented without labels.

The series of eight lines was presented to subjects a number of times in successive random orders. Subjects in condition 1, therefore, became increasingly familiar with the relationship between labels and lengths of lines. Results showed that they exaggerated the differences in lengths between categories A and B considerably more than those in the two control groups. Also, as the subjects in condition 1 became more familiar with the relationship between the lengths of lines and labels (A and B), they further exaggerated the differences between the categories. There was also a tendency for subjects in condition 1 to judge the lines within each category to be more similar to one another than did the subjects in the other two conditions.

The Categorization of Social Stimuli. There seem to be certain outcomes of the categorization process that are present both when the stimuli categorized are social and when they are nonsocial. These "continuities" link Tajfel's earlier work on the categorization of nonsocial stimuli and his later work on social categorization and intergroup behavior. Categorizing people does, however, have some unique properties.

In categorization experiments using nonsocial stimuli, subjects do not necessarily relate to the categories through reference to a system of norms and values. For example, in the Tajfel and Wilkes (1963) experiment, the eight lines did not have social significance for the subjects, and subjects did not act upon any system of social norms and values when estimating their lengths. However, if the stimuli used in a categorization experiment were social, then the subjects would be linked to them through values and norms. For example, if subjects were given the task of grouping various other people into different categories, then the choices they made might depend on the values they ascribed to these various others. A subject who was racially prejudiced probably would not place white others in the same group as blacks because of the different values he or she ascribed to blacks and whites.

Another factor that intervenes when subjects are asked to categorize people is that they sometimes identify with certain of the people they are categorizing, and their own statuses thus become affected by the choices they make. For example, if we take the case of the racially prejudiced white person, when grouping black and white others, such a person would identify with the white group and any racial mixing that took place would, from that person's perspective, negatively affect his or her status. Such a person would try to make sure not to mistakenly place any blacks in the white group, with which he or she identifies. This concern with racial purity has been evident in various societies, the classic examples being Nazi Germany and present-day South Africa. Pettigrew, Allport, and Barnett (1958) used an innovative experimental method to demonstrate this type of behavior in the context of South Africa.

Pettigrew et al. (1958) presented pairs of photographs of faces and asked subjects to identify the race of each. The subjects were Afrikaners, English-speaking whites, Coloreds, Indians, and Africans. Through using the perceptual phenomenon of binocular rivalry, which was caused in this case by showing a picture of a different face to each eye, considerable uncertainty was introduced into the task of recognizing the race or ethnic group of each face. The Afrikaner subjects (the dominant group in South Africa, who assume themselves to be racially superior) showed much greater caution in placing faces in the European category, and a greater tendency to place faces in the "extreme" group of African rather than the "neutral" group of Colored or Indian. It seems that, rather than risking one of the non-Europeans slipping through and endangering the purity of their own white group, the Afrikaners preferred to adopt a strategy of overexclusion from the European group and overinclusion in the African group. They were, it seems, acting to achieve as clear-cut a distinction as possible between their own group, which they assumed to be high-status, and low-status others. They achieved this distinction by using the extreme category of African more often, so that the categories which fall between African and European (Coloreds and Indians) became less populated.

The experiment by Pettigrew et al. (1958) demonstrates in a rather dramatic manner two points we wish to clarify at this stage: first, when people are grouping other people, values and norms influence their choices, and second, when the person making choices is identified with one of the groups, his or her own status is affected by the outcomes of the groupings. When this identification takes place, there seems to be a tendency to try to achieve intergroup distinctiveness.

The prejudiced behavior of subjects in the study conducted by Pettigrew et al. (1958) took place in a context rich with social norms and values. But what would be the minimum conditions required for subjects to show a desire for intergroup differentiation? For example, if the subjects did now know the identity of others they were categorizing, but only that some of these others belong to the same group as themselves, and some belong to different groups, how would they react? Would this be a sufficient basis for subjects to identify with their own group, and try to differentiate between it and the other groups? As we saw from our discussion of realistic conflict theory in Chapter 3, the usual conditions for intergroup conflict include two groups that are clearly categorized according to some important value dimensions and that have a history of competition and confrontation over some important resources. What if these conditions were only minimally met? Following Tajfel and Wilkes's (1963) experiment that used eight lines as stimuli, and found that labeling the four shorter lines A and the four longer ones B leads to inter-category differentiation and perceived intracategory uniformity, would the mere fact that unidentified others are labeled A and B, and the subject is in B (for example), lead to the subject's differentiating between the two categories? These are the kinds of questions that led to the now classic minimal group experiments.

The minimal group experiments on social categorization and intergroup behavior carried out by Tajfel and his associates during the late 1960s and 1970s are simple in design, but complex in the method they adopt for identifying and measuring intergroup bias. These experiments were designed to isolate social categorization as an independent variable and measure its influence, if any, on intergroup behavior. There are two distinct parts to the minimal group experiment: during the first part, social categorization takes place on a trivial criterion and unidentified others are placed in the same category as the subject or in a different one; in the second part, subjects allocate rewards to these others, some of whom are in the same category as themselves.

The method used for assessing intergroup bias in the minimal group paradigm involves a specially designed set of matrices, developed to identify and measure various strategies, such as fairness and in-group favoritism, that people might use in an intergroup context. Alongside these matrices there have developed a set of specialized terms that must be comprehended if the experimental analyses and results are to be understood. In order to clarify the design of the minimal group paradigm and illustrate the mechanisms used to assess intergroup bias, we shall first describe an example of a typical minimal group experiment and then illustrate how the matrices can be used to measure intergroup bias.

Tajfel and his associates set out to define an intergroup situation where two social categories are created but where none of the other conditions usually associated with intergroup conflict are present. That is, for example, none of the conditions associated with realistic conflict as discussed in Chapter 3 should be operating. The criteria they set included the following:

1. There should be no face-to-face interaction whatever between subjects in the in-group, in the out-group, or between groups.
2. Complete anonymity of group membership should be preserved.
3. There should be no instrumental or rational link between the criteria for inter-group categorization and the rewards subjects would allocate to in-group and out-group members.
4. The rewards should not have any utilitarian value for the subject making them.
5. Subjects should be presented with a number of different options in terms of how they allocate rewards to in-group and out-group members. The options should include the following:
    a. Fairness (F)—equal rewards are allocated to in-group and out-group members.
    b. Maximum joint profit (MJP)—rewards are allocated in such a way that there is a maximum payoff for both in-group and out-group members.
    c. Maximum in-group profit (MIP)—rewards are allocated in such a way that the in-group member receives the highest reward possible, independent of what the out-group member receives.
    d. Maximum difference in favor of the in-group (MD)—rewards are allocated in such a way that the difference between what the in-group member receives and what the out-group member receives is greatest in favor of the in-group member.
6. Last but not least, the rewards should be made as important as possible to the subjects. They should consist of real decisions about the distribution of concrete rewards (and/or penalties to others rather than some form of evaluation of others).

The First Minimal Group Experiment. The subjects in the first minimal group experiment (Tajfel 1970; Tajfel, Flament, Billig & Bundy, 1971) were 64 British schoolboys, aged 14–15. The experiment was in two main parts.

The experiment began with subjects doing a dot-estimation task. They were then assigned to one of two conditions, with different instructions. In the neutral condition, subjects were told that findings show that in dot-estimation tasks some people tend to consistently overestimate, while others tend to consistently underestimate the number of dots, but these tendencies are unrelated to accuracy. In the value condition, subjects were told that some people are consistently more, and some less, accurate at dot-estimation. It was hypothesized that greater in-group favoritism would occur in the value than in the neutral condition.

In part 2, subjects were told that the experimenter wished to take advantage of their presence to conduct an investigation involving a completely different kind of judgment task. For the purpose of convenience, they would be divided into groups on the basis of their performance at dot-estimation. In fact, however, the division of subjects into groups was done on a random basis. Subjects were told their group membership privately and were not aware of the group membership of others. Next, subjects in the neutral condition were told that they would be assigned to a group on the basis of whether they underestimated or overestimated the number of dots. Those in the value condition were told that groups would be formed on the basis of dot-estimation accuracy. The more accurate would be in one group and the less accurate in another.

The second judgment task required subjects to allocate rewards to in-group and out-group members. This amounted to allocating rewards and penalties, in real money, to others who were identified only by code numbers. Subjects were taken to separate cubicles, informed privately of their own group identity, then instructed on the format for making allocations.

The most important aspects of the allocations made by subjects in this first experiment were the following:

1. On no occasion would subjects be rewarding or penalizing themselves; their choices determined only the outcomes of others.
2. They would know only the group identity, and not the personal identity, of the individuals they were rewarding.
3. The amount of money each person received would depend on how much others had rewarded him or her.
4. Everyone was guaranteed a standard sum of money for taking part in the experiment.
5. There were three types of allocation decisions:
   (a) subjects were allocating for two members of the in-group other than themselves;
   (b) subjects were allocating for two members of the out-group; (c) subjects were allocating for a member of the in-group, other than themselves, and a member of the out-group.

The results of this experiment demonstrated that when subjects were faced with a choice between an in-group member and an out-group member, they favored the in-group at the expense of the out-group. That is, they endorsed a combination of MD and MIP strategies most often. The nature of this discrimination did not differ significantly between the two (value and neutral) conditions. On the choices where subjects were giving rewards to two out-group members or two in-group members, they showed no bias and instead endorsed the "fair" option most often.

On the basis of the discrimination showed by the subjects, which favored the in-group and was biased against the out-group, Tajfel and his associates concluded that group formation and discriminatory intergroup behavior had developed as a result of social categorization per se, without the presence of any of the normal conditions associated with intergroup bias.

Extensions of the Basic Minimal Group Findings. By the mid-1970s considerable evidence had been gathered to support the proposition that social categorization per se, as far as it could be isolated experimentally, can, under certain conditions, be a sufficient basis for intergroup discrimination (for example, Allen & Wilder 1975; Billig 1973; Billig & Tajfel 1973; Doise, Csepeli,

Dann, Gouge, Larsen & Ostell, 1972; Tajfel 1974a; Tajfel et al. 1971; Turner 1975). In explaining these findings, Tajfel and his associates emphasize social categorization and social comparison processes as the psychological processes "intrinsic to or stimulated merely by ingroup-outgroup divisions which tend to create discriminatory social relations" (Turner 1981, p. 77). However, among the features of the minimal group paradigm that we need to examine more closely are the relative importance of self versus group interests and the importance of the "trivial" basis for social categorization.

An important question that arises with respect to the minimal group paradigm is to what extent subjects in experiments are showing bias toward self-interest rather than group interest. This issue was not tested by Tajfel et al. (1971) because subjects were placed in a position where they could reward only the in-group or the out-group directly; there was no opportunity to reward the self directly. However, a number of studies were later carried out to test the relative importance of self versus group interests in the minimal group context (Turner 1975, 1978a; Turner, Brown & Tajfel, 1979).

In the first experiment (Turner 1975, 1978a), subjects first indicated their degree of liking for a set of pictures. Similarity between subjects was defined in terms of these aesthetic preferences. In the second part of the experiment, subjects awarded money to others, using the Tajfel matrices. There were three conditions. In condition 1, the control condition, there was no explicit mention of groups by the experimenter. Subjects would allocate rewards to themselves and similar/dissimilar others (similarity was on the basis of picture preferences). Each person was to receive all the money allocated to himself or herself. In condition 2, subjects were ostensibly categorized on the basis of similarity (on picture preferences). They made choices for themselves and others, the others being in-group and out-group members. Each person was to receive all the money awarded to himself or herself. In condition 3, subjects were ostensibly categorized into two groups on the basis of similarity (on picture preferences). However, they were told they would receive an equal share of the money their in-group received.

Thus, in condition 1 there was no categorization; in condition 2 there was categorization, but the individual could reward himself or herself directly; in condition 3 there was categorization, but the individual could not reward himself or herself directly (only the in-group could be rewarded). The results demonstrated that whenever possible, subjects were biased toward themselves. Only in the third condition, where self-interest was directly linked to that of the group, was there in-group favoritism. The predictions of how subjects would like others, if their identities were revealed, also showed that there was in-group favoritism only in condition 3.

The same trend of bias toward the self, rather than the in-group, was found by Turner in a second experiment (1975, 1978a). However, this bias was modified when subjects first allocated money to in-group and out-group members, and afterward had the chance to allocate rewards to themselves directly. It seems that when subjects had the chance to act in terms of group membership, they developed some level of loyalty to the in-group; this meant they were prepared to make sacrifices and modify their bias toward the self in order to reward the whole group. However, their basic self-bias persisted.

On the same theme, Turner et al. (1979) tested the hypothesis that subjects would be willing, to some degree, to sacrifice group and personal monetary profit in order to achieve positive group distinctiveness. Results reveal that some degree of sacrifice was made in the predicted manner, but that the trend of bias toward the self found by Turner (1975, 1978a) still existed.

These findings are of fundamental importance, since they seem to indicate that subjects have a preference for improving the position of the self, although the strength of this bias can be modified when group loyalty develops. This kind of behavior seems to be present in real work settings when individual workers agree to place the interests of an entire labor union ahead of their individual interests, and move toward better working conditions through collective action. That is, instead of aiming for rewards that might benefit them more individually, workers are influenced by group loyalty and agree to make their individual demands subservient to collective needs.

Minimal group studies have typically involved groups with equal power, in that the allocation of rewards has been undertaken by members of different groups with equal power (see Ng 1980). Such equality among groups is a rare phenomenon in real intergroup settings. A series of experiments by Ng (1982) on groups with unequal power suggests that members of majority groups tend to discriminate more than members of minority or equal power groups. While the experiments by Ng (1982) did not meet the criteria of the minimal group paradigm, Sachdev and Bourhis (1984, 1985) conducted a series of experiments specifically to explore the independent effects of power differences between groups on patterns of intergroup behavior in the minimal group paradigm. Their findings support those of Ng (1982) in that members of dominant groups were more discriminating. However, they also found that discrimination by "high power" groups (not having total control) was more extreme than discrimination by "absolute power" groups (having absolute control). However, the absolute power groups were more discriminating than "no power" and "low power" group members, and at least as discriminating as the "equal power" groups. The "absolute power" group seemed to be more secure in their positive social identity, and thus more willing to allow out-groups to "bask in the glow" of their positive identity. An example of this kind of "benevolent paternalism" in real life might be the upper-class members of the white Anglo-Saxon Protestant (WASP) majority in North America who show liberal attitudes toward ethnic minorities, whereas lower-class WASPs tend to show relatively more negative prejudice toward ethnic minorities (Lambert & Taylor 1986).

The "Trivial" Basis of Social Categorization in the Minimal Group Paradigm

An important aim of Tajfel and his associates was to minimize the importance of the criteria used as the basis for social categorization in the minimal group paradigm. Criteria typically used as a basis for social categorization have been performance on a dot-estimation task (Tajfel 1970) and aesthetic preferences (Turner 1975). These have been referred to by Tajfel as being "unimportant" (Tajfel 1978d, p. 439) and "trivial" (Tajfel 1978c, p. 77), and similar descriptions have been used by Turner (1981, p. 75). However, it needs to be appreciated that in this context such terms as "trivial" and "unimportant" are not correct in a literal sense. In terms of the influence that they have on intergroup behavior, such criteria cannot be said to be "trivial" or "unimportant," since they are sufficient to evoke strong and consistent intergroup bias. Indeed, there is evidence to suggest that the effect of such criteria can be as powerful as "important" criteria in the context of the minimal group paradigm (Moghaddam & Stringer 1986).

Moghaddam and Stringer (1986) tested the hypothesis that there would be no difference between the influence of two criteria of different real-world importance when each is used independently as the only criterion for social categorization in the same minimal group setting. In condition 1, social categorization was on the basis of a dot-estimation task, a "minimal" criterion. In condition 2, social categorization was on the basis of the participants' schoolhouse system, a highly important criterion from the perspective of participants. Results showed that while participants in both conditions were biased toward the in-group, supporting the findings of Tajfel et al. (1971), there was no significant difference between the levels of bias shown across conditions. The profound impact of social categorization is underlined by the findings.

This finding is in line with evidence from field studies which suggest that individuals will ascribe importance to what may be in most contexts a "trivial" phenomenon and exaggerate certain characteristics of their in-group or of relevant out-groups in order to achieve a clearer and more meaningful basis upon which to differentiate between themselves and others. From anthropological studies it is apparent that the boundaries of ethnic groups are sometimes objectively blurred, but subjectively perceived as distinct and prominent, in order to preserve and legitimize a certain status hierarchy. For example, Maquet (1961) reports that in Ruanda, the height difference between two major groups, the Tutsi and the Hutu, were emphasized and exaggerated. This exaggeration helped to achieve intergroup differentiation, and also had certain value connotations. The Tutsi were the dominant group, and their exaggerated height superiority played an important part in defining and maintaining their higher social status. LeVine and Campbell (1972, pp. 81–113) provide a useful review of anthropological evidence on ethnic boundaries that reveals how in many cases the boundaries between ethnic groups can be seen as arbitrary and trivial when viewed objectively, but are ascribed importance in order to play a crucial role in interethnic differentiation.

There are also many examples from modern industrial settings where a criterion for social categorization might seem trivial from the perspective of outsiders, but assumes great importance from the perspective of group members. For example, soccer might be viewed as being "just a game," and the fact that Pat and Mick support different soccer teams might not be of great significance in the work setting. However, when they enter the soccer stadium to support their rival teams, the previously "trivial" basis for social categorization can suddenly become highly important—as demonstrated by the tragic deaths of British and Italian soccer fans at Brussels in June 1985.

FOUR CENTRAL CONCEPTS IN SOCIAL IDENTITY THEORY

> Oh, if I had done nothing simply from laziness! Heavens, how I should have respected myself, then. I should have respected myself because I should at least have been capable of being lazy; there would have been one quality, as it were, positive in me. . . . Question: What is he? Answer: A sluggard; how pleasant it would have been to hear that of oneself! It would mean that I was positively defined . . . I should then be a member of the best club by right, and should find my occupation in continually respecting myself.
>
> Fedor Dostoevsky (1821–81)
> *Notes from the Underground*

The first series of results from experiments using the minimal group paradigm were interpreted by Tajfel and his associates, using the concept of "generic norm" (see Billig 1972; Tajfel et al. 1971). This proposed the presence of a social norm of in-group favoritism that subjects perceived to be relevant to the minimal group situation. However, an explanation based on the concept of generic norm was of little value once the behavior under question became other than simple in-group favoritism. Thus, the need for an explanatory model that could account for more complex behavior patterns in the minimal group and other contexts led to the evolution of social identity theory.

Four major concepts developed out of the minimal group experiments: (1) social categorization, the segmentation of the world so as to impose an order on the environment and provide a locus of identification for the self; (2) social identity, that part of the individual's self-concept which derives from knowledge of his or her membership in a social group, together with the value and emotional significance attached to that membership; (3) social comparison, the process through which characteristics of the in-group are compared to those of the out-group; (4) psychological group distinctiveness, assumed to be the state desired by individuals in which the in-group has an identity that is perceived by the group members as being both distinct and positive vis-à-vis relevant comparison groups. In briefly elaborating upon the intellectual roots of these concepts, we shall argue that psychological group distinctiveness is the most innovative and probably the most important contribution made by social identity theory to social psychology. Since we have already discussed social categorization at some length in the context of the minimal group experiments, we shall not elaborate further on the concept at this stage.

Social Identity

In social identity theory, the knowledge that one belongs to certain groups and the value attached to group membership, in positive and negative terms, represent the individual's social identity. The two essential features of the concept are that group membership is viewed from the subjective perception of the individual, and that the value-laden nature of group membership is highlighted and given importance.

The idea that groups have social values and that one acquires certain values through group membership has influenced research in social psychology since its early days. This is demonstrated, for example, by the early studies reporting the phenomenon of black children devaluing their own group and preferring the white out-group (Lasker 1929), a phenomenon later described as "misidentification." By describing this behavior as "misidentification" (see Milner 1975), researchers are suggesting that subjects are defining their group membership in a way that does not correspond to the material realities of the group situation, with the aim of being part of the high-status out-group. These processes—the subjective structuring of the social environment and the need to belong to a positively valued group—are also incorporated in social identity theory.

In postulating that humankind has a need to achieve a positive social identity, Tajfel and his colleagues were working according to a long accepted idea that people desire to be positively evaluated (Goffman 1963). This desire seems to be responsible for the preference people have been shown to have for favorable rather than accurate evaluations of themselves (Eiser & Smith 1972). People's attitude seems to be "don't tell me the truth about how I am doing, just tell me how well I am doing." It is interesting that much of the critical debate about the "cooperative subject" and "experimenter bias" in the psychology experiment has centered on the assumption that subjects wish to be favorably evaluated by the experimenter (A. G. Miller 1972). Critics of the experimental approach have argued that subjects look for cues in the experimental situation that will tell them what the experimenter expects them to do, then comply with these expectations because they want to be favorably evaluated.

Thus, the basic proposition that individuals are motivated to achieve a positive social identity is supported by evidence from a wide range of studies. Social identity theory has extended this idea to the intergroup level, in order to propose that individuals are motivated to belong to positively evaluated groups. This extension opens the way to explorations of possible behavioral strategies that might be adopted when an individual perceives his or her social identity as inadequate.

Social Comparison

> The only "reality" tests that matter with regard to group character-istics are tests of social reality. The characteristics of one's group as a whole (such as its status, its richness or poverty, its skin color, or its ability to reach its aims) achieve most of their significance in relation to perceived differences from other groups and the value connotation of these differences. (Tajfel 1978a, p. 66)

While the desire for a positive social identity is viewed by social identity theory as the psychological "motor" behind the individual's actions in the intergroup context, the social comparison process is seen as the means through which the individual obtains an assessment of his or her group's social position and status. The role of social comparison as an explanatory concept in social psychology has gained considerable importance since Festinger (1954) introduced his theory of social comparison. Festinger concerned himself only with comparisons of opinions and abilities on which, it was hypothesized, people need to evaluate themselves. The motivation for such evaluations, he argued, was the need to reduce uncertainty and achieve accuracy in self-evaluation.

However, there is an impressive body of evidence to suggest that social comparisons involve much more than opinions and abilities (see Manis 1972, for example). Festinger's assumption that social comparison is a less preferred means of self-evaluation than "objective" comparison, and is used only when objective comparison is not available, is negated by evidence (R. L. Miller 1977). In line with these more recent findings, Tajfel and his associates have assumed a far more extensive range of application for social comparison processes than did Festinger. More specifically, they have asumed that it is through the social comparison process that individuals achieve an understanding of the relative status and value of their own group and, thus, the status and value they acquire through membership in their group. Consequently, Tajfel and his associates have proposed that social comparisons at the intergroup level play an important role in shaping the actions of individuals.

Psychological Group Distinctiveness

As an alternative to the "nice person" model of humankind, European social psychologists could rely upon an intellectual tradition, influenced by Marx and Freud, that presents a model of self-centered, irrational humankind struggling to improve their position in a conflict-based society. Such human beings would show an almost neurotic concern with their own identity, and one of their key traits would be an idiosyncratic view that shows the self in a positive light. The participation of such persons in intergroup life would be characterized by competition rather than cooperation, and by a strong desire to achieve distinctiveness, to stand apart from other groups, rather than to converge and become more similar. In social identity theory it is postulated that group members will desire to achieve an identity for their group that is both distinct from, and positive in comparison with, other groups.

The idea of a need for distinctiveness had already been elaborated in biological and socioeconomic analyses; what social identity theory introduced is the idea of a need for psychological distinctiveness. The concepts "diversification of life-style," "vacant spaces," and "competition," stemming from the work of Darwin and adapted to interpret social life by Durkheim (1960), among others, are part of a general theoretical orientation that shows the processes of competition and innovation leading to greater diversification of life-styles and to the creation or discovery of new "vacant spaces." The influence of this theoretical orientation can be seen in present-day social research (see Lemain and Kastersztein 1971–72). For example, it influenced Mulkay and Turner's (1971) outline of the relationship among overproduction, scarce resources, and innovation in three different social settings: the saints in North African Islam, French painting in the 19th century, and the 20th-century scientific community. The work of Lorenz (1966), which explores the role of aggression in achieving space allocation, is influenced by the same principles.

Ecologists and ethologists, among others, have focused upon the use of material resources, so that the vacant spaces with which they are concerned are principally food and territorial space. However, in social psychology a tendency has developed, fully crystallized in social identity theory, to extend the same principle to include use of social identity and the need for groups to find (or create) vacant (distinct) identities for themselves to occupy. While basic biological needs are seen as a drive behind animals' moving to find the vacant spaces that make food and territory available to them, psychological motives are postulated by social identity theory to be the drive behind attempts by groups to find identities that show them in a distinct and positive light.

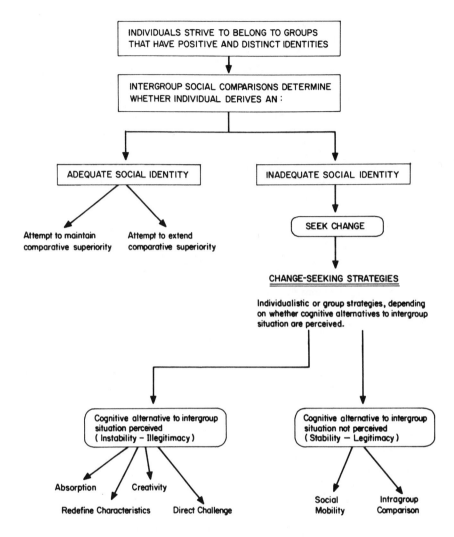

Figure 4.1 Schematic Representation of Social Identity Theory

SCOPE OF SOCIAL IDENTITY THEORY

Social identity theory is fairly extensive in scope, compared with other social psychological theories of intergroup behavior (see Figure 4.1). Specifically, the theory attempts to provide answers to the following questions, some of which have already been addressed in terms of the four key concepts:

1. Why individuals desire to be members of high-status groups.
2. Why individuals desire to belong to groups that have distinct identities.
3. In what conditions group members will act as a group in order to try to change situations with which they are dissatisfied.
4. What strategies group members will adopt in order to improve their group position.
5. In what conditions and through which strategies group members will act individually in order to try to improve their own (individual) position rather than adopt group strategies to try to improve the position of the whole group.

The theory begins with the four basic concepts we have already described. Categorization is conceived of as a basic cognitive tool that allows individuals to structure the social environment and define their place in it. The knowledge that he or she belongs to certain groups and the value attached to group membership, in positive and negative terms, represent the individual's social identity. This component (social identity) forms an important part of the self-concept.

It is hypothesized that individuals wish to belong to groups that compare favorably with, and are distinct from, other groups and that lead to positive evaluations for themselves.

Through intergroup comparisons, individuals will come to view their own group as psychologically distinct and, in relation to relevant comparison groups, they will try to make the in-group more favorable. The attempt to achieve a comparatively superior position for the in-group, on the basis of valued dimensions, is the key factor leading to discriminatory intergroup behavior.

The dynamic nature of this theory becomes apparent when it deals with situations involving potential social change. Change will be desired by individuals whose group membership provides them with inadequate social identity; "inadequate" in this context refers to either a negative social identity or a social identity that is not as positive as one with which the individual is satisfied. Clearly, members of disadvantaged or minority groups will fall into this category. Members of the dominant group will want to maintain or extend their comparatively superior position. Members of the disadvantaged group will wish to achieve some change in the intergroup situation, so that their social identity can be comparatively improved. These contradictory aims result in competition and conflict, with a move by one group being met by reactions from the other group. Since only through social comparison is social identity meaningful, it is the relative position of groups that is important. Therefore, competition and conflict are seen as an essential aspect of the intergroup situation.

THE IMPORTANCE OF COGNITIVE ALTERNATIVES

An inadequate social identity is not by itself enough to motivate a group to change its position. The presence of perceived cognitive alternatives to the existing intergroup situation is required in order that a strategy for achieving social change is embarked upon. Unless members of disadvantaged groups are aware of cognitive alternatives, they will not attempt to act upon their dissatisfactions and change their intergroup situation. For example, during the late 1960s and early 1970s, a number of Third World countries saw the possibility of changing their power relations with the West by using oil as an economic weapon. Once the idea became recognized by other Third World countries, they attempted as a group to organize and to challenge the Western powers, partly by implementing the 1973 oil embargo. Whether such cognitive alternatives are perceived depends upon two factors: the extent to which individuals believe the present intergroup situation can be changed and their position in the hierarchy can be altered (stability–instability), and the extent to which the present intergroup situation and hierarchy are seen as just and fair (legitimacy–illegitimacy).

When a group with an inadequate social identity does perceive cognitive alternatives to the present intergroup situation, any one or a combination of four different strategies for achieving intergroup change may be adopted. First, a group may attempt to be absorbed into the dominant group. This strategy requires fundamental cultural and psychological change to become successful. For example, an immigrant arriving in North America might try to "lose" completely his or her original national/cultural identity and become "an American." A second strategy might be to redefine the previously negatively evaluated characteristic of the group, so that it is now positively evaluated (for instance, "Black is beautiful"). A third strategy involves the creation and adoption of new dimensions for intergroup comparison and evaluation—dimensions that have not previously been used and on the basis of which the group has a greater chance of defining itself more positively. For example, the "native peoples" of Canada might refer to their ancient traditions and cultures, in comparison with which the history of the "new Canada" might seem unimpressive. The fourth strategy involves direct competition with the dominant group. That is, a negatively evaluated group might directly challenge the position of the relatively positively evaluated group or dominant group in the status hierarchy. This strategy is most likely to lead to direct conflicts and clashes. All four strategies, adopted by a group with inadequate social identity, will lead to dominant group(s) members reacting and adopting strategies to maintain or increase their dominance.

When members of disadvantaged groups do not perceive cognitive alternatives to the present intergroup positions, they will do nothing to change their group situation, but may well adopt individualistic strategies to improve their individual positions. An individual may, as one strategy, attempt to exit from the disadvantaged group and join a more positively evaluated group. This is the strategy of social mobility, but it is available only when the group is an open one and exit is available as an option (cf. Hirschman 1970). If exit is not possible because, for example, the individual cannot change his or her skin color, or sex, the individual may choose the strategy of comparing himself or herself with others within his or her own group (see Smith 1985, p. 171). This form of interpersonal intragroup comparison is less likely to lead to unfavorable evaluation of the individual.

SOCIAL MOBILITY AND SOCIAL CHANGE

This account of intergroup behavior places considerable importance on whether the individual perceives social mobility or social change as possible. Social mobility consists of a ". . . subjective structuring of a social system" (however small or large the system may be) in which the basic assumption is that the system is flexible and permeable, that it permits a fairly free movement of the individual particles of which it consists (Tajfel 1974b, p. 5). Social change is at the other extreme:

> . . . the subjective modes of structuring the social system in which the individual lives. It refers basically to his belief that he is enclosed within the walls of the social group of which he is a member; that he cannot move out of his own into another group in order to improve or change his position or his conditions of life; and that therefore the only way for him to change these conditions (or for that matter, to resist the change of these conditions if he is satisfied with them) is together with his group as a whole, as a member of it rather than someone who leaves it. (Tajfel 1974b, pp. 5–6)

Earlier in this chapter, we referred to the ideological reasons for an attempt to develop a European social psychology that places greater emphasis upon intergroup behavior and large-scale social change. The incorporation of the concept of social change reflects this European approach. Social change necessarily involves intergroup confrontation, since one group's efforts to improve its position vis-à-vis the dominant group will be met by a reaction from those attempting to maintain or improve their own relatively favorable position. Social mobility, by contrast, does not threaten the relative position of groups.

STUDIES THAT HAVE TESTED SPECIFIC HYPOTHESES

The development of social identity theory took place after the basic minimal group paradigm had been tried out—indeed, the theory was developed partly to explain the findings of experiments using the minimal group paradigm. After the formal elaboration of the theory, a number of studies were carried out to test specific hypotheses derived from it. However, some research findings seriously challenge a number of the basic propositions of social identity theory. We shall discuss two such examples. First, we discuss the findings of a study by Brown, Wade, Mathews, Condor and Williams (1983) that tested the hypothesis, central to social identity theory, that there should be a positive association between the degree of group identification and the extent of positive intergroup differentiation.

According to social identity theory, the stronger the identification of the individual with the group, the more he or she will attempt to achieve intergroup differentiation. Brown et al. (1983) tested this prediction in three different settings: a bakery, a department store, and a paper mill. The subjects' strength of identification with the in-group was measured, and their attitudes toward other groups in the organization were assessed. On the basis of these attitudinal measurements, indexes of intergroup differentiation were computed and correlated with measures of group identification. Results showed that in different groups within each organization, very different relationships between identification and differentiation emerged, ranging from significantly negative (contradicting the prediction of social identity theory) to significantly positive (as predicted by social identity theory). The overall relationship between strength of identification and intergroup differentiation was only weakly positive. Clearly, a very central assumption entailed in social identity theory is challenged by these findings.

However, not all researchers have interpreted the propositions of social identity theory to mean that strength of identity should necessarily correlate with intergroup differentiation. For example, Smith (1985) has argued that the theory deals mainly with salience and security of social identity in intergroup relations, and he presents a case for viewing salience, security, and strength as distinct constructs. From this perspective, the findings of Brown et al. (1983) do not necessarily contradict the propositions of social identity theory.

Social identity theory proposes that whether disadvantaged group members attempt to adopt group or individualistic strategies to improve their position will depend on the presence, or absence, of cognitive alternatives. When cognitive alternatives do not exist, no possible change in the status quo is conceived. In such situations, members of disadvantaged groups are said to have secure identities (Tajfel 1978b). The presence of cognitive alternatives depends on two factors: perceived legitimacy/illegitimacy and stability/instability. A number of experimental studies have attempted to vary levels of perceived legitimacy and stability in order to test the effects of these variables on intergroup behavior (Caddick 1981; Commins & Lockwood 1979a, 1979b; Turner & Brown 1978). This relationship has also been investigated by field studies (Brown & Williams 1983; Skevington 1980). The findings of the experimental and field studies have not, however, been in agreement. There is evidence from the experimental studies that perceived illegitimacy of the status relationship of two groups leads to intergroup discrimination. However, this finding is not supported by evidence from field research (see Brown & Williams 1983, for example). Also, increased perceived instability does not seem by itself to lead to greater intergroup discrimination (see, for example, Turner & Brown 1978). This evidence seriously challenges important predictions in social identity theory.

CRITICAL REVIEW OF SOCIAL IDENTITY THEORY

Surely a theory should be evaluated not only on the basis of how valid its predictions prove to be, but also on the criterion of how effective it is in stimulating fruitful research. Social identity theory should probably be judged as being more successful on the second criterion, since it has inspired an impressive amount of important research since the mid-1970s (see Tajfel 1978b, 1982a, 1982b for reviews), but certain of its major predictions have been seriously challenged by research findings.

Having been significantly affected by the movement to develop a distinctly European social psychology, the influence of social identity theory has tended to remain confined to Europe, although it began to make some headway in North America by the end of the 1970s (see Austin & Worchel 1979).

Among the positive attributes of this theory, there are two that are probably most important. First, social identity theory is relatively extensive in scope, dealing with a large range of individual and collective responses that disadvantaged group members could make in the position of their group vis-à-vis more advantaged groups (the social mobility-social change continuum). Second, social identity theory has once again placed "identity" as a, if not the, central issue of research on intergroup behavior.

By incorporating the concept of social change, social identity theory has highlighted the important role social psychologists could have in explaining the behavior of the individual in the grand arena of the social order. In particular, the concepts of legitimacy/illegitimacy and stability/instability link the perceptions people have of the social order, and what they are likely to do in the face of these perceived social realities. This link is very important, but almost completely neglected by social psychologists. It bridges the gap between the sociopolitical order and the actions of individuals. For example, if I see the present social order as legitimate and stable, then I am very unlikely to try to change it through intergroup confrontation or any other means. On the other hand, I might very well try to improve my individual position by working toward such things as a better job and a bigger house, and thus effectively work to strengthen the present social order.

An important issue referred to in passing by social identity theory is where the individual gets his or her perceptions of legitimacy and stability. Social identity theory makes passing reference to ideology to answer this question, the idea being that the dominant ideology will influence the perceptions that people have in terms of legitimacy and stability. The strength of social identity theory is that it leads us at least to raise such issues, although to date it does not provide satisfactory answers to them.

Apart from the fact that some of its major assumptions seem to be challenged by research evidence, social identity theory has a number of other limitations that we should address. First, it fails to specify the priorities individuals will have in deciding what to do in the intergroup context. To clarify this point, it is useful to refer to the flowchart of the major behavior paths predicted by the theory (Figure 4.1). A number of particular strategies are set out, but at each stage there is no indication of whether the individual will show a priority for one strategy or another. For example, we reviewed experimental evidence (Turner 1975 1978a; Turner et al. 1979) suggesting that when subjects are given a chance to reward the self directly in the intergroup setting, they will show bias toward the self, although this bias will be modified if they first make allocations to other in-group and out-group members. Given this finding, and given the individualistic, competitive nature of modern societies, particularly Western capitalist societies, we could argue that individuals will always show a priority for adopting individualistic rather than group strategies for improving their position. This could be the case regardless of whether cognitive alternatives exist. However, social identity theory does not incorporate such a leaning toward this perhaps more realistic individual mobility strategy.

To give another example of the need to specify priorities with respect to the strategies, if an individual is part of a group wanting to adopt group strategies to achieve social change, what he or she will do will depend largely on what his or her priorities are with respect to the strategies available for action (such as absorption, redefine characteristics, creativity, direct challenge). It is not enough simply to specify the strategies available and, in some cases, to go further and specify the prerequisites for being able to adopt such strategies; it is also necessary to specify how motivated people are to adopt each strategy relative to other available strategies. The priorities of individuals in the intergroup context need to be clarified.

The theory would be strengthened if it were extended to deal with another important kind of social mobility: that on a purely psychological level. It may be recalled that, according to social identity theory, when an individual does not perceive cognitive alternatives to the existing intergroup situation, and at the same time has an inadequate social identity, the individual may attempt to change his or her individual situation through social mobility—that is, by moving out of the present in-group and trying to get into a higher-status group, which would lead the individual to acquire a more adequate social identity. If exit from the group is not possible, then the theory predicts that intragroup social comparisons will take place, so that the individual can try to achieve adequate social identity through this means. However, in many cases, minority group members may not be able to leave the ingroup physically but may be doing this on a purely psychological level. The "misidentification" of black children with the white outgroup is a classic example of this kind of exit (see Milner 1975).

CONCLUSION

Social identity theory focuses on social psychological processes to explain intergroup behavior, defining the group in terms of the person's perceptions of group membership. It is a theory dealing with extensive ranges of behavior, from social mobility to social change. In all these features, it is fairly distinctive as a social psychological theory of intergroup behavior. However, partly because this theory evolved as part of a European social psychology, its influence in North America has remained relatively limited. The dynamism of this theory, its truly psychological nature, together with the impressive body of research it is stimulating, will ensure that its influence will spread to North America.

SUGGESTED READINGS

Tajfel, H. 1970. Experiments in intergroup discrimination. *Scientific American*, *223* (5), 96–102.

———. (ed.). 1982b. *Social Identity and Intergroup Relations*. Cambridge: Cambridge University Press.

Tajfel, H., and J. C. Turner. 1979. An integrative theory of intergroup behavior. In W. G. Austin and S. Worchel (eds.), *The Social Psychology of Intergroup Relations*, pp. 33–47. Monterey, Calif.: Brooks/Cole.

5   Equity Theory

Scope: Equity theory deals mainly with relations between individuals, but has implications for both advantaged and disadvantaged groups in the context of intergroup relations. Equity theory specifies the conditions associated with intergroup conflict and offers hypotheses about how these might be resolved.

Assumptions: A fundamental assumption is that individuals strive to maximize rewards for themselves. However, in pursuit of this end, individuals learn that they must conform to certain norms of justice in their dealings with others.

Propositions: Equity theory proposes that people strive for justice in their relationships and feel distressed when they perceive injustice. A relationship is judged to be just when the ratio of one group's inputs and outcomes are equal to those of the other involved in the relationship. Where the ratios are unequal, psychological distress will be experienced by both groups, and steps will be taken to restore justice by actually or psychologically adjusting the inputs and outcomes of one or both groups in the relationship.

In this chapter we will be focusing on equity theory, the most prominent of a number of theories that deal with justice in human relationships. Why a chapter on justice when the theme of the present volume is intergroup relations? Whenever minority or disadvantaged groups in a society take action, there is a persistent theme in the accompanying rhetoric. Phrases such as "our fundamental rights have been violated," "the treatment we receive is unfair," and "we have legitimate claims" are typical. In short, justice seems to be central to conflict, and for this reason theories whose main focus is justice in interpersonal relationships can have important implications for intergroup relations.

Justice can be viewed as a socially defined standard for the evaluation of resource distribution in human relationships. Research in social justice is currently dominated by equity theory, although significant contributions have also been made by Lerner's (1977) "just world" theory, and Deutsch (1975, 1985), Leventhal (1979), Sampson (1975), and Austin (1979) have elaborated a number of fundamental concepts in the area of justice.

> Essentially, equity theory deals with two questions: (1) What do people think is fair and equitable? and (2) How do they respond when they are getting far more or far less from their relationships than they deserve? How do they react when they see their fellows reaping undeserved benefits—or enduring undeserved suffering? (Walster, Walster, and Berscheid, 1978, p. vii).

It is this second question that most explicitly links equity theory to issues in intergroup relations, such as the preconditions for conflict, the form conflict might take, and how conflicts are resolved. It is equity theory's focus on the evaluation of fairness, and responses to it, that make it a potentially heuristic theory in the present context.

There are additional features of equity theory that make it a potentially valuable source of insights into social behavior generally and intergroup relations in particular. First, there is an elegant simplicity and parsimony to its fundamental propositions that provides a focus and coherence to hypotheses that emerge from it. Second, the theory is comprehensive, claiming at least to provide the beginnings for a badly needed general theory of social behavior. Finally, the theory makes certain nonobvious predictions that offer new insights into social behavior. These aspects of the theory provide some indication of why it has assumed such an important position in current social psychology generally. It may also explain why, as of 1978, the theory had generated over 400 studies in diverse areas of social behavior.

An important comprehensive review of equity theory is provided by Walster and her associates (Walster et al., 1978). Current notions of equity lean heavily on earlier formulations as far back as Aristotle, and more recently include Homans (1961), Blau (1964), and the extensive work of Adams (1965). Central to the theory is its focus on relations among people rather than on the individual in isolation. However, the theory is essentially individualistic in the sense that it tends to focus on individuals interacting with other individuals. In describing the theory it will constantly be necessary to extrapolate to the group level, and the reader should bear in mind that such inferences are problematic at best.

The chapter is divided into five main sections. In the first section, an outline of equity theory is presented. It becomes clear from this outline that equity theory presents a model of the individual as a rational being who computes the inputs and outcomes for the self and others, then compares the derived ratios, to arrive at a notion of justice. The second section is a relatively detailed account of an experiment prototypic of research on equity theory. As is illustrated by the experiment, the conditions leading to such rational behavior can be fairly readily simulated in controlled, laboratory conditions. In such controlled conditions, inputs and outcomes can be accurately varied and estimated, and the hypotheses derived from equity theory can be tested relatively accurately. The task of defining equity theory concepts, such as "inputs" and "outcomes," is far more difficult, however, in the context of the real world.

Equity theory has a number of interesting implications with respect to the behavior of advantaged and disadvantaged groups, and we describe the most important of these in the third and fourth sections, respectively. By definition, advantaged and disadvantaged groups have conflicting interests, since the former will have to lose its advantaged position if the latter is to achieve equality. However, many disadvantaged groups seem to perceive their position vis-'a-vis the advantaged group as just. Equity theory provides an explanation for this rather curious attitude, using psychological processes as the basis for its explanation. Furthermore, equity theory can be used to explain differences in the strategies used by advantaged and disadvantaged groups, and to account for how both of these different strategies can help strengthen the position of the advantaged group(s).

Equity has a number of fundamental limitations as a theory of intergroup behavior, and we discuss the most important of these in our critical analysis of the theory. Equity theory presents a model of the individual as a rational being in a marketplace context: a being who works through estimates of inputs and outcomes, in order to calculate ratios, and then to compare his or her ratio with that of others in order to arrive at a notion of justice. This approach reflects North American cultural values, particularly with respect to the emphasis that the model places upon individuals rather than groups. The North American culture, which gives priority to self-help and individual responsibility, leads to justice being seen more in terms of the individual than of the group.

This approach is based on the assumption that it is the qualities of the individual, in terms of such traits as courage, hard work, and intelligence, that will determine an individual's progress. Group membership, be it male or female, black or white, rich or poor, is judged to be a secondary factor. Inputs and outcomes, together with justice and injustice, are therefore discussed in terms of the individual. In extending equity theory to the intergroup context, we find that equity theory in its present form does not adequately account for a number of important types of behavior.

AN OUTLINE OF EQUITY THEORY

Simply stated, equity theory proposes that people strive for justice in their relationships and feel distressed when they perceive an injustice (see Figure 5.1).

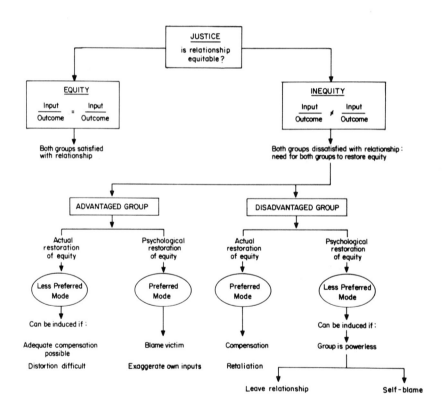

Figure 5.1   Schematic Representation of Equity Theory

People define justice on the basis of an analysis of the inputs and outcomes for those involved in a relationship. Inputs are contributions that persons (or groups) make in the form of attributes, abilities, or efforts, and outcomes are rewards (or punishments) that may be tangible (such as pay, services) or intangible (such as status, liking). Justice exists when the ratio of inputs to outcomes for one person (or group) is equal to the input/outcome ratio of the other. This ratio is calculated through the following formula:

$$\frac{\text{Outcomes for person (group) X}}{\text{Inputs by person (group) X}} = \frac{\text{Outcomes for person (group) Y}}{\text{Inputs by person (group) Y}}$$

Crucial to the idea of equity theory is that for justice to exist, the outcomes for those in a relationship need not be equal; rather, it is the *ratio* of outcomes to inputs that must be equal. Some concrete examples may help our understanding of this most fundamental proposition of equity theory. Because the emphasis is on ratio rather than on outcome, it is possible to have a perfectly equitable relationship in which, for example, a man treats a supposedly intimate relationship very casually while the woman invests her life in it. What makes it a just, and therefore satisfactory, relationship from an equity theory perspective is that the man in our example puts little into the relationship but gets little out of it. The woman, by contrast, may put much more in, but as long as she gets proportionally more out of the relationship, justice will be perceived to prevail. Similarly, the fact that there are substantial pay differences between laborers and professionals does not necessarily lead to a perception of injustice. As long as those in professional occupations are judged to be making proportionally more inputs (such as education, responsibility) than laborers, the situation is judged to be fair.

Having established the basic concept of ratios involving inputs and outcomes, it is necessary to be a little more precise in our formula for equity. We began with the basic formula $Ox/Ix = Oy/Iy$ because it most clearly emphasized the ratio concept that is basic to equity. However as Walster, Berscheid and Walster (1973) point out, the formula does not consider inputs that may be negative. Take the case of two persons (X and Y) in a relationship such that the inputs and outcomes are as follows: input x $= 5$, outcome x $= -10$, input y $= -5$, outcome y $= 10$. Using the basic equity formula, the relationship would appear to be equitable, since the resulting ratio is (-2) in both cases. But intuitively this makes little sense: Person X contributes positive inputs to the relationship but receives negative outcomes, whereas person Y receives positive outcomes even though his or her inputs were negative.

Walster et al. (1973) address this problem by proposing a formula that maintains the fundamental conceptual definition of equity but permits negative inputs and outcomes:

$$\frac{Ox - Ix}{/Ix/} = \frac{Oy - Iy}{/Iy/}$$

In this formula /Ix/ and /Iy/ denote the absolute value of inputs for x and inputs for y. If the numbers used in the earlier example are applied to the present formula, the results now make intuitive sense. The result for person X is (− 3), whereas for person Y it is (+ 3), showing clearly that person Y is getting undeserved rewards from the relationship with X. In fact, the formula has been refined even further (see Walster et al. 1978) but the essential rationale remains unchanged.

According to equity theory, people have notions about the ratios of outcomes to inputs with reference to their various social relationships. These notions are presumably achieved through a number of steps (see Anderson 1976): (1) the ratio of outcomes to inputs for the self has to be calculated; (2) the ratio of outcomes to inputs for the other (comparison) person has to be calculated; (3) these two ratios have to be compared. The assumption that people have such a rational approach to arriving at an idea of whether their rewards are (comparatively) just seems to contradict other models of social behavior. For example, as we saw in Chapter 2, Freud placed a relatively greater emphasis on the nonrational tendencies of people. Furthermore, the successful making of equity judgments requires the ability to make proportional logico-mathematical operations. As Hook and Cook (1979) point out, this ability does not develop in North American children until they are 13 years old. However, this does not seem to preclude children younger than 13 years old from having a notion of equity.

However, although equity theory assumes that people move forward along rational paths to arrive at a definition of justice, it does not assume that the notion of justice achieved necessarily corresponds with objective reality. It is subjective perceptions, influenced by emotional needs as well as irrational judgments of justice, that form the basis of social action; and such subjective perceptions can, and often do, deviate from objective reality. For example, in the case of the laborer who compares the ratio of his or her own outcomes and inputs with that of the lawyer, it is how the laborer subjectively estimates the four main variables—(1) own inputs, (2) own outcomes, (3) the lawyer's inputs, (4) the lawyer's outcomes—that is important and influences the laborer's behavior, not necessarily the objective status of these four variables. The laborer might imagine that his or her inputs in terms of training are equal to those of the lawyer when, in fact, they may be far less; or the laborer may assume that the outcomes received in terms of "enjoyment from life" are far more than what the lawyer gets when, in fact, they are far less. This emphasis on subjective perceptions and social comparison processes, through which ratios of outcomes and inputs are compared, makes equity theory very much a psychological theory of social behavior.

When an analysis of inputs and outcomes leads to the perception that equity is not attained, psychological discomfort is felt by the person making the analysis. The person experiencing the discomfort of inequity may be either or both of the individuals in a relationship—or, indeed, an outside observer of a relationship—and the key is the individual's subjective analysis of the ratio of inputs and outcomes. This discomfort is felt as psychological stress or tension that is highly unpleasant. As a response to the discomfort generated by the perception of inequity, the person takes steps to restore equity to the relationship, thereby removing the psychological distress. A person experiencing the distress of inequity can restore equity in one of two ways: (1) the actual restoration of equity, whereby the inputs or outcomes of one or both parties in the relationship are changed so that the ratios are made equal, or (2) the psychological restoration of equity, whereby the reality of the inputs and outcomes is cognitively distorted so that the ratios are made equal. For either the actual or the psychological restoration, there are four basic elements in the equity equation that can be changed: the inputs or outcomes of one person in the relationship, or the inputs and outcomes of the "other" (or any combination of these).

Thus, in a case where women in the face of inequity on the job attempt the actual restoration of equity, there are four basic elements that can be adjusted to produce equity: women can be paid more, men can be paid less, women can be asked to make less work input, or men can be required to put in more work. Alternatively, using a psychological restoration strategy, equity can be restored by coming to believe that women do work less, and so forth for each of the inputs and outcomes. Even where women have apparently identical inputs—as when they hold the same jobs as men—psychological restoration can be achieved by believing, for example, that women are not as dedicated to the job.

Equity theory has a number of important political implications, which we can highlight by elaborating upon the above example. Keeping in mind that a person experiencing the distress of inequity can restore equity either actually or psychologically, the question arises as to why some disadvantaged groups, such as women, seem willing to use the second strategy and cognitively distort the reality of the inputs and outcomes, so that the ratios for them and the dominant group (men) would come out equal. Obviously, such cognitive distortion is materially harmful to the disadvantaged group. If women who are doing the same job as men accept the idea that they are putting less into it, when in fact they are putting in just as much, or even more, then they are more likely to accept less material rewards than they deserve. Among the political implications of this process are that advantaged groups, in this case men, might try to create conditions in which the disadvantaged group, women, will attempt to restore equity through psychological rather than actual means. The claim by some women's liberation advocates that men's control of the educational and mass communications systems has given them power to manipulate women and make many of them feel content with their disadvantaged position can be usefully seen in this light.

Billig (1976) uses the term "groups-for-themselves" to describe groups whose ideology accurately reflects their material conditions, and the term "groups-in-themselves" to describe groups whose ideology reflects a false consciousness. Linking this terminology to equity theory, groups-for-themselves would attempt to use an actual restoration of equity, since they would have an accurate picture of their material conditions vis-à-vis other groups, and only actual changes that lead to greater, or full, justice would satisfy them. Groups-in-themselves, such as perhaps women in the past, have a false picture of their material conditions. Such a false picture could both be the result of, and lead to, the psychological restoration of equity, whereby inputs and outcomes are cognitively distorted and justice is seen to exist, when in fact there is injustice.

At first glance it would seem that equity theory makes a fundamental assumption about humankind that is at odds with most current psychological thought. That is, most psychological theories assume that individuals are self-interested or, in equity terms, will try to maximize their outcomes. Equity theory seems to imply that people are not motivated by self-interest but, rather, by fairness. However, Walster et al. (1978), and in a clearer manner Lerner (1977), claim that theories of justice do not in fact challenge the assumption of self-interest. Rather, equity theorists argue that people need an agreed-upon set of norms for exchange precisely so they can maximize their own rewards. That is, individuals need a shared understanding of contingencies in their universe so they can direct their behavior toward maximizing their own outcomes.

An elegant example of this is provided by Sampson's (1976) reference to Hardin's (1968) "tragedy of the common." The "common" is traditionally open pasture land where all villagers can freely allow their animals to graze. The system works to perfection until one individual decides to add one animal to the herd, thereby increasing his or her personal gain. The addition of one animal by itself is harmless, but when all villagers attempt personal gain by increasing their herds, everybody loses. The common is now so overgrazed that no herd can survive. Thus, the individual maximization of outcomes requires a shared set of social norms, and hence some form of equity. This argument would therefore suggest that equity theory fits easily into most modern conceptions of the nature of humankind.

However, it is instructive that the "common" example represents a case where people have similar, rather than conflicting, interests. The common can be used by all villagers, and everyone has equal rights of use. The rational approach to using such a facility would be through a shared set of social norms allowing maximum use of the facility by each individual while preserving it. However, in most, or perhaps all, societies there are real differences of ownership level, as well as conflicts of interests, between individuals and groups, and the status quo tends to favor the relatively advantaged. Equity theory suggests that both the advantaged and the disadvantaged groups seek to maximize their own outcomes, and what they need for this is a shared understanding of contingencies in their universe. It may be, however, that at times the disadvantaged group will not act according to this rational model of humankind, but will reject the established social norms and seek fundamental social change.

Nowhere is the paradox involving the collective and individual maximization of rewards described by the "common" fable more striking than the nuclear arms race. Nation-states compete with one another in order to gain maximum rewards at the expense of the other. However, it could be that an individual nation really gains little or nothing by having the greatest nuclear capability. Even the weakest competitor in the arms race is capable of destroying the entire planet, and so without norms of justice the biggest common of all, the planet, may be lost to everyone.

Finally, it is important to point out that equity theory involves an integration, first made by Adams (1965), of two important traditions in social psychology: behavioristic notions of social exchange (Thibaut & Kelley 1959) coupled with a motivation for cognitive balance (Heider 1946; Festinger 1957). Consistent with a behaviorist perspective, relationships are viewed in terms of exchange in which the relationship is maintained by the capacity of each participant to provide reinforcement for the other. Further, the focus on apparently calculable inputs and outcomes is consistent with the mechanistic view of human behavior often associated with behaviorist thinking.

The idea that inequity is associated with psychological distress grows directly out of principles, such as cognitive dissonance, that have played an important role in social psychology. Festinger (1957) conceived of dissonance as psychological distress that resulted from an incompatibility of cognitions, attitudes, or behaviors within the individual. With equity the distress still lies within the person but arises out of dissonance in resource distribution between people. The fact that equity theory is rooted in principles that have already enjoyed a lengthy tradition in psychology no doubt partly explains its pervasive influence in mainstream social psychology.

Having presented equity theory in summary form, we are now ready to formulate some of the interesting hypotheses that bear directly on intergroup relations. From equity theory it can be hypothesized that a group which receives less than it feels it deserves will feel distressed—hardly a novel prediction. Of greater interest is the prediction that an overbenefited group will feel psychological distress and be motivated to restore equity. A number of experiments lend credence to this hypothesis (such as Adams & Rosenbaum 1962). Prototypic of such experiments is one by Austin and Walster (1974).

A TYPICAL EXPERIMENT STIMULATED BY EQUITY THEORY

Austin and Walster (1974) conducted an experiment in which they addressed two important hypotheses relevant to the present context. First, it was hypothesized that persons who are given an equitable reward will be less distressed than persons who receive an inequitable reward (that is, persons who are either underrewarded or overrewarded). A second interesting hypothesis was that when persons are treated inequitably, they will experience less distress if they expected overreward or underreward than if they did not.

College students, who were normally paid $2 for participating, believed they were taking part in a decision-making experiment. Upon arriving at the laboratory, the subject discovered that he or she and another subject (really a confederate) would be paid by a third subject (another confederate) chosen at random to be the decision maker. The workers were asked to proofread simple material. They turned their work over to the decision maker, who checked their proofreading and then decided how $4 would be distributed between the two workers.

In order to manipulate expectations, the experimenter returned to the laboratory and told the worker who was the only real subject in the experiment that the decision maker had corrected the proofreading, that both the real subject and the other worker had correctly identified 94 percent of the errors, and that the decision maker planned to pay them. Some of the subjects were told the plan was to pay them $1 and the other worker $3, others were told $2 and $2, and still others would receive $3, while their co-worker would receive $1.

A little later the decision maker arrived and actually paid the subject $1, $2, or $3, meaning that sometimes the subject received more than was equitable ($3), less than was equitable ($1), or equitable pay ($2). This meant that the amount a subject received was more, less, or exactly what he or she expected. After being paid $1, $2, or $3, subjects answered a mood adjective checklist that was designed to assess their positive and negative feelings at that time.

The results confirmed both hypotheses. Those paid $1 or $3 were less satisfied than those receiving $2. Beyond this, subjects in all three conditions were more content when what they received was what they expected.

Our purpose here is to describe the type of experiment that equity theorists devise, but it is also important to appreciate the implications of the findings for intergroup relations. First, it seems that advantaged groups may well feel distress, and hence be motivated to make a fairer distribution of resources among societal groups. Second, but more disconcerting, it would seem that disadvantaged groups who expect to be treated inequitably accept such treatment to a greater extent than those who do not expect it..

With these suggestive findings as an example of the potentially interesting hypotheses that arise from equity theory, we can turn our attention to a more careful analysis of the implications of the theory for advantaged and disadvantaged groups.

ADVANTAGED GROUPS

In extrapolating and generalizing the findings obtained in the above experiment to real intergroup situations, it is tempting to be optimistic about the ultimate resolution of situations where advantaged groups exploit those who are disadvantaged. This optimism becomes tempered when we examine equity theory's predictions about how an over- or underbenefited person will restore equity. Faced with inequity, people can actually or psychologically restore equity. These two strategies have very different practical outcomes.

Psychological Restoration of Equity

Naturally, advantaged groups, motivated out of self-interest, will be more likely to use a psychological strategy, avoiding the necessity of actually having to compensate the disadvantaged group, and perhaps compromise their advantaged position in the process.

Thus, advantaged groups are more likely to cognitively distort relative inputs and outcomes in order to restore equity. Of particular interest for intergroup relations is the tendency to distort the disadvantaged group's inputs or, in Lerner's (1971) terms, derogate or blame the victim. If the advantaged group can convince itself that disadvantaged group members' inputs (such as intelligence, willingness to work) are proportionally lower than their own, then relatively fewer outcomes can be justified and less distress alleviated. Ryan (1976) describes this process eloquently in the context of racism. He describes two forms of blaming the victim:

> The old-fashioned conservative could hold firmly to the belief that the oppressed and the victimized were born that way—"that way" being defective or inadequate in character or ability. The new ideology attributes defect and inadequacy to the malignant nature of poverty, injustice, slum life and racial difficulties. But the stigma, the defect, the fatal difference—though derived in the past from environmental forces—is still located within the victim, inside his skin.(p. 7)

From an equity perspective then, Ryan's analysis involves advantaged group members' psychologically restoring equity by devaluing the inputs of disadvantaged group members. Also, whether disadvantaged group members are born with less input potential or have less input potential because of environmental circumstances, the results are the same.

Actual Restoration of Equity

The situation has now turned 180 degrees. Advantaged individuals or groups may experience distress but can conveniently use psychological rather than actual means of restoring equity. Does this mean that advantaged groups will never truly compensate victims and restore actual equity? Certain hypotheses arising out of equity theory indirectly suggest that there are conditions which at least raise the probability of an actual, as opposed to a psychological, restoration strategy. There is some evidence that exploiters will resist either inadequate or excessive compensation and favor adequate compensation (see Berscheid & Walster 1967). Specifically, if advantaged groups can be led to see a mechanism for actual compensation that is adequate, it raises the likelihood of such a strategy being adopted. Walster et al. (1978) point out in speculative fashion the subtle implications in an intergroup relations context:

> If we generalize shamelessly from the preceding findings, we might speculate that a more effective strategy for the blacks might have been to minimize their description of their suffering, and to make it clear that if available compensations were extended it would completely eliminate the debt owed to them. While this is not true, it may have been a profitable strategy, since it would have insured that the blacks would have at least received minimal compensation. (p. 38)

Beyond this, equity theorists propose that the less exploiters have to distort reality, the more successful are psychological restoration techniques. Indeed, Rosenberg and Abelson (1960) have shown that individuals prefer to distort reality as little as possible. Thus, the exploiter may well be pressured into actual compensation for the disadvantaged if confronted with objective and visible information about inputs and outcomes that leave little room for cognitive distortion.

A further proposition bears directly on the likelihood of psychological restoration techniques being used by exploiters. The hypothesis is that anticipation of future interaction with another inhibits the use of distortion (see Pannen 1976). The idea, of course, is that continued interaction raises the probability of the exploiter having continually to confront himself or herself with distortions, whereas with no anticipated contact the exploiter will not have to face the results of inequity. The message is clear for disadvantaged minorities: Do not separate socially, and thereby allow exploiters conveniently to avoid confronting inequity. Instead, constantly, through interaction, make inequalities salient and psychological distortions unacceptable. In this manner, the chances for actual restoration are heightened.

In summary, equity theory offers the novel proposition that overbenefited participants in a relationship feel psychological stress and the need to restore equity. While cognitive distortion offers exploiters a way out, there would seem to be conditions that at least heighten the probability of there being an actual redistribution of resources. If there is any validity to this proposition, mobilization of disadvantaged groups against injustice may indeed reap important rewards.

DISADVANTAGED GROUPS

Actual Restoration of Equity

The choice between actual and psychological strategies for restoring equity that affect advantaged groups have profound implications for disadvantaged groups. Just as members of the advantaged group prefer psychological restoration techniques, so members of disadvantaged groups naturally prefer the restoration of actual equity. We can go one step further and expect that within the context of actual restoration, compensation would be preferred to retaliation. That is, equity theory leads us to conclude that victims or disadvantaged groups would prefer that their own outcomes were increased (compensation) rather than those of the exploiter or advantaged group's being decreased (retaliation).

However, once again this "rational" approach to conflict solving predicts behavior patterns that only a "rational" person would follow. There are many instances (such as race riots, through which material destruction takes place) where the victims or disadvantaged group members are out to avenge what they see as wrongdoings and unjust behavior, and they seek to do this by harming the advantaged group rather than by getting compensation for themselves. Such destructive, "irrational" behavior, which seeks to harm the advantaged group rather than to compensate the disadvantaged group, is difficult to explain through equity theory or extrapolations from it.

The use of violence, or the threat of violence, by a disadvantaged group in order actually to restore equity has important implications for intergroup relations. Donnerstein, Donnerstein, Simon and Ditrichs (1972) conducted a particularly interesting experiment using white subjects who feared retaliation for injustice by blacks. The researchers were interested in the level of shocks white subjects would deliver to black subjects when the experiment was designed so that the black subject did not know who was delivering the shock as opposed to when the white subject was known to the black target. Second, in one condition the white knew the black would have a chance to retaliate, whereas in the other condition it was clear no retaliation was possible. The results showed clearly that whites gave higher levels of shocks to blacks when the black subjects were anonymous and when there was no fear of retaliation from the black subject. Anonymity or retaliation made no difference when white subjects shocked fellow white targets. Of course, for ethical reasons, although subjects believed they were shocking a target person, no shocks were actually delivered.

The social implications of these findings are, of course, far-reaching. As Donnerstein et al. (1972) conclude, "the variables of nonanonymity and expected retaliation might act to promote racial equality by minimizing aggressive behavior by white persons initially and/or by arresting justification techniques after aggressive action has terminated" (p. 244).

Psychological Restoration of Equity

Despite the possibility for retaliation, disadvantaged groups face a particular problem with actual restoration techniques, in that both compensation and retaliation presuppose the power and capability to bring about equity. Being disadvantaged, the group of course by definition lacks the fundamental resources needed to bring about actual equity. Thus, often the only option for the disadvantaged group is to restore psychological equity, which really means coming to believe that their disadvantaged position is deserved. If disadvantaged group members can downgrade their own inputs or exaggerate those of the advantaged group, then differential outcomes are justified. Although such a view does not serve the interests of the disadvantaged group, there are two powerful forces that enhance the probability of its adoption. First, the disadvantaged group needs to restore equity in the face of no power actually to redistribute inputs and outcomes. Second, the advantaged group has a vested interest in propagating this victim-blame perspective.

These two powerful forces combine to explain an important puzzle: How is it that disadvantaged groups often do not immediately and directly take collective action aimed at obtaining a more favorable distribution of society's resources? From an equity perspective, such inaction is understandable, and it is even possible to understand how such a group might come to believe its disadvantaged position is right and just.

A final strategy open to those who suffer from inequitable treatment is to escape the distress of inequity by leaving the relationship. This exit option has not received much attention in the equity literature but is one that may be central to relations between groups. A cursory glance at the number of separatist movements, be they political or psychological, is striking. In Canada, Quebec separation is the most salient, although strains of western separation also linger. A similar theme emerges to a greater or lesser extent among the Basques of Spain, the Welsh and Scots of Great Britain, native peoples in North America, and some militant feminists who advocate a world without men.

The exit option has received little research attention from social psychologists. An interesting exception is a study by Valenzi and Andrews (1971), who conducted a realistic field study in which clerks were hired for a six-week period at the same hourly rate. When the clerks returned for work on the second day, a new pay structure, designed by the experimenters to produce inequity, was introduced. Among the findings reported is that while none of the overpaid and equitably paid clerks left, 27 percent of the underpaid clerks left the job. Such data are important because in most laboratory investigations, subjects will usually continue for the sake of the experiment despite inequitable treatment. A further example of psychological separation comes from an experiment by Schmitt and Marwell (1972). They gave workers a choice that put them in a dilemma: They could work in a group and be paid inequitably or work alone and be paid equitably but much less than they would have received in the group. Despite the obvious economic loss, many opted to work by themselves for equitable pay, thereby psychologically removing themselves from the distress generated by the group relationship.

Presumably, although direct evidence is lacking, disadvantaged persons or groups opt for separation when they have no realistic hope of restoring equity—often, we might suppose, because of a lack of power to induce a fairer distribution by the advantaged group. Leaving the relationship or separating may well provide groups with the opportunity to strengthen their resources and to strategically reenter the relationship only when they feel they are in a position to demand and receive actual equity.

This brief description of advantaged and disadvantaged group strategies for maintaining and restoring equity permits some appreciation of how equity theory provides possible insights into certain persistent puzzles in the area of intergroup relations: the mechanisms by which advantaged groups maintain their power, and how they can at times be induced to instigate a fairer redistribution of rewards, are explained; and how disadvantaged groups come at least to tolerate their situation can be appreciated. We now turn our attention to those conditions, specified by equity theory, whereby disadvantaged groups may take dramatic action, and what form that action might take.

When the Best of Intentions Backfire

Members of the advantaged establishment, especially those in political office, often express frustration at the current social unrest that is typical of North American society and of many others. The frustration is expressed in the form of "The more we do to make the distribution of resources more equitable for disadvantaged groups, the more discontent they express and the more militant they become." This unexpected reaction may deter any charitable desires that advantaged groups may have, and thereby create a vicious circle. Some interesting extrapolations from equity theory have led to thought-provoking experiments in this context. One in particular was conducted by deCarufel and Schopler (1979). As part of a larger experiment, they had subjects in a simulated industrial setting perform a clerical task. Subjects believed that their pay was being determined by a student who was chosen to be the allocator. After the first series of work sessions (part 1), the allocator created inequity by keeping more than half of the money he had been given to divide with the worker-subject. After a break the allocator made a decision about a new pay structure (part 2). In the "constant" condition the worker was again treated with inequity; in the "equity" condition the money was divided equally; and in the "overcompensation" condition the allocator gave the worker more than half the money.

The finding of particular interest here is how those in the equity and overcompensation conditions reacted. We might expect that those in the overcompensation condition would be more satisfied (subject received 14¢ or 15¢; allocator kept 10¢ or 9¢) than those in the equity condition (subject received 12¢; allocator kept 12¢). Surprisingly, the findings were opposite to this prediction; satisfaction was lower in the overcompensation than in the equity condition.

How might this be explained? The authors speculate that the allocator may have been the instigator of dissatisfaction in the worker by his or her zeal to overcompensate. That is, perhaps the allocator, through a distribution of overcompensation, was unknowingly communicating a message. In the equity condition the message would be "There should be fairness from now on [referring to the allocations for part 2], and I have accomplished that by dividing the money equally." In the overcompensation condition the allocator may well have been communicating to the subject "You deserve not only equal pay in part 2 but compensation for part 1 of the experiment." This would trigger an expectation of compensation on the part of the subject that was not met. The pay differential favored the subject, but was not enough totally to make up for the inequity of part 1. Hence, a degree of dissatisfaction.

The implications for intergroup relations are significant. Advantaged groups that initiate social programs may well be triggering rising expectations in disadvantaged groups. These expectations may be of the form "We not only want what is equitable now, but what will make up for the past."

CRITICAL REVIEW OF EQUITY THEORY

Equity theory suffers from a number of limitations, which we review in this section. The most important are that equity theory is not specific about inputs and outcomes; it tends to be culturally biased; and it is vague about the social comparison process assumed to be involved in judgments of fairness. We will review each of these limitations in some detail, since there have been a number of attempts to overcome them, and many have rather direct implications for the operation of justice in relations between groups.

Specifying Inputs and Outcomes

A particularly thorny problem for equity theory is its ability or lack of ability to specify the appropriate inputs and outcomes in a particular relationship (see Deutsch, 1985). Take the case of an advantaged professional group that justifies its high average income on the grounds that its members spend more years obtaining a higher level of education than do those who receive far less income and have fewer educational requirements. An important test for any theory of intergroup behavior is whether it can predict how a group, in this case professionals or workers, will feel and respond to their situation. An analysis of inputs (education) and outcomes (salary) might predict that members of both groups will feel the relationship is equitable, and therefore be satisfied with the status quo. Suppose, however, that a study of worker satisfaction is conducted, and feelings of anger and resentment surface. Does this finding mean that equity theory is wrong? It could, but it could also mean that important inputs and outcomes were forgotten when the prediction was being made. Perhaps outcomes like prestige and security, along with inputs such as boredom, physical exertion, and shift work, were not considered in the original prediction. If they had been included, then the inequity might have been obvious and the prediction changed to one of dissatisfaction.

This example highlights an important problem: No matter what prediction is tested, equity theory can never be proved wrong, because other inputs and outcomes can always be found later to explain whatever results were obtained. This circularity of argument poses a fundamental difficulty. It means it is virtually impossible to predict how advantaged and disadvantaged groups will react to their situation—instead, we must wait until the reaction takes place, and then identify and calculate the inputs and outcomes that were central.

In discussing the criteria according to which hypotheses should be evaluated, the philosopher Karl Popper (1959) gives considerable importance to the criterion of "falsifiability." That is, in order for a hypothesis to be judged useful, it must be specific enough to be falsifiable. For example, if the hypothesis is "There are pink elephants," it is not falsifiable, since it does not specify exactly where and when pink elephants are found. If we wanted to test a hypothesis that simply states "There are pink elephants," we could search the whole of Africa and Asia and still be unable to prove this hypothesis wrong, since there are plenty of other places (such as the Amazon, Siberia, the planet Venus, or another galaxy, for example) where pink elephants might be.

In the same way, on the criterion of falsifiability, equity theory is not a theory that can be easily tested in its present form, since it does not define key concepts, such as inputs, in a precise enough manner to allow for a fair test of the theory. Just as the pink elephant could always have been hidden in a secret valley, out of reach of explorers, there could always be another neglected input, not accounted for by the researcher but influential on the subject's behavior nevertheless. This neglected input could always be cited to account for behavior that had not orginally been predicted on the basis of equity theory. Of course, this criticism of falsifiability is to some extent also relevant to the other major theories of intergroup relations discussed in this volume. However, we raise the issue in this chapter because equity theory seems to be particularly vulnerable when assessed according to the criterion of falsifiability.

It is hard to believe that inputs and outcomes are a purely random process. The problem is that we are not yet able to predict with a significant degree of accuracy how people arrive at an understanding about which inputs and outcomes are crucial to a particular relationship. Further research is needed to clarify this process, and would greatly enhance the predictive power of equity theory.

The question of specifying inputs and outcomes is also related to the types of experiments typically conducted in this area. Nowhere is the need to complement laboratory research with field studies so acute as in the testing of equity principles. The typical laboratory study, as we have seen, is carefully designed to allow for the test of a specific hypothesis. This means that conditions are set up that severely restrict subjects. For example, in order to study the effects of inequity, researchers will place subjects in a situation where they all have the same qualifications and do the same amount of work, thereby fixing the inputs. What varies are the specific rewards that subjects in different conditions receive, and these differences are designed to produce inequitable conditions. Subjects are then given a limited range of options to deal with the inequity thus created, such as expressing negative feelings or retaliating in subsequent trials.

In real life, of course, the inputs, outcomes, and responses are not fixed in this manner. For example, few subjects in an experiment leave it, rebel against the researcher, or sabotage the experiment. After all, they agreed to participate in the experiment. In real life intergroup relations, these are some of the more interesting strategies that groups use to cope with inequity. Beyond this, it is important to appreciate that in real life there are at least four basic elements that can be juggled either psychologically or actually in order to produce equity: one's personal or one's group's inputs and outcomes, and those of the other person or group. Experimentally the strategy is to fix three of the four options and then make predictions about how the fourth will vary systematically as a result of a number of predetermined factors.

Field studies, of course, do not permit the fixing of various inputs and outcomes. It is, therefore, impossible to make unequivocal causal statements about any results obtained. What it does permit is some appreciation of which elements are used naturally by people, collectively or in isolation, to deal with issues of equity. Beyond this, field studies provide hints as to which social variables may be systematically related to different inputs and outcomes. Data from such field studies can then be used as a basis for designing more controlled laboratory conditions to test certain hypotheses, hopefully with some confidence that the factors which the experimenter chooses to fix or leave free to vary have some basis in reality.

In summary, the problem of defining inputs and outcomes makes predictions about intergroup relations from an equity perspective problematic. However, a combined field and experimental approach to the question may lead to a situation where equity can have predictive power. Then we may be able better to predict whether a disadvantaged group will accept its position, demand compensation, or lower its own inputs in response to its undesirable situation.

Culture Bias

Martin and Murray (1983) argue that there is a fundamental bias to the manner in which equity theory is formulated: "Distributive justice theory represents well the opinions of those people who are relatively advantaged beneficiaries of the current system of distributing economic goods" (p. 175). Thus, they feel that equity ". . . represents the perspective of those who find current exchange norms to be fair. It particularly excludes the perspective of those who find such exploitation less than justifiable" (p. 177). An important point raised by Martin and Murray is that this bias restricts the scope of issues equity theory might address, and precludes certain questions that might be raised from a disadvantaged group's perspective. Specifically, for example, such a perspective may influence the inputs and outcomes that are deemed appropriate, and it may even explain why the theory postulates a fundamental need for the maintenance of equity. Such a motive surely would be expected from a perspective that seeks to maintain the status quo.

Equity theory is conceived within a North American context, and therefore tends to reflect the cultural values of that society. Specifically, equity theory and research deal with individuals rather than groups. This is not to say that groups do not conform to equity principles, but to assume so is naive. The added complexity of relationships at the group level and the nature of inputs and outcomes that are important for groups must be addressed. Indeed, the very nature of the relationship is different with groups, since much of it is not face-to-face.

Equity, through this individualistic bias, ignores a number of processes directly related to intergroup relations. Leventhal (1979) cites a number of examples that illustrate the point. He notes that when a group is in conflict, the normal concerns for justice within the group are affected. Attention focuses on the threats related to conflict rather than on fairness within the group. Further, conflict produces in-group solidarity that includes greater agreement among individuals and subgroups about the justice of how resources are distributed within the group. Finally, individual or subgroup concerns about justice are suppressed in favor of evaluating fairness in terms of what is best for the group. These issues illustrate a few of the many ways in which much is lost when principles of equity at the individual level are extrapolated directly to the level of the group.

We can further clarify the above points by discussing a recurring historical phenomenon. National leaders have learned that there is one sure way to distract attention from problems at home, and that is to start a fight with an enemy abroad, or at least to make the enemy abroad appear dangerous and threatening. When disadvanted groups exert pressure for reform and political forces mobilize against injustices, a common response from reactionary leaders has been to mobilize the army and put the nation on war alert against a foreign enemy. This trick seems to divert attention away from injustices at home and to lead to national solidarity. Dahrendorf (1964, p. 58) analyzes the East-West conflict in terms of the tendency for human groups to react to external pressure by increased internal coherence, and the consequence of this process on human liberty:

> In the East-West conflict, each society finds itself in . . . a position of pressure from without . . . [that] may lead the liberal societies of the West to restrict internal liberties in the name of resistance to totalitarian pressure . . . [resulting in] the paradoxical possiblity that democracy can be destroyed while it is being protected.

The most compelling analysis of the differences involved in justice at the interpersonal and intergroup levels is provided by Watson (1985). She postulates that human relationships can vary along a social continuum ranging from intimate, to role, to group relationships, and that the operation of equity may be quite different, depending upon the type of relationship involved. Watson (1985) found that the conception of justice associated with equity theory applied only when subjects evaluated role (work) relationships; it did not apply for intimate or group contacts. Specifically, in a series of laboratory and field studies Watson found that at the group level the rules of justice were much more strictly applied than in intimate relationships. For example, in one study

> . . . subjects who had described an injustice in their relationships with a close friend perceived these incidents as less unjust and less serious than subjects who had described injustices in a work setting. Incidents in this latter context were, again, perceived as less unjust and serious than those in a group setting. (Watson 1985, p. 275)

Beyond this, Watson also found evidence to suggest that for intimate relationships, inputs in the form of the person's intentions are a primary concern, whereas in the intergroup context the focus is more on outcomes.

Finally, at the group level attention must be paid not only to the distribution of rewards or outcomes but to procedures of justice as well. We can all think of unjust outcomes that arise from just procedures, as when an innocent defendant is judged guilty through a fair jury trial. Conversely, unjust procedures can generate just distributions, as when a dictator is benevolent and distributes goods with fairness and compassion.

The cultural context of North America, with its individualistic bias, is reflected in the application by equity theory of economically based concepts to all human relationships. The very terms used by equity theorists—"inputs," "outcomes," "rewards," "costs," "profits," and "investments"—reflect this orientation. Deutsch (1975), in recognizing this issue, notes that "this focus is a natural one in a society in which economic values tend to pervade all aspects of social life" (p. 137). Similarly, Sampson (1975) argues that "non-economic forms of human relationship—including, for example, relationships of liking, loving, helping, harmony, and so forth—arise from the trend to mimic the economic form" (p. 48).

One of the important consequences of such a marketplace or economic view of human relations is that the very assumption that equity forms the basis of all relationships needs to be challenged. Deutsch (1975) argues that equity operates only where the relationship is competitive and the goal is economic productivity. However, where the aim is to maintain or foster enjoyable social relations, equality will be operative. That is, when the aim is harmony among people, all should receive the same outcomes. Finally, a needs principle of justice will operate where the primary goal is personal welfare. For example, children are given not what they deserve but what they need.

Undoubtedly the nature of the distribution achieved in a society is influenced by social norms such as distributive justice. However, equity is only one of many possible rules of justice, and one that reflects North American cultural traditions. In other cultures such rules as equality and needs might have greater influence. To complicate matters further, it is clear that different rules operate even within the same society. The North American value system clearly illustrates this point. Everyone is "guaranteed" equality of opportunity to achieve whatever station in life their talents and efforts permit (equity), but those in genuine need will be helped by specially designed welfare and assistance programs.

The whole issue of which rule of justice operates in what circumstances is a complicated one, but an example may serve to point out its potential importance for intergroup relations. A number of experiments have examined how boys and girls distribute resources (for instance, Leventhal & Lane 1970). The usual procedure is to have a group of boys or girls perform a group task in which individual members make differential inputs to the completion of the task. One of the members is then given a sum of money and asked to take the responsibility for dividing it among the group members. Boys typically allocate according to an equity rule, those boys who contributed most to the task receiving the most, and others receiving an amount consistent with their input. Girls, on the other hand, tend to follow an equality rule; independent of different contributions, the money is divided equally among all members.

Applying Deutsch's (1975) analysis, we might explain the results as follows. Boys are socialized to be cooperative where possible, but to put a special premium on productivity. Thus, they operate on the basis of equity. Girls, by contrast, may be more concerned with good social relationships than with productivity, and therefore use equality as the basis for resource distribution. If this is true, we have two groups whose different value systems lead to completely different perspectives on the distribution of resources. One can only speculate about the extent to which various societal, racial, cultural, or occupational groups have such different value systems, and the complexities involved when two groups whose values diverge attempt to negotiate an acceptable basis for the just distribution of resources.

Equity Theory and Order of Comparisons

Although equity theory assumes that a great deal of often complex information must be processed in order for individuals to arrive at notions of inputs, outcomes, and equity, the theory has little to say about the way in which this information processing takes place. However, implicit in the theory are a number of ideas about the order in which comparisons are made by an individual who is assessing his or her inputs and outcomes. Specifically, equity theory implies that two intrapersonal comparisons take place between an individual's outcome and input, and that these are followed by one interpersonal comparison of the two outcome/input ratios.

The sequence of comparisons implied by the equity equation involves an assumption about psychological processes that has been experimentally tested by Anderson and Farkas (1975) and by Anderson (1976). Evidence from these experiments suggests a reverse order of comparisons: two interpersonal comparisons are first made, one between the two persons' inputs and another between their outcomes; the two resulting interpersonal ratios are then compared, with the new equity equation being the following:

$$\text{Outcomes B}/(\text{Outcomes A } + \text{ Outcomes B}) = \\ \text{Inputs B}/(\text{Inputs A } + \text{ Inputs B})$$

Thus, it seems that the actual sequence of comparisons involves comparing input with input, and outcome with outcome, rather than the more demanding route of comparing outcome with input. Reviewing the evidence regarding the sequence of comparisons, Ng (1984) has suggested that "The equity equation should be rewritten accordingly if it is intended to represent the cognitive processes of comparisons even though, mathematically, the original and revised equations are equivalent" (p. 633).

A more general criticism is that equity theory does not pay sufficient attention to information processing and the social comparisons that are assumed to be involved in it. In the intergroup context, in particular, it is important to know not only the sequence of social comparisons but also, more specifically, the range of "others" chosen as targets for social comparison. What are the motivations influencing the selection of "others" for social comparison when an individual is assessing his or her inputs, outcomes, and equity ratio? This important issue has not received sufficient attention on the part of equity theory.

CONCLUSION

These limitations notwithstanding, equity theory specifically, and justice theories more generally, make an important contribution to intergroup relations. Equity theories are to be commended for attempting a broadly based theory of social behavior. Insights into persistent puzzles are offered and a framework is provided for addressing new issues. In the context of intergroup relations, an especially important new question must be how small groups with meager resources cope with large, powerful groups. Terrorism and hostage-taking represent creative, if frightening, solutions. Perhaps the challenge is for theorists interested in intergroup relations to examine how individualistic processes of equity apply to situations involving groups.

SUGGESTED READINGS

Lerner, M. J. 1977. The justice motive: Some hypotheses as to its origins and forms. *Journal of Personality, 45,* 1–52.

Messick, D. M., and K. S. Cook, (eds.). 1983. *Equity Theory: Psychological and Sociological Perspectives.* New York: Praeger.

Walster, E., G. W. Walster, and E. Berscheid, 1978. *Equity: Theory and Research.* Boston: Allyn & Bacon.

6   Relative Deprivation Theory

Scope: Relative deprivation theory deals mainly with disadvantaged individuals and, by implication, groups. The theory specifies the conditions associated with feelings of discontent.

Assumptions: The major assumption is that a person's or group's satisfaction is not related to the objective situation but, rather, to the situation relative to other persons or groups.

Propositions: Theorists agree that discontent arises from comparisons with a "better off" other. They disagree, however, about the other conditions that must be met in order for relative deprivation to be experienced. Among the other conditions postulated as necessary for feelings of discontent are that people must believe it is possible to attain a better situation, and that they feel they deserve to do so.

Everyday experience provides us with a number of shocks to our sense of rationality and justice when we try to comprehend exactly what makes people satisfied with their life situations. Mary is unwaivering in her affection for her boyfriend, Paul, even when he stands her up, verbally abuses her in public, and generally makes unreasonable demands. A corporate president is unhappy, while a factory worker whistles at his work. Bob is thrilled with his third-hand car, while even with his new Jacuzzi, John can't seem to shake the blues. At the group level human satisfaction is equally mysterious. North Americans express great discontent about their economic status while many in Third World nations are starving. Unions demand more and are increasingly dissatisfied. In the meantime, executives and professionals complain about their expense accounts and fringe benefits.

What these examples underscore is that when it comes to people's feelings, there is no isomorphic relation between their objective situation or status, and subjective experience. This dictum has been recognized for centuries, but it was not until 1949 that the concept of relative deprivation was formalized by Stouffer and his colleagues.

The fundamental idea is that it is a person's relative status that determines his or her sense of satisfaction, not the objective situation. The deprivation component of "relative deprivation" signals a concern for when people feel relatively poorly off, rather than situations where they are relatively advantaged. From this description the potential value of relative deprivation theory for understanding intergroup relations is evident, especially as it pertains to disadvantaged groups responding to groups that are more advantaged.

The basic idea of relative deprivation allows us to understand some of the complexities involved in predicting people's reactions to various objective circumstances. Thus, using our initial examples, Mary may be poorly treated by Paul, but compared with the loneliness she felt previously, life is relatively good. For Bob, having a third-hand car beats walking, and working-class North Americans will feel deprived when they compare their own situation with that of affluent groups, either as they are in reality or as they are depicted in the steady stream of television shows about rich, powerful, and successful people.

The insights gained by recognizing the relative basis of human satisfaction leads to some particularly thorny issues. For example, a person can make comparisons with any number of others. And since a comparison with a "worse off" other leads to a very different reaction from one with another who is "better off," it will be crucial to be able to make a precise prediction about whom a person chooses as the target for comparison. This is but one of the enduring issues associated with relative deprivation that we raise here in order to appreciate that while the relativity concept is a powerful theoretical advance, there is much yet to be done.

We begin our outline of relative deprivation theory by describing the basic findings of Stouffer and his colleagues. The purpose is to make clear, by empirical example, what types of discontent can be explained through the concept of relative deprivation. Next we focus on a 1976 article by Crosby, who provides an excellent integration of the state of the theory to that point. This is followed by a discussion of recent research that bears directly on relative deprivation in the context of intergroup relations. Finally, we present a critical analysis of relative deprivation theory. An important theme here will be the extent to which the focus of theory and research has been on the individual and his or her experiences of deprivation. All too quickly these findings from this individual perspective are extrapolated to the group level. It is also important to bear in mind that unlike equity theory (Chapter 5), for example, relative deprivation theory focuses on disadvantaged individuals and groups. The interest of theorists is in the feeling of disconcent that arises when comparisons are made with "better off" others.

OUTLINE OF RELATIVE DEPRIVATION THEORY

On December 8, 1941, Stouffer and his colleagues (Stouffer, Suchman, DeVinney, Star & Williams, 1949) initiated a large-scale research project designed to assess the attitudes of the American soldier. This was a landmark study, since for the first time the methods of social science were judged to be potentially valuable in the context of the U.S. Army, replacing the subjective opinions of military personnel who made only brief visits to the field and reported on the morale of military units on the basis of a few casual conversations. One of the most important concepts to emerge from this vast research project, published ultimately in four volumes, was relative deprivation.

The concept proved invaluable for reconciling paradoxical findings from the study. For example, complaints about promotion were expressed more vehemently in the air force than in the military police. This was a surprising finding, since the air force had numerous corporals and sergeants, whereas the vast majority of soldiers in the military police were privates. Relative deprivation provided a possible answer. Most men in the air force got promotions. Those who did not felt relatively aggrieved. By contrast, few in the military police received promotions. The result was that those who were not promoted did not feel deprived by comparison, and thus were less likely to feel aggrieved.

Black soldiers in the southern United States were expected to feel particularly bitter given the history of extreme racism in that region. However, the morale of these soldiers was as good as, and at times better than, that of blacks stationed in the North. The data indicated that the high morale of those in the South was a function of comparisons they made with black civilians in the South, who were treated very poorly. But northern blacks felt relatively frustrated, because their judgments were relative to civilian blacks in the North, who were earning higher wages in the war-related factories.

These are but two of the examples from Stouffer's work that illustrate how the concept of relative deprivation can provide insights into apparently irrational feelings. It is important to note, however, that it is not possible to make a specific prediction about feelings by using relative deprivation. It is possible to explain the feelings only after the fact. How can we know beforehand that black soldiers in the South will compare themselves with civilian blacks? It is equally logical for them to compare themselves with blacks in the North or with white soldiers stationed in the South. Clearly, an important issue for the predictive power of relative deprivation is to be able to establish the mechanism by which people choose a comparison other.

Pettigrew (1978) is even harsher in his criticism on this point:

> Relative deprivation as an explanatory concept has often been invoked in *post hoc* fashion, its causal relationships left ambiguous, its measurement varied and questionable, and its application confused by the failure to specify precisely its operation at both the individual and social level of analysis. (1978, p. 32)

A QUARTER-CENTURY OF RESEARCH ON RELATIVE DEPRIVATION

The concept of relative deprivation flourished over 25 years, following the initial work of Stouffer and his colleagues, but much of the work was centered on sociology and political science, not social psychology. Gurr (1970), for example, was a political scientist who nevertheless relied on important psychological concepts, especially relative deprivation, in order to explain political violence. A summary of his propositions is presented here because they serve to illustrate the type of advancement made following the initial work by Stouffer et al. (1949).

Gurr (1970) proposed that ". . . the potential for collective action varies strongly with the intensity and scope of relative deprivation among members of a collectivity" (p. 24). Relative deprivation was defined as an individual's perception of a discrepancy between his or her value expectations and value capabilities. By "value expectations" Gurr meant anything a person believes he or she deserves to have, and "value capabilities" refers to those things a person believes it is possible to obtain.

Gurr (1970) distinguished three types of relative deprivation, each of which is a predisposing pattern for political violence. In the first, decremental deprivation, value expectations remain relatively constant, but value capabilities begin to fall, leading to a discrepancy between the two. For example, the middle class might come to expect a certain life-style that is based on their income. If disposable income is steadily reduced because the government continues to increase income taxes, then decremental deprivation may arise as the gap between expectations and income increases.

The second pattern, aspirational deprivation, involves a situation where value capabilities remain relatively constant but value expectations rise. For example, those in power might appeal to certain ethnic minority voters by promising them better opportunities and conditions. This, of course, will raise value expectations, and unless value capabilities meet these expectations, the result will be relative deprivation.

Progressive deprivation, the third pattern, is really a special case of aspirational deprivation and occurs when value capabilities are rising, and as they rise, so do value expectations. Any society will show such a pattern during a period of economic growth: people have more, and so come to expect more. The "crunch" comes when value capabilities level off or even decline (things cannot improve forever), but value expectations continue to rise. The outcome of this process is relative deprivation.

Our brief discussion of Gurr's (1970) elementary propositions is designed to provide an example of how the basic idea of relative deprivation developed into a much richer theoretical concept. It would be difficult, and perhaps not very useful, to discuss the numerous elements of relative deprivation that emerged during this period. However, in 1976 Faye Crosby, a social psychologist, published an important paper that not only outlined her own theoretical position but also attempted to integrate into her work other major positions on relative deprivation. Thus, reviewing certain of Crosby's propositions allows us to trace developments in the field of relative deprivation generally.

Before analyzing her model, it is important to address a definitional ambiguity about the concept of relative deprivation. The term has been used in two distinct ways. Some theorists focus on the cognitive component of relative deprivation, the perceived differential between one's own treatment and that of a comparison other. The key cognitive judgment would be the magnitude of the differential.

Other theorists emphasize the emotional component of relative deprivation, which would include feelings of anger, outrage, and grievance. From an emotional perspective, intensity would be the main variable. Our concern in this chapter is with what makes people, especially in a group context, feel in ways that would potentially lead to protest or militant action—in short, with hostile feelings. Thus relative deprivation will be viewed here as an emotion. The cognitive aspect, the magnitude of the differential between self or own group and another person or group, can be viewed as one possible precondition for the feelings of anger and grievance we will associate with relative deprivation.

It should be stated at the outset that Crosby's model attempts to explain relative deprivation as it pertains to the individual. She makes no claims about how the process might operate in groups. The most important feature of her model is that she boldly attempts to specify the necessary and sufficient conditions for relative deprivation to be experienced. Specifically, she proposes that for the negative emotions of relative deprivation to be experienced, a person must see that someone possesses X, want X, feel entitled to X, feel that it is feasible to attain X, and not feel personally responsible for the lack of X.

Before providing a brief description of each precondition, it is important to understand what is meant by X. X for Crosby stands for anything a person may have or acquire, from good looks to a higher salary. And X may be concrete or abstract. To use an intergroup example, X may include concrete rewards, such as natural resources, education, and jobs, or more abstract commodities, such as power, status, and moral rights. Again it is essential to recognize that, for Stouffer et al. (1949), comparison with a better-off other was sufficient to evoke relative deprivation; for Crosby (1976), every one of the five preconditions must be met. If any are missing, the feeling may be negative, such as disappointment, but the anger and outrage associated with relative deprivation will not be experienced.

The first precondition requires that a person see that someone possesses X. Obviously, it is necessary for a person to be aware that X exists in order to analyze his or her own situation with respect to X. The bigger issue here, of course, which Crosby does not address, is how to determine, among the many others who may possess X, or differing amounts of X, precisely which other will be used as a basis for comparison.

Next, the person must want X. This important precondition highlights the emotional or feeling aspect of relative deprivation. Knowing someone possesses something you don't value will not make you angry or upset. Only when someone possesses something you want will relative deprivation be experienced.

A more interesting and complex precondition is that the person must feel entitled to X. The basic idea is that even if you see someone who possesses something you want badly, this does not necessarily mean anger will be experienced. Only if you feel you deserve X, or that it is right and fair that you have X, will relative deprivation be experienced. As Crosby notes, the student who is given a D on an exam but feels he or she deserved a D, may feel disappointment or inadequacy, but not the anger and outrage of relative deprivation. If, however, the student is given a D but feels that he or she deserved a C or higher, then relative deprivation will be experienced.

The complexity of the entitlement precondition arises because it requires an answer to the prior question: How does a person assess the deservedness, fairness, or justice of his or her situation? As we have seen from our discussion of equity theory in Chapter 5, this in itself is a complex issue.

The feasibility precondition is complex as well. If a person knows he or she will obtain X, then no relative deprivation is experienced. At the other extreme, if there is absolutely no way that X can be obtained, then it is unlikely that relative deprivation will be experienced. This latter experience can perhaps best be described as wishful thinking. James Bond has a life-style that makes mine look dull by comparison, but it isn't realistic for me to think in his terms, so the comparison does not evoke anger in me, only envy.

The final precondition requires that the person not blame himself or herself for not having X. In one important respect this precondition is contained in precondition 3, the feeling of entitlement. If a person does blame himself or herself for not having X, then he or she is really saying that he or she doesn't deserve X or that the lack of X is just. Thus, like precondition 3, it is essential that the lack of X be judged unfair for relative deprivation to be experienced.

Empirical research to test the validity of each of these preconditions is vital for the insights it may provide into individual's or, if we extrapolate, groups' responses to inequality. For example, think of the outrage that women, Native Americans, French-speaking Québecois, gays, blacks, and Hispanics in North America have expressed. Perhaps in these cases all five preconditions for relative deprivation have been met. But think of working-class North Americans, certain Indian groups of relatively low caste, colonial Africans (until very recently), or certainly newly arrived immigrant groups in western Europe or North America. The apparent acceptance of the unequal treatment they receive surely has nothing to do with not seeing that others are better off or not wanting the rewards that society has to offer. Instead, it may be because there is the perception that the inequality is fair or that equality is totally unfeasible from the outset. The point here is that the presence or absence of any precondition is hypothesized to have a dramatic impact. In the highly speculative examples offered here, the range is from acceptance to collective and militant protest—in the extreme, the contemplation of the separation of a province from the rest of the country.

Crosby's initial 1976 model is the most explicit and complete in terms of spelling out the precise preconditions for relative deprivation. As such, it serves as an excellent reference point for considering other theories. Davis (1959) was the first to describe a formal theory of relative deprivation (see Cook, Crosby, and Hennigan 1977). Adopting Crosby's format, we will translate Davis' (1959) theory to propose that the necessary preconditions are that someone does not possess X, wants X, and feels entitled to X. However, he includes certain subtleties that are important. First, he considers with whom people make comparisons, proposing that people compare themselves with similar others, a view consistent with Festinger's (1954) fundamental hypothesis of social comparison theory. Thus, members of a disadvantaged group may not compare themselves with an extremely advantaged group, simply because there is insufficient basis of similarity. Of course, questions as to precisely how people define similarity still remain (see Suls & Miller 1977).

Because comparisons are made with similar others, Davis believed this automatically made people feel entitled to the X in question. Thus entitlement is contained in the fact that the first precondition is that the person sees that a similar other possesses X.

Runciman (1966) agreed on the three preconditions proposed by Davis but added the feasibility condition. Like Crosby, he felt that relative deprivation required coping with reality-based aspirations.

However, Gurr (1970) made the opposite prediction. He focused on what gives rise to a sense of grievance and believed that when people do not think attaining X is feasible, this contributes directly to a sense of grievance and, thereby, feelings of deprivation.

Thus various theorists include some but not all of the preconditions outlined by Crosby (1976). Beyond this, there would seem to be a fundamental disagreement about the role of feasibility. Crosby (1976) and Runciman (1966) believe it is the perception of X as attainable, and Gurr (1970) argues that it is perceiving that the attainment of X is not feasible that leads to relative deprivation.

Before completing discussion of relative deprivation theories, it may be instructive to examine two other theories in terms of how they would deal with the preconditions proposed by Crosby (1976). The two theories in question are frustration/aggression theory and equity theory, both of which were described in earlier chapters.

Frustration/aggression theory (Dollard et al. 1939) focuses on the individual, and hypothesizes that whenever goal-directed behavior is blocked, frustration will be experienced, which will lead to aggression. The interesting aspect of the theory is its attention to the psychoanalytic concept of displacement. Thus, when a powerful person or force blocks goal-directed behavior, the frustrated person may displace his or her aggression from the rational target onto a related but weaker targer. The man whose boss has made him angry may not confront the boss, but instead take out his aggression on the boss's secretary, his own wife, and even the family pet. The concept of displacement has been important in explaining why powerless minority groups are so often the target of aggression.

Placing the theory in relative deprivation terms generally, and in Crosby's model in particular, the person must want X and believe it is feasible to obtain X. Presumably people do not pursue goals they don't want or don't think are possible to achieve. No reference is made to seeing that others or similar others possess X, or that entitlement, deservedness, and responsibility are necessary conditions.

The essence of equity theory, which was discussed in detail in Chapter 5, involves social comparison and entitlement. People judge the satisfaction of relationships on the basis of the ratio of inputs to outcomes for both participants in the relationship. Naturally a person sees the other's inputs and outcomes—in Crosby's terms, the X—and makes social comparisons. Equity theory makes very explicit predictions about whom one makes comparisons with—the other person in the relationship.

Also implied in equity theory are the preconditions associated with entitlement. Equity explicitly defines this in terms of the equality of ratios of inputs to outcomes for both partners. Thus, in Crosby's terms equity theory involves seeing that another possesses X, wanting X, feeling entitled to X, and not feeling responsible for the lack of X. Not mentioned is the controversial feasibility precondition.

With each theory having its own constellation of preconditions for relative deprivation, it would be crucial to put each of the theories to the test. Fortunately, Bernstein and Crosby (1980) have done just that. This research is important not only for the findings that emerged but also because the studies typify the two kinds of methods that have been used most widely in social psychological research on relative deprivation.

Before describing these methods, it may be helpful to organize and summarize the predictions about the specific preconditions that each theory makes. Table 6.1 uses Crosby's (1976) preconditions as a format and lists the other theories in terms of the precise preconditions each specifies.

Table 6.1   Summary of Preconditions for Relative Deprivation Specified by Various Theories

THEORISTS	OTHER POSSESSES X	WANT X	ENTITLED TO X	FEASIBLE TO ATTAIN X	LACK OF RESPONSIBILITY FOR LACK OF X
CROSBY	✓	✓	✓	✓	✓
DAVIS	✓	✓	✓		
RUNCIMAN	✓	✓	✓	✓	
GURR	(✓)	✓	✓	–	
FRUSTRATION / AGGRESSION		✓		✓	
EQUITY	(✓)	✓	✓		✓

   – means the absence of precondition

   ( ) means precondition necessary but with important qualifications

Source: F. Crosby & M. Bernstein (1978). Relative Deprivation: Testing the Models. Paper presented at the meeting of the American Psychological Association, Toronto. Reprinted by permission of the authors.

The studies conducted by Bernstein and Crosby (1980) and Crosby (1982) are prototypic of social psychological research on relative deprivation. The first used a more experimental procedure involving 528 university students as subjects. The subjects were asked to read a number of carefully prepared vignettes about an individual who lacked a desired X. Different variations of the vignette described the individual as someone who (a) did or did not see another who possessed X; (b) did or did not feel entitled to X; (c) had or had not attained X in the past; (d) did or did not think it likely to attain X in the future; and (e) did or did not assume personal responsibility for current failure to possess X. After reading the vignette, subjects rated, on modified Likert-type scales, the extent to which the central character would have experienced resentment, dissatisfaction, anger, and unhappiness.

Subjects made judgments about a large number of vignettes where every possible combination of the presence or absence of each precondition was presented. In this way the effect of each precondition could be assessed in terms of its importance for relative deprivation. However, the "wanting" component was not manipulated.

A concrete example will make the procedure clearer. The following is one of the vignettes used by Bernstein and Crosby:

> John is a sophomore in college. At the beginning of this semester, when he was registering for courses, John had to choose course X or course Y, which both interested him and which met at the same time. He decided to take course X. When he signed up for the course, he felt that his chances of obtaining a very high grade were excellent. Secretly, he wanted to earn an A in the course. Now the course is half over and John's grade so far is a B – . His best friend, who is also taking the course, has an A average. John realizes that his own work has *not* been outstanding and that on the basis of the work he has done so far he deserves no more than a B. Since there is only one small paper still due in the course, he now feels that he stands almost no chance of reaching his goal. Although he sometimes wonders if he should have signed up for course Y, he knows that he could not have foreseen how events would turn out. Therefore, he does not blame himself for the situation he is in. (1980, p. 446)

The independent variables or preconditions were manipulated in the following ways:

Comparison-other was absent or present. For comparison-other absent, the story read: "All of the other students in the course also seem to have about a B average." For comparison-other present, it read, "His [her] best friend, who is also taking the course, has an A average."

Entitlement was absent or present. For absent, the story read: "John [Jane] realizes that his [her] own work has *not* been outstanding and that on the basis of the work he [she] has done so far he [she] deserves no more than a B.'' For entitlement present, it read: ''John [Jane] feels that his [her] own work has been excellent and that he [she] too deserves an A.''

Past feasibility was low or high. Low past feasibility stories read: ''When he [she] signed up for the course, he [she] felt his [her] chances of obtaining a very high grade were rather poor.'' In the high past feasibility condition, the sentence ended: ''. . . were excellent.''

Future feasibility was low or high. In the low condition, stories read: ''Since there is only one small paper still due in the course, he [she] feels that he [she] stands almost no chance of reaching his [her] goal.'' High stories read: ''Since there are two more papers due in the course, he [she] feels that he [she] [still] has an excellent chance of obtaining an A by the end of the semester.''

Personal responsibility was absent or present. Personal responsibility absent stories concluded: ''Although he [she] sometimes wonders if he [she] should have signed up for course Y, he [she] knows that he [she] could not have foreseen how events would turn out. Therefore, he [she] does not blame himself [herself] for the situation he [she] is in.'' Personal responsibility present stories concluded: ''He [she] also feels that if he [she] had signed up for course Y, his [her] goal would have been realized. Therefore, he [she] blames himself [herself] in large part for the situation he [she] is in.''

An interesting pattern of results emerged. Consistent with all the theories, seeing that others possess X and feeling entitled to X were strongly related to the negative emotions of relative deprivation. However, the finding related to feasibility supported Davis (1959) and Gurr (1970), but not Runciman (1966) or Crosby (1976) herself. The findings showed that relative deprivation was not severe when it was not feasible to obtain X. Equity and frustration/aggression theory were shown to be incomplete in that they do not deal with feasibility.

Finally, the results for the personal responsibility precondition were exactly opposite to the prediction: relative deprivation was highest when people blamed themselves for not having X. Does this mean that this whole precondition must be reevaluated, or is there a possible methodological problem? One limitation of the vignette is that it tells us about the main character but not about other specific persons who might be blamed in the situation. Perhaps the self-blame finding arose because the vignette offered no real alternatives.

Bernstein and Crosby (1980) produced an elegant demonstration of how the specific preconditions of relative deprivation can be operationalized and experimentally studied. The cost of such an experimental approach is that the subjects were not asked about their feelings about a real and involving personal topic. Of relevance to this issue is a fairly comprehensive study conducted by Crosby (1982) with over 400 participants that focused on relative deprivation and working women. One of the key features of this study is the effort made to deal with issues of high personal importance to participants.

Women with relatively low- and high-prestige jobs, as well as a sample of homemakers, were asked about their feelings concerning their individual work situation, the work situation of women in general, and their own home life. The questions focused generally on their feelings of relative deprivation, and specifically on each of the preconditions that various theorists have hypothesized to be associated with relative deprivation. The comprehensive nature of the study permitted multiple tests of the role of various preconditions. Unfortunately, no clear pattern of preconditions emerged consistently, and hence none of the theories of relative deprivation received strong support. However, two themes did emerge in virtually every analysis: wanting and deserving.

This led Crosby (1982) to revise her original model, in which she hypothesized five preconditions. She now posits two preconditions for relative deprivation: (1) a discrepancy between actual outcomes and desired outcomes (want), and (2) a discrepancy between actual outcomes and the outcomes deserved. Unfortunately, the simplicity of these two preconditions hides a real complexity. The key elements in the two preconditions are actual outcomes, desired outcomes, and deserved outcomes. The first, actual outcomes, is concrete and relatively easy to deal with. Determining desired outcomes and deserved outcomes is more problematic. Assessing desired outcomes involves the complex issue of who serves as the target for social comparisons. That is, what we desire is based on what others have. However, it is not just what anyone has that is important, but what those with whom we compare have. Now we are back to the complicated question: With whom does a person compare?

Similarly, "deserved outcomes" raises the question of how justice and fairness are determined. As we saw from Chapter 5, this is no small task. Thus, Crosby's two apparently simple preconditions for relative deprivation contain a number of hidden complexities.

Despite our having to weave a complex story of interacting and differing numbers of preconditions, there has been progress with the concept of relative deprivation. We have learned that though the feelings of relative deprivation are subjectively defined, it is not enough merely to have a negatively based social comparison. In addition, the concept of deservedness or fairness is central. The challenge now is to define these precisely, so we can predict when relative deprivation will be experienced.

RELATIVE DEPRIVATION AND INTERGROUP RELATIONS

Runciman (1966) was the first to explicitly address the question of relative deprivation in a collective or group context, by distinguishing between egoistical and fraternal deprivation. Egoistical deprivation involves the traditional case, in which an individual feels deprived because of his or her position within a group. When dissatisfaction arises because of a person's group's status vis-à-vis other groups in society, fraternal deprivation is experienced. Runciman (1966) felt that a person could experience either or, at times, both forms of deprivation. This might occur, for example, when a woman feels that her personal earnings are less than those of other women at her place of work and that women as a group earn less than men at the same place of work.

The importance of Runciman's (1966) distinction is best captured in a study by Vanneman and Pettigrew (1972). The focus was on relative deprivation and its relation to the attitudes of whites toward voting for black mayoralty candidates in major cities in the United States. The study was explicitly designed to operationalize Runciman's distinction between egoistical and fraternal deprivation. White respondents were asked to judge "their own economic gains" in relation to (1) their in-group (whites) and (2) the relevant out-group (blacks). Figure 6.1 describes how respondents would be classified on the basis of their answers to these two questions.

The findings reinforce the need for a distinction between individual and collective relative deprivation. The greatest reluctance to vote for black mayoralty candidates, and the most negative images expressed regarding these black politicians, came from those who felt fraternal deprivation. Egoistical deprivation did not produce such negative attitudes; those who felt it, surprisingly, were most favorable to the black candidates.

There is a second implication to Runciman's (1966) distinction that is directly relevant to the issue of intergroup relations. We might expect that a person who experiences egoistical deprivation would be prone to take some form of individualistic action. By contrast, collective or group action would be anticipated in the case of a person who experiences fraternal deprivation.

Guimond and Dubé-Simard (1983) addressed precisely this hypothesis in the context of French-speaking Québecois's perceptions of inequality in the

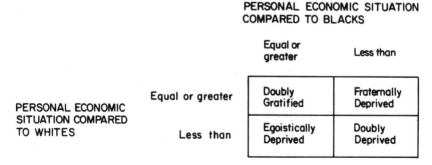

Figure 6.1   Four Types of Relative Deprivation

province of Quebec. Their study was limited to the expression of collective, nationalistic attitudes but showed that it was fraternal deprivation, not its egoistical counterpart, that was directly related to a positive attitude toward the collective Quebec nationalist movement.

Runciman (1966), however, did not deal with fraternal deprivation in any real depth, and important ambiguities remain. For example, one way to distinguish egoistical from fraternal deprivation is in terms of the target for social comparison. Thus, a comparison with members of one's own group (similar others) would be related to egoistical deprivation; a comparison with members of a "better off" group (dissimilar others) would involve fraternal deprivation. Martin and her colleagues (Martin & Murray 1983; Martin, Price, Bies, and Powers, 1979) examined this distinction by having secretaries view a tape and slide show depicting executives and secretaries in a company similar to their own. Secretaries were then told what pay they would receive and were asked whose pay they would be interested to learn about. The subjects were most interested in the highest-paid secretary and showed less interest in the pay of executives. Thus, comparison was egoistical, with a similar other, not with the dissimilar other (executive). At one level such findings might be interpreted to mean that individual comparisons are primary and more frequent than group comparisons. We should not, however, be too hasty in drawing this conclusion. Instead, we should reexamine the definition of group or fraternal deprivation.

By the definition described above, even the group comparison is individualistic, in the sense that it is the individual comparing himself or herself with another individual who happens to represent a different group. It is an individual secretary comparing with an individual executive. What about the more usual case, where, as a member of a group, I compare my group with another group? Thus, in the Martin et al. (1979) experiment, the question would not be "Does the secretary compare herself with another secretary or an executive?" but, rather, "Does she compare secretaries as a group with executives as a group in terms of salary?"

Crosby's (1982) study of working women points to the fundamental importance of this distinction. The women in her sample were asked about their personal feelings regarding their specific work situations, as well as about the situation of women in general. Surprisingly, Crosby did not obtain the same responses to these two questions. The women responded that on the whole they were satisfied with their personal work situations. However, they expressed considerable discontent about the position of working women as a group in the United States. Moreover, the women who expressed the most dissatisfaction about the role of women in general were those in high-prestige jobs. Why this should be the case, and why women report satisfaction with their own personal situations but dissatisfaction about the position of women in general, needs to be explored (see Taylor & Dubé 1986). Clearly, the distinction between egoistical deprivation and fraternal deprivation has important implications for people's feelings, but experiencing one of these does not necessarily mean that the other one is experienced as well.

Finally, Martin, Brickman and Murray (in press) expressed dissatisfaction with current definitions of deprivation in group terms and conducted interesting experiments to examine the variables affecting feelings of relative deprivation and their relation to action. Again, a business context was used. Subjects were presented with information about a fictitious company that had different salary levels for men and women. The variable manipulated was the number of women in the company whose salaries were equal to those of the men. The findings indicated that feelings of collective relative deprivation correlated with the magnitude of salary inequities. However, these feelings did not necessarily translate into collective action. Another feature of the experiment was that subjects were asked to judge the extent to which they would engage in various collective actions, such as attending meetings, engaging in work slowdowns, or making deliberate errors in work. However, the amount of felt deprivation did not produce differential willingness to engage in these forms of collective action.

Clearly, work on the feelings associated with collective deprivation is just beginning and, at least for the immediate future, research on this topic is likely to be somewhat uncoordinated. There are a number of reasons for this. First, there will continue to be research at the individual level that is extrapolated directly to the group. Second, fundamental issues regarding the social comparison process remain to be resolved, such as when people make comparisons and which targets people choose for their comparisons. Research on these topics at either the individual or the group level will be important. Finally, there are no systematic attempts to outline the features unique to collective relative deprivation. Hence, research will, in the short term at least, be exploratory and therefore unfocused. The hope is that with an increased awareness of group issues and the insights gained from exploratory research, a clearer definition of the issues will emerge.

CRITICAL REVIEW OF RELATIVE DEPRIVATION

We have already noted that an important limitation of relative deprivation theory is its individualistic emphasis. Aside from Crosby (1982), Guimond and Dubé-Simard (1983), Martin (1986), Pettigrew (1978), Runciman (1966), and Walker and Pettigrew (1984), collective deprivation has not been appreciated. This is a serious limitation, in that relative deprivation is invoked so often to explain collective discontent in society. We cannot assume that individualistic and intergroup deprivation are isomorphic. They may well serve different functions, serve very different needs, and lead to very different emotions and behavioral reactions. Echoing this point, Pettigrew notes that ". . . analyses of relative deprivation *have* too often stressed individual comparisons and perceived deprivation at the expense of the societally and politically more crucial group comparisons and perceived deprivations" (1978, p. 32).

This brings us to the next limitation, which Martin et al. (in press) were probably the first to raise. What is the relationship between relative deprivation and the behavioral response it generates? Under what conditions are a person's feelings translated into action, and how do we determine whether the reaction is individualistic or collective? As the research of Martin et al. (in press) demonstrates, feeling relative deprivation does not guarantee action of any kind. Martin found that the key was not relative deprivation itself, but whether a course of action was open to individuals. Taylor, Wong-Rieger, McKirnan and Bercusson (1982) examined the relationship between feeling threatened and whether an individualistic or collective response would be preferred. The participants were Anglophone Quebecois, and the focus was on the language situation in Quebec. Potential individual threats, such as the inability to communicate in French on the phone or one's son or daughter marrying a French-speaking person, were contrasted with possible collective threats, such as the lack of opportunity for advancement at work for Anglophones, or hostility between Francophones and Anglophones. The overriding hypothesis was that individual threats would be associated with individually based coping strategies, and that collective action would be the anticipated response to group threats.

Surprisingly, this hypothesis was not confirmed. The Anglophone participants in the study consistently preferred an individualistic strategy for coping with threats even when these were defined as group-based. Why might this be the case? Perhaps the Anglophone community in Quebec is not a well-defined social category that is accustomed to taking collective action. Or maybe there was, at the time of the study, no obvious leadership around which to organize collective action. Again, perhaps there is a feeling that taking collective action would only make matters worse and ultimately produce a worsening of intergroup relations. Whatever the reason, it is clear that there is no simple relationship between the feeling of relative deprivation and the response it generates. It will be essential for theories of relative deprivation to address this issue, especially when it involves application of the theory to collective action.

A third and final limitation brings us to certain of the fundamental underpinnings of relative deprivation. Specifically, there are two questions that must be resolved for relative deprivation to gain true predictive power. First, when do people make social comparisons? Second, how is a target for comparison selected? These are themes we have alluded to throughout the chapter, but progress on these questions is essential if relative deprivation theory is to be considered seriously in the domain of intergroup relations.

In a recently completed research project (Taylor, Moghaddam, & Bellerose, 1987), we set out to examine, in the context of intergroup relations, what types of comparisons people make. Our operating hypothesis contrasted sharply with that expressed by Pettigrew (1978). He feels that the issue of what types of comparisons people make is simpler to address in a group context. His argument is that "when groups are the referent, as opposed to individuals, the number of possibilities are sharply reduced. And reference groups tend to be reciprocally paired much in the manner of social roles: white-black; native-immigrant; blue-collar-white-collar. Even in polyethnic states, groups often form two political factions" (1978, p. 36). We began with an opposite prediction: that multiple comparisons not only are possible, but actually are made in a group context.

Our starting assumption was that members of one group do not always make comparisons with the same out-group. Rather, we believe that the target of comparison changes according to the purpose of the comparison. Our hypothesis was that when members of a group are seeking information, with a view to evaluating their position, they make comparisons with a number of potentially "better off" and "worse off" out-groups. However, when the aim is to bolster group morale, a "worse off" comparison group is chosen. Finally, when the aim is to appeal to some authority for more resources, a much "better off" other is chosen as the comparison group in order to maximize the effectiveness of the appeal.

The participants in this study were Anglophones from the province of Quebec, and the focus was on the threats they feel from language legislation in the province that has made French the official language. From a pilot study we found eight major groups with whom Anglophones spontaneously make comparisons on the issue of language rights. These are listed in Table 6.2 along with the average rating a sample of 82 Anglophones gave on a ten-point scale anchored at one end by "much worse off" (0) and at the other by "much better off" (10). From the table we can determine whether a particular comparison is upward (any group with a rating above 5) or downward (any group with a rating below 5).

In order to test the hypothesis that the comparisons people make change according to the purpose, and that the purpose will determine whether the comparison is upward or downward, we gave our sample of Anglophones written scenarios. One scenario dealt with making comparisons in order to ascertain one's own or one's group's position. This is the purpose relative deprivation theorists assume operates on a normal basis. The scenario read: "Well, the point I am making is that if you really want to know how Quebec Anglophones are being treated and really want to analyze what we deserve, you have to compare Quebec Anglophones with _____ ."

The respondent read the scenario and filled in the blank with whatever group or groups he or she felt were appropriate from the list in Table 6.2. In

Table 6.2   Ratings by Anglophones of Extent to Which Various Comparison Groups Are Better Off (0) or Worse Off (10) Regarding Language Rights

Anglophones in other provinces	9.2
Anglophones in Quebec in the past (prior to Bill 101 and 22)	7.5
Francophones in Quebec today	6.6
Francophones in Quebec in the past (prior to Bill 101 and 22)	5.3
Other language groups in other provinces	5.1
Francophones in other provinces	4.9
Other language groups in Quebec	3.9
Badly treated minorities in other countries	2.1

Source: Taylor, Moghaddam, and Bellerose. 1987.

accordance with the hypothesis, respondents did not choose one specific group as the target of comparison. More than any other scenario, respondents tended to make comparisons with a number of other groups. Such a strategy is perfectly reasonable. When the person's aim is to evaluate his or her own position or that of his or her group accurately, the more information available, and hence the more comparisons made, the better. It is interesting to note, however, that relative deprivation theory does not address this possibility. It assumes there is only one target of comparison, and that any feelings a person might have arise out of that single comparison.

Our Anglophone respondents had a very different social comparison strategy when the purpose shifted from one of evaluation to boosting morale. The "morale" scenario read: "Yes, I certainly agree that we Quebec Anglophones are getting a bad deal. But then there are some groups, like _____, who are in a worse situation. It sure makes me feel better about the deal Quebec Anglophones are getting when I compare our situation to theirs."

The three popular comparison groups were "badly treated minorities," "other language groups in Quebec," and "Francophones in other provinces," the three groups judged from Table 6.2 to be "worse off" in comparison with Anglophones. As predicted, when people are motivated to protect or enhance their morale or sense of well-being, they choose a "worse off" other with whom to make a comparison (Ashby-Wills, 1983).

The third scenario of interest was one involving an appeal for greater equality: "We Quebec Anglophones have a perfect right to be fed up. While everyone agrees that _____ are much better off than us, it is also true that they are really no different from us, and so we should both be treated equally."

The two popular selections here were "Francophones in Quebec today" and "Anglophones in other provinces." As we can see from Table 6.2, these are two of the three groups rated as "better off."

Thus these results, preliminary though they may be, underscore certain of the complexities involved in determining people's reactions to a particular situation. Our Anglophone respondents made very different comparisons, depending upon their needs and purpose. Moreover, these results challenge certain assumptions of current relative deprivation theory, especially those expressed by Pettigrew (1978). First, respondents do not make a comparison with one other person or group when evaluating their situation. Their need for information seems to provoke comparisons with a variety of "others." And the comparisons are not merely with similar others. Sometimes, when the aim is to boost morale, extremely worse off others are chosen; and when an appeal is being made, extremely better off others are the focus. In both cases the comparison others are quite dissimilar.

In summary, relative deprivation suffers because its application to intergroup relations has only begun to be studied directly. The second limitation involves the target for comparison, which strikes at the heart of relative deprivation. This second limitation is thus more serious, in the sense that it likely accounts for why the momentum that began with the research on the American soldier has not been sustained. The need, then, is for fundamental research on the basic principles of relative deprivation, as well as on its application to intergroup relations.

CONCLUSION

Relative deprivation theory can be usefully considered as a special case of social comparison theory that deals with disadvantaged individuals and groups. Its strength is in offering insights into some persistent puzzles associated with intergroup relations. Why is it that groups which are well off in terms of objective criteria can sometimes feel most dissatisfied? Why do extremely disadvantaged groups sometimes accept their difficult position?

The recent upsurge of interest in relative deprivation theory no doubt is partly due to the challenge posed by such questions—questions that must be answered in order for relative deprivation theory to fulfill its early promise. Specifically, theorists still have to identify the various conditions for relative deprivation, extend the theory to fully cover intergroup relations, and tackle the difficult issue of the selection of target comparisons.

SUGGESTED READINGS

Crosby, F. 1976. A model of egoistical relative deprivation. *Psychological Review, 83*, 85–113.

_____ . 1982. *Relative Deprivation and Working Women.* New York: Oxford University Press.

Olson, J. M., C. P. Herman, and M. P. Zanna (eds.). 1986. *Relative Deprivation and Social Comparison: The Ontario Symposium.* Vol. 4. Hillsdale, N.J.: Erlbaum.

7   Elite Theory

Scope: Elite theory attempts to explain relations between majority and minority groups, with special emphasis on the conditions that lead minority group members to instigate collective action.

Assumptions: The major assumption is that every society is governed by an elite, and that intergroup conflict does not fundamentally change the structure of society, since a new elite simply replaces the old one.

Propositions: All societies are composed of elites and nonelites. Where these groups are open and circulation between them is allowed, talented individuals move up into the elite and those with insufficient talent move down into the nonelite. However, where circulation is not permitted, talented members of the nonelite form counterelites and eventually overthrow the governing elite. Once in power, the new elite takes on the powers and privileges of the old governing elite.

Elite theory is a dynamic social psychological theory of intergroup relations that has had an important influence on the work of sociologists and political scientists, but not of psychologists. Its dynamic nature is reflected by the predictions it makes about changes in group membership and intergroup relations, while its social psychological character is reflected by the pivotal role it ascribes to the abilities and motives of individual group members in determining intergroup behavior.

Five central assumptions underlie elite theory: First, that the elite and the nonelite form distinct groups in all societies. Second, all societies are governed by an elite. Third, in conditions where access to the elite is open, circulation between the elite and nonelite will be in terms of individuals; but where access is closed, circulation will be in terms of groups. Fourth, in conditions where entrance into the elite is closed, it is the most talented members of the nonelite who will instigate the formation of counterelites and mobilize the nonelite against the governing elite. It is under these circumstances that intergroup conflict arises, with the possibility of power changing hands and a new elite gaining control of key power positions. Fifth, although governing elites may be toppled and replaced by counterelites, the basic structure of society will not change and there will always be an elite that rules and a nonelite that is ruled. This basic two-tier social structure will remain the same in all societies, irrespective of labels, such as "democratic" or "Marxist," that may be used to describe particular political systems. Thus, from the perspective of elite theory, intergroup conflict and even revolution can lead to changes in, but not the disappearance of, the governing elite.

The social psychological nature of elite theory, particularly as outlined by Pareto and his followers, is explicitly reflected by the definition of the elite group and the assumed basis of elite/nonelite group formation. While Pareto has been almost completely ignored by psychologists (for some exceptions see Billig 1982; Lambert 1956; McDougall 1935), he himself gave considerable importance to psychology: "Clearly psychology is fundamental to . . . all the social sciences . . . . . Perhaps a day will come when the laws of social science can be deduced from the principles of psychology" (Pareto 1971, p. 29). His definition of the elite group is psychological, since he assumes its formation to be determined principally by the abilities of individuals:

> Let us assume that in every branch of human activity each individual is given an index which stands as a sign of his capacity, very much the way grades are given in the various subjects in examinations in school. The highest type of lawyer, for instance, will be given 10. The man who did not get a client will be given 1—reserving zero for the man who is an out-and-out idiot. . . . And so for all

branches of human activity . . . . So let us make a class of the people who have the highest indices in their branch of activity, and to that branch give the name of 'elite'. (Pareto 1935, III, pp. 1422–23)

An enlightening question, particularly since it reflects upon the nature of psychology itself, is why elite theory has been neglected by psychologists. One possible explanation for this neglect could be that elite theory does not have anything positive to contribute to psychology. Allport adopts this position when he describes Pareto's *The Mind and Society* as ". . . a vast treatise on sociology from the point of view of an irrationalist social psychology" (1968, p. 21), and claims that Pareto ". . . was only saying, in different and complicated terms, what irrationalist social psychologists have previously said," and that Pareto was ". . . unacquainted with the history of social psychology" (1968, pp. 20–21). Writing much earlier, McDougall (1935) had stretched this argument to an extreme and claimed that Pareto ignores all psychology from Aristotle on. The invalid nature of this claim is clearly demonstrated by Pareto's critical writings on French collective psychology (see Billig 1982, p. 84, n. 128). Also invalid is the claim that irrationalistic social psychologists had preempted Pareto, since, as we shall demonstrate, the dynamic theory of intergroup behavior developed by Pareto and other elite theorists entails features that can make original and important contributions to the social psychology of intergroup behavior.

The real reasons for the neglect of elite theory by psychologists may well be its explicit political connotations. Psychologists have traditionally endeavored to present their profession and research as scientific and apolitical. The adoption of a theory that has had explicit links with political ideologies might jeopardize the fragile image of psychology as a science.

Elite theory was developed principally by Vilfredo Pareto and Gaetano Mosca, two Italian theorists writing mainly in the first part of the 20th century. Pareto's apparently anti-democratic and pro-fascist sentiments have been responsible for openly politicizing elite theory and making it "unsafe" from the viewpoint of psychologists concerned with achieving an apolitical image. It should be noted, however, that psychologists have been less concerned about adopting theories that are implicitly political and reactionary but that are camouflaged by a cloak of scientific neutrality (see Billig 1976, 1978, 1982; Sampson 1981). Mosca was more favorably inclined toward democracy and, indeed, took pains to demonstrate the compatibility of elite theory and democracy. Probably for this reason, his work is ascribed more importance by contemporary elite theorists (for instance, Dye & Zeigler 1970). It would be misleading, however, to view elite theory solely in the context of early 20th-century social sciences.

The tradition of extolling the virtues of the talented elite, in contrast with the belief in the common man, can be traced directly back to Plato. As

Friedrich noted, ". . . the elite is a modern version of Plato's guardian class" (1942, p. 251). In *The Republic*, Plato argues that government should be in the hands of a specially trained group of philosopher kings, particularly because of their wisdom and lack of desire for power (see Adam 1963). Plato's historical influence on the minds of the Western elite have ensured the survival of his views on elites and power. Interestingly, Pierre Trudeau, Canada's prime minister for almost 16 years, cited Plato when asked about his own motivation for power:

> Warner Troyer (reporter): How badly do you want to be prime minister?
>
> Trudeau: Not very badly. But I can give you another quotation, from Plato—that men who want very badly to head the country shouldn't be trusted. (CBC-TV interview, Toronto, March 26, 1967)

As the movement toward democratization gained momentum during the 18th and 19th centuries, fear of rule by the masses brought about a more determined and well-defined effort by supporters of elite doctrines. For example, in works such as *Heroes, Hero-Worship and the Heroic in History* (1841), Carlyle described democracy as meaning despair of finding any heroes to govern you in a world devoid of heroism. The writings of Ruskin and Macaulay in England, John Adams and John Calhoun in America, and Nietzsche in Germany echoed the same sentiments. Thus, elite theory should be viewed from the perspective of a general concern on the part of those who feared the outcome of "radical reform" and "democratization," and argued in favor of the "wisdom of the elite" as opposed to the "wisdom of the common man."

However, the critical target of modern elite theory has not been democracy, but Marxism. Marx had predicted a gradual transformation of the structure of society. From the capitalist state would emerge a proletariat that would acquire class consciousness and perceive themselves as a distinct class with interests that conflict with those of other classes. Acting on the basis of this perception, the proletariat would mobilize as a class and defeat the ruling class. Marx predicted that the proletarian revolution would gradually lead to a classless society, and that the state would eventually dissolve and disappear. Thus, Marxism predicts structural changes in society, leading to the defeat of the rulers by the ruled, and the eventual disappearance of rulers as a privileged class.

By contrast, elite theory predicts that there will always be an elite ruling class and a nonelite that is governed. This two-tier structure is proposed as unchanging and present in all societies.

Both elite theorists and Marxists give importance to the role of the elite in revolutions, but for different reasons and with different predictions for the outcomes of interclass relations. Elite theory assumes that counterelites will lead the masses in the struggle to overthrow the governing elite, only to take the place of the governing elite. Thus, the masses are mobilized, used to topple the governing elite, and then put back in a subordinate position. Marxists also see revolutionary movements as being led by elites: ". . . no revolutionary movement can endure without a stable organization of leaders that maintains continuity" (Lenin 1973, pp. 152–53). However, from the Marxist perspective, the elite-led revolution will ultimately lead to the elimination of the elite as a privileged governing class.

In one sense, it is not surprising that the elite theory account of intergroup behavior has been neglected by social psychologists, since intergroup behavior is itself a largely neglected topic of study in social psychology (see Chapter 1). However, there has been renewed interest on the part of both European and North American researchers in this area, and there are at least four important reasons why the elite theory account of intergroup behavior should receive serious attention from researchers.

First, elite theory is dynamic, with change being its central concern. Probably more than any other social psychological theory, it focuses upon changes in group membership and the effects of such changes upon intergroup relations.

Second, elite theory concerns itself with large social groups, macro social changes, and long time periods. This is a welcome change from the almost exclusive tendency in social psychology to deal with small groups and behavioral processes at the micro level.

Third, elite theory has had considerable influence on sociological and political science research, a fairly unusual situation among social psychologically based theories. Researchers from different social science backgrounds have paid special attention to governing elites (Wilkinson 1969) and elite recruitment (Eulau & Czudnowski 1976). A number of widely read texts on the U.S. political system adopt the elite theory perspective. An important example is Dye and Zeigler's *Irony of Democracy*, whose opening sentence boldly states: "Elites, not masses, govern America" (1970, p. 1). The most important modern work influenced by elite theory remains C. Wright Mills's *The Power Elite* (1956). However, neither Mills nor any other researcher has yet developed and utilized the social psychological account of intergroup behavior entailed in elite theory.

The fourth important reason why elite theory should receive more serious attention from social psychologists is that the account of intergroup behavior it offers seems largely to correspond with the beliefs and perceptions of many lay people. A significant number of people seem to see society the way elite theory says it is, and this is surely an important quality for a theory of social behavior to have. Mosca (1939) argued that "In practical life we all recognize the existence of this ruling class [elite] . . . we all know that the management of public affairs is in the hands of a minority of influential persons, to which management, willingly or unwillingly, the majority defer" (p. 50). Very few social psychological theories can make a similar claim of corresponding closely with the way lay people view society.

Elite theory and research have been critically discussed in a number of fairly comprehensive texts (for instance, Prewitt & Stone 1973), and it is not our intention here to conduct another review. Our main objective is to identify and highlight the social psychological aspects of elite theory, and to outline a social psychological account of intergroup behavior from the elitist perspective. We begin this task by providing an outline of elite theory. This outline will be organized in five parts, each part dealing with one of the five fundamental propositions of elite theory: the existence of elite and nonelite groups in all societies; the inevitability of elite rule; circulation of the elite; counterelite formation; the static nature of the social structure.

A number of fundamental gaps exist between elite theory and the social psychology of intergroup behavior. The most important theoretical and practical aspects of these gaps are discussed in the second section. While certain propositions of elite theory probably need modification in order to be tested through the experimental methods of social psychology, in certain other respects it would probably prove beneficial if existing social psychological perspectives on intergroup behavior moved closer to that of elite theory. This is particularly so with respect to the elite theory's tendency to deal with large social groups and intergroup processes over long time periods.

Finally, a critical review of elite theory is presented. Once again, our aim will not be to conduct an exhaustive review on the basis of existing social science elite research, but to limit our concerns to key matters related to the task of developing a social psychological model of intergroup behavior based upon elite theory.

AN OUTLINE OF ELITE THEORY

The elite theory account of intergroup behavior postulates a number of processes that can vary considerably in terms of time scale and size of social unit involved: from short-term, intra-personal processes to long-term processes involving entire societies and spanning centuries.

The Elite and the NonElite

"So we get two strata in a population: (1) A lower stratum, the *non-elite* . . . then (2) a higher stratum, the *elite*, which is divided into two: (a) a governing *elite*; (b) a non-governing *elite*" (Pareto 1935, III, p. 1424).

The first fundamental psychological assumption of elite theory is that the elite and the nonelite form two distinct groups in society, the elite being composed of the more talented individuals. The elite is further divided into governing and nongoverning categories; most elite theorists have concerned themselves primarily with the latter.

Differences in quality of membership between the elite and nonelite groups is assumed to lead to important differences in the behavior of the two groups, particularly in terms of group organization, cohesiveness, and consciousness. The power of the elite minority is seen to arise principally from its superior organizational abilities and its greater group cohesiveness. The nonelite is seen as a mass of individuals whose forces are unconnected and dispersed. The nonelite can be organized only by the elites, either the governing elite or the counterelites.

Thus, elite theory proposes that the elite is a distinct group because of its psychological, rather than its social, characteristics. It is the superior abilities of individual members of elites, rather than their social traits such as social class, ethnicity, and religion, that ensure elite superiority. In fact, if the elite group loses its superior psychological characteristics and elite membership becomes exclusive to those who, for example, are born into a particular class or ethnic group, then elite theory would predict a decline of the governing elite and the rise of a counterelite. Given the central role elite theory ascribes to psychological factors, the testing of some of the theory's major propositions necessarily requires a psychological approach.

Every Society Is Governed by an Elite

> In all societies—from societies that are very meagerly developed and have barely attained the dawnings of civilizations, down to the most advanced and powerful societies—two classes of people appear—a class that rules and a class that is ruled. The first class, always the less numerous, monopolizes power and enjoys the advantages that power brings, whereas the second, the more numerous class, is directed and controlled by the first. . . . (Mosca 1939, p. 50)

The assumption that every society is necessarily ruled by an elite is central to elite theory. The "necessity" of elite rule stems from the superior organizing abilities of the elite. Discontent among the masses could lead to the downfall of the governing elite, but ". . . there would have to be another organized minority within the masses themselves to discharge the functions of a ruling class. Otherwise, all organization and the whole social structure, would be destroyed" (Mosca 1939, p. 50). It is not difficult to see how such concern for the survival of the social structure, viewed as fragile and vulnerable, could lead some elite theorists to argue vehemently that the best government is a strong centralized one, firmly entrenched in the hands of a talented minority that possesses the will to rule. It is in this context that one should evaluate Pareto's support for the "rule of the strong" (1935, IV, p. 1525).

Two contrasting viewpoints can be identified among elite theorists in regard to the role of the elite in democracy, the first personified by Pareto and the second by Mosca. The first viewpoint is more conspiratorial, seeing democracy as a smokescreen that allows the elite and counterelites to monopolize power without the "interference" of the nonelite. The second viewpoint is more influential among modern elite theorists and sees elite rule as compatible with democracy. Both viewpoints rely upon complex psychological interpretations of interpersonal and intergroup behavior.

Like Marx, Pareto assumed a sharp distinction between reality as it is propagated in society and objective reality. While most actions in society are nonlogical from an objective viewpoint, in that they do not use means appropriate to ends and do not logically link ends to means, they are propagated and perceived as logical. Thus, the need to ". . . tear off the masks nonlogical conduct is made to wear and lay bare the things they hide from view" (Pareto 1935, I, p. 171). Once Pareto "tears off the mask," he finds that democracy is merely a tool used by the elite to keep the nonelite in a disadvantaged position while retaining power for itself. As for concepts such as "the equality of man," these are merely the ". . . means commonly used, especially today, to get rid of one aristocracy and replace it with another" (Pareto 1971, p. 93).

In passages that preempt Festinger's (1954) cognitive dissonance theory, Pareto argues that people interpret the world in a way that will make their own actions appear logical. While society is governed by an elite that is motivated purely by self-interest, concepts such as "equality of man" and "equal rights" are used to camouflage this reality and make the social order appear rational:

> Men follow their sentiment and their self-interest but it pleases them to imagine that they follow reason. And so they look for, and always find, some theory which, *a posteriori*, makes their actions appear logical. If that theory could be demolished scientifically, the only result would be that another theory would be substituted for the first one, and for the same purpose. . . . (Pareto 1971, p. 95)

In contrast with the viewpoint presented by Pareto, contemporary elite theorists agree more with Mosca's argument that elite theory and democracy are, in important ways, compatible. This compatibility is assumed on the basis of two intergroup processes: the first involving the transfer of pressure and discontent from the nonelite to the elite, which leads to intergroup influence and accountability, and the second being the circulation of the elite.

Mosca (1939) argued that the governing elite cannot remain outside the influence of the nonelite: "Whatever the type of political organization, pressures arising from the discontent of the masses who are governed, from the passions by which they are swayed, exert a certain amount of influence on the policies of the ruling . . . class" (p. 51). Counterelites play a key role in the transfer of this pressure from the nonelite to the elite by organizing and mobilizing the masses and giving voice to their discontent.

While political pressure ensures that the governing elite responds, to some degree, to the demands of, and is accountable to, the nonelite, "circulation of the elite" provides talented people with the opportunity to move up the social hierarchy and join the elite. From the perspective of theorists who view elite theory and democracy as compatible, the equal opportunities offered to all in democratic societies ensure that free circulation of elites takes place. This is seen as essential for the survival of the system.

Circulation of the Elite: Groups and Individuals

"Circulation of the elite" is the pivotal concept in elite theory. The term refers to the circulation of both individual elites and groups of elites (see Figure 7.1). Elite theory predicts that in conditions where entrance into the elite group is open, circulation of individuals will occur. That is, individuals who are members of the nonelite, but have the abilities to move up and join the elite, will first attempt to move up as individuals. Elite theory predicts that if the talented members of the nonelite find that entrance into the elite group is closed to them, they will then form counterelites, moving to challenge and eventually topple the governing elite. Thus, in conditions where entrance into the governing elite is closed, circulation will be in terms of groups.

Circulation of the elite in terms of individuals refers both to the upward movement of individuals from the nonelite to the elite group and to the downward movement of individuals from the elite to the nonelite group. A critical assumption in elite theory is that the only way an elite can ensure its survival is to keep its doors open to talented members of the nonelite, and to discard individuals who are nominally in the elite group but do not have the abilities to function adequately as elite group members:

> The governing class is restored not only in numbers, but—and that is the more important thing—in quality, by families rising from the lower classes and bringing with them the vigour and the proportions of residues necessary for keeping themselves in power. It is also restored by the loss of its more degenerate members. If one of these movements comes to an end, or . . . if they both come to an end, the governing class crashes to ruin. . . . Potent cause of disturbance in the equilibrium is the accumulation of superior elements in the

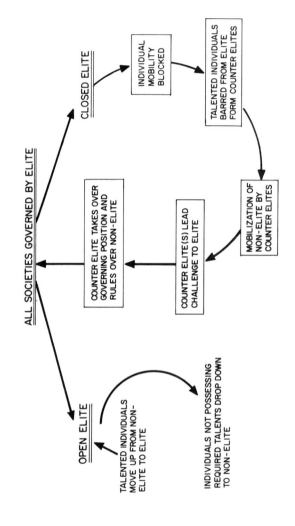

Figure 7.1   Schematic Representation of Elite Theory

lower classes and, conversely, of inferior elements in the higher classes. (Pareto 1935, III, pp. 1430–31)

Pareto's famous statement "History is a graveyard of aristocracies" (1935, III, p. 1430) is a reflection of the elite theory's belief that all governing elites eventually make the mistake of ending the conditions in which circulation of individuals can occur freely, and bringing about conditions in which only circulation of groups is possible. By closing its membership, or restricting it too much, every governing elite eventually digs its own grave.

Mosca saw democratization as a means of facilitating the circulation of the elite and strengthening the governing elite: "It [the democratic tendency] enables ruling classes to be continually replenished through the admission of new elements who have inborn talents for leadership and a will to lead . . ." (Mosca 1939, p. 416). This theme is also of critical importance in the work of modern elite theorists, particularly those concerned with protecting the democratic system in the face of radical challenges. For example, Dye and Zeigler (1970) make the following point in favor of free circulation:

. . . a certain amount of circulation of elites is essential for the stability of the elite system. Openness in the elite system siphons off potentially revolutionary leadership from the lower classes, and an elite system is strengthened when talented and ambitious individuals from the masses are permitted to enter governing circles. (p. 4)

"Elite circulation" is also one of the means through which the elite and the nonelite are linked and mutually influenced. In moving from one group to another, an individual ". . . generally brings with him certain inclinations, sentiments, attitudes, that he has acquired from the group from which he comes . . ." (Pareto 1935, IV, p. 1426). Thus, individuals moving up from the nonelite to the elite, and those dropping down from the elite to the nonelite, are acting as instruments of intergroup influence. By examining where an individual comes from and which processes have been passed through, modern elite theorists attempt to better understand and predict how the individual will behave in the new social group. This is the area known as "political recruitment," defined by Marvick (1976) as the study

. . . of politics with a special eye to how participants got there, where they come from and by what paths, and hence what ideas and skills and contacts they acquired or discarded on the way. Its payoff as a mode of inquiry comes when it helps the observer to anticipate what viewpoints are likely to be introduced into the political context by virtue of the presence of political actors with particular kinds of credentials. (p. 30).

Counterelites

Counterelites are composed of individuals who are talented enough to be effective members of the elite but are barred from elite membership. Counterelites are formed for the explicit purpose of challenging the governing elite, overthrowing it, and taking its place.

Whether counterelites form is assumed to depend upon the open or closed nature of the elite. In conditions where the elite is an open group and circulation between the elite and the nonelite occurs freely, social mobility takes place individually, with the most able individuals moving up to join the elite group (see Figure 7.1). However, in conditions where the elite is a closed group, potential elite members form counterelites.

The success of counterelites in their challenge for power depends principally upon two factors: the quality of individuals belonging to the elite and the counterelites, and the relative will of the elite and the counterelites to use force in order to achieve power. The quality of group members refers to the proportion of members who are nominally in a group but do not possess the personal abilities required to function effectively in it. However, the will to be in power is also important, since a group may possess the necessary talents but be unwilling to use all the necessary means, including force, to achieve and retain power. Thus, Pareto states that

> Revolutions come about through accumulation in the higher strata of society of decadent elements no longer possessing the residues suitable for keeping them in power, and shrinking from the use of force; while meantime in the lower strata of society elements of superior quality are coming to the fore, possessing residues suitable for exercising the functions of government and willing enough to use force. (1935, III, p. 1431)

The central role ascribed to the will to achieve and retain power, through force in particular, points to the importance of ideology among the elite. Unity and commitment to an ideology are seen by elite theory as essential qualities if an elite is to survive. For this reason, the process of elite recruitment necessarily involves both screening and socialization, particularly in modern times: ". . . only those non-elites who have demonstrated their commitment to the elite system itself and to the system's political and economic values can be admitted to the ruling class" (Dye & Zeigler 1970, p. 4).

The Static Structure of Society

Elite theory has profound implications for our understanding of social development, since it assumes the structure of human society to be unchanging. From the perspective of elite theory, every society is, and always will be, ruled by an elite. Counterelites that topple the elite do so merely to take their place, not to change the system:

> . . . every time the democratic movement has triumphed, in part or in full, we have invariably seen the aristocratic tendency come to life again through efforts of the very men who had fought it. . . . Everywhere, those who have reached the top rungs on the social ladder have set up defences for themselves and their children against those who wished to climb. (Mosca 1939, p. 417)

Counterelites get support from the masses by tricking them into believing that their aim is to change the stratified nature of society, and end all or the most significant inequalities of power and wealth. The counterelite is "inevitably" led to act in this conspiratorial manner, because if it were to clearly and simply

> . . . proclaim its intentions, which are to supplant the old elite, no one would come to its assistance, it would be defeated before having fought a battle. On the contrary, it appears to be asking nothing for itself, well knowing that without asking anything in advance it will obtain what it wants as a consequence of its victory. . . . (Pareto 1971, p. 92)

This cyclical, and perhaps cynical, model of social evolution advanced by elite theory has its counterparts in both popular and classical literature, as well as in beliefs held by lay people. The view that inequality will always be present, and that the reformers and revolutionaries of today become the conservatives and tyrants of tomorrow, is both very ancient and very prevalent. It is an outlook well encapsulated by the poet William Butler Yeats:

> Hurrah for revolution and more cannon shot!
> A beggar on horseback lashes a beggar on foot.
> Hurrah for revolution and cannon come again!
> The beggars have changed places, but the lash goes on. (1968, p. 190)

THE SOCIAL PSYCHOLOGY OF INTERGROUP BEHAVIOR AND ELITE THEORY

At both the theoretical and the practical level, fundamental gaps exist between the social psychology of intergroup behavior and elite theory. At the theoretical level, the social psychology of intergroup behavior has thus far typically involved extrapolations from the level of individual and small group behavior to that of large groups and macro-social processes. For example,

extrapolations have been made from research involving the behavior of individuals in the laboratory gaming context (Deutsch 1973) and from small
group behavior in realistic field research contexts (Sherif 1966) to the level of
international conflicts (see Chapter 3). It has been assumed that the influence
of key social psychological factors in the development of peaceful or conflictual
relations is largely the same, if not identical, at the interpersonal, intergroup,
and international levels. This assumption has been the basis upon which social
psychologists studying the processes leading to peace and conflict have focused
upon relations between individuals and small groups. In contrast, elite theory
has focused on large groups and macro social processes.

The application of elite theory to the level of interactions between small
groups, such as those traditionally studied by social psychologists, will probably require certain refinements in the theory. Consider, for example, a study
that focuses upon interactions between workers and managers in a factory
context. How do we define the elite and nonelite in this setting? Do all the
managers automatically belong to the elite group, or only some of them, or
perhaps even none of them? This specific example illustrates an issue of
general importance: does the elite always have to be defined in terms of national or international hierarchies, or can we regard "local elites" as sharing
essentially the same key psychological characteristics as the national elite?
What, if any, are the psychological differences in intergroup behavior between
the national elite and the nonelite, and the local elites and the nonelites? These
are crucial issues, since social psychologists have tended to deal with local
elites, which have been advantaged groups in small settings, while elite theory
deals with national elites.

At the practical level, social psychologists face the major challenge of devis-
ing effective ways to test the propositions of elite theory. In particular, the
dynamic nature of elite theory makes the experimental testing of its propositions a challenging task. Elite theory predicts changes both in the membership
of elite and nonelite groups, and in the relationship between the groups. While
these changes are assumed to stem from intrapersonal factors (the personal
talents of group members and changes in human resources of elite and
nonelite groups), the changes themselves are large-scale and are postulated to
involve the entire governing and governed groups in society.

Given the gaps that exist between elite theory and the social psychology of
intergroup behavior, we should seriously address the question of how the experimental methods of social psychology can be effectively used to test the
propositions of elite theory. A first step in this direction might be to consider
the kind of research carried out on elite theory by other social science
disciplines, and to evaluate how social psychology might contribute to our
understanding of the phenomena under investigation.

Although elite theory incorporates a social psychological account of intergroup behavior, its major propositions have not been tested by social

psychologists. However, significant research on various aspects of elite theory has been carried out by sociologists and political scientists, as well as by other social scientists. We shall briefly describe a representative study from this literature, then point out the contributions that social psychologists could make to better understanding of the processes involved in the behavior of elites and nonelites.

The compatibility of elite theory and democracy is probably the most important underlying theme of contemporary elite research. Supporters of the view that the two are compatible have rested their case principally on two concepts: accountability of the elite and circulation of the elite. Following Lasswell (Lasswell & Kaplan 1950), emphasis has been placed on the relationship between the elite and the nonelite, and the accountability of the former to the latter. From this perspective, since the democratic system ensures that the elite is accountable to the nonelite, it is not the number of the few who govern that is seen to be important, but the nature of the influence exerted by the nonelite on the elite. The elite and the nonelite are assumed to share power through accountability.

Following Mosca (1939), elite theorists have proposed that the democratic system strengthens the elite, since it ensures the free circulation of elites. In democracies, suitably talented individuals are, theoretically at least, able to move up the social hierarchy and reach positions of power, thus preventing the stagnation of the elite group.

Accountability of the elite and circulation of the elite both entail assumptions that require empirical verification, and a major part of the research effort by elite theorists has been to this end. Kaltefleiter (1976) reports a study investigating circulation of the elite in Germany. This study is of particular interest from our perspective, since it attempts to complement sociological research methods with social psychological ones. However, we shall point out a number of ways in which the social psychological method of inquiry adopted could have been very usefully and effectively extended to produce a fuller understanding of the topic under investigation.

Kaltefleiter begins his investigation with an interesting set of questions about the modern elite in Germany, questions that reflect typical concerns among elite theory researchers:

> Does this elite represent the "ruling class" of a traditionally autocratic political culture, which today is acting behind the facade of a formally democratic constitution? Or is it an integrated part of an open and democratic society based on effective political competition, equal opportunities, free interchange among elites and nonelites and intergenerational mobility. (1976, p. 239).

He then addresses these questions by analyzing the recruitment of political elites in Germany. Kaltefleiter's principal research method is to investigate the social characteristics of the elite and to identify changes in these characteristics over time. The spectrum of social classes and ethnic and religious groupings from which the elite is recruited will, he assumes, cast light upon the openness and accessibility of the political elite. Thus, the first important question he addresses is "Where does the elite come from?" The answer he arrives at, after comparing the social class origins of the political elite at a number of stages since 1925, is that "Even given the difficulties of comparing the different data, the trend is obvious: from a highly upper-class recruitment to a middle-class recruitment, which slowly tends to become open to the lower class" (1976, p. 242).

Another question addressed by Kaltefleiter is "What stations do the elite pass through before joining the elite group?" Most important, elites have to pass through a high level of formal education. This requirement proves to be more important than any other. The traditionally important effect of religious affiliation on elite group membership was found to be diminishing, with the underrepresentation of Catholics decreasing, although a slight overrepresentation of Protestants was found still to be present among the German political elite.

Kaltefleiter also investigated certain perceptions of the political elite, thus complementing his sociological investigations with psychological ones. Specifically, he investigated whether holders of elite positions view their advancement to, or retention of, these positions as the result of strong competition. The assumption underlying this approach was that in an open system, where the elite is accessible, a large percentage of the elite would perceive access to the elite group and the maintenance of the elite position as involving a hard struggle.

Kaltefleiter found that 66 percent of the political elite, as opposed to 55 percent of the nonpolitical elite, mentioned that they had to fight hard for their successes; 37 percent of the political elite, compared with 20 percent of the nonpolitical elite, believed that they had to struggle constantly or frequently to maintain their elite positions. The higher percentages of the political elite reporting that they had to struggle to achieve or maintain elite positions, or both, is interpreted by Kaltefleiter as evidence that democratic processes are ensuring the openness of the political elite, at least relative to other elites. He concludes that "The recruitment process, which demonstrates tendencies towards an open and highly competitive elite, operates according to the theoretical assumptions of a democratic system" (1976, p. 260).

Kaltefleiter's research method rests on the assumption that the perceptions of political elite members regarding how hard a struggle it has been to achieve and maintain their positions of power, necessarily reflect the accessibility of the political elite. Much social psychological evidence exists to suggest that once a person has behaved in a certain manner and has invested in a certain position, that person will interpret social reality in a way that justifies his or her present position (see Festinger 1957, 1964). It may be that just as large a percentage of the nonelite will report that they have had to struggle to reach and maintain their present positions. Alternative, and possibly just as valid, interpretations of Kaltefleiter's findings may also exist. For example, it may be that a higher percentage of the political elite reports having had a hard struggle to reach and maintain their elite positions simply because they are the elite most concerned about their public image, as well as the most talented in presenting a selected public image.

A more important and theoretically more interesting set of issues, not addressed by Kaltefleiter, concerns the social attributions and comparisons made by the elite and the nonelite in interpreting their past and present positions. To what factors do the elite attribute their top positions, and to what factors do the nonelite attribute their exclusion from the elite? With whom do the elite and the nonelite compare themselves when justifying their present position? How do new elite members interpret and justify their leaving the nonelite, breaking ties and loyalties, and joining the elite while their former group receives relatively low rewards? These are some of the basic questions that could usefully be addressed to achieve a more complete picture of elite circulation.

CRITICAL REVIEW OF ELITE THEORY

Although offering a dynamic social psychological theory of intergroup behavior that treats social mobility and social change in a fairly comprehensive and intuitively appealing manner, elite theory has a number of important limitations that need to be addressed. First, classical elite theory, as developed principally by Pareto and Mosca, is deterministic. Second, it has not developed a generally accepted and satisfactory definition of the elite. Third, since elite theory categorizes the social world into two groups, the rulers and the masses, the role of the new middle classes is left rather vague.

Determinism

Elite theorists replaced the Marxist notion of a ruling class that governs by virtue of its economic power with that of an elite group that rules by virtue of the superior qualities of its members. But they also replaced the economic determinism entailed in Marxism with an equally iron form of social determinism. Bottomore (1966) has clarified this point eloquently:

> The fundamental argument of the elite theorists is not merely that every society has been divided into two strata—a ruling minority and a majority which is ruled—but that all societies *must* be so divided. In what respect is this less deterministic than Marxism? For

whether men are obliged to attain the classless society or are necessarily prevented from ever attaining it, are they not equally unfree? It may be objected that the cases are not alike: that the elite theorists are only excluding one form of society as impossible while leaving open other possibilities . . . whereas the Marxists are predicting that a particular form of society will necessarily come into existence. But one might equally well say that the elite theorists—and especially Pareto—are claiming that one type of political society is universal and necessary, and that the Marxists deny the universal validity of this "law of elites and masses" and assert man's liberty to imagine and create new forms of society. (p. 19)

Once we accept as valid the assumption that all societies must be governed by an elite, we lose the opportunity to explore the conditions in which other forms of social structure can arise. It may be the case that all societies are presently ruled by elites; it may even be the case that most people perceive the governing elite to have achieved its position through legitimate means and superior individual talents. But the elite rule and perceptions of the elite may themselves be an outcome of certain forms of social construction and ideology that are presently dominant but may be changed. While it is important to explore social psychological phenomena within the present social system and its dominant ideology, the theories we adopt should not close our minds to the possibilities of fundamental changes in the system or to implications of change for individual behavior in any particular social context.

Defining the Elite

How one might usefully define the elite is a particularly thorny problem, and that has not been addressed with any degree of success in the literature. There has been a tendency to use circular definitions. To the question "Who are the elite?" we receive the reply "Those who govern;" while inevitably those who govern are described as the elite. At the operational level, the challenge facing researchers has been that of identifying those who really govern. This is essentially the challenge Mills took up in his classic work *The Power Elite* (1956). For Mills, the elite are people with the power to make effective decisions, those who are able to realize their will even if others resist it. These individuals are found at the helm of the most powerful institutions, and they are supposedly characterized by common psychological and social traits. However, whereas Pareto defines the elite in terms of their superior, inborn personal characteristics, Mills defines them more in terms of characteristics acquired through common socialization experiences.

On the question of definition, an issue of critical importance, from the social psychological perspective, is "Do the elite perceive themselves to be a distinct and cohesive group?'' This is not necessarily the same as asking if they actually form a distinct, cohesive group. Reflected here is the difference between the social psychological and the sociological perspectives. Adopting the sociological perspective, Mills argued that there are three major elite groups—the economic, the political, and the military—and that they form a cohesive power force. From the social psychological perspective, we might begin by asking: Do those who have been identified as elite members from the sociological perspective actually perceive such a group to exist and themselves to belong to it?

Elite and Nonelite: A Need for a Third Category?

While Marxism proposes a gradual historical development toward the polarization of two social classes, the proletariat and the ruling class, elite theory proposes an unchanging division of society into two social categories, the elite and the nonelite. Marxism focuses upon the consciousness of the proletariat, proposing that there will ultimately be open class war because the proletariat will come to see itself as a distinct group with interests that contradict those of the ruling class. Elite theory focuses upon the consciousness of the elite group, proposing that there will never be open conflict between the elite and the nonelite, because the elite and the counterelites realize that it is in their interest to compete for power between themselves, and also because they have the ability always to outmaneuver the nonelite and keep it in a disadvantaged position.

The respective emphases of Marxism and elite theory on the consciousness of the proletariat and the elite group reflect the different ideological underpinnings of the two theories. While Marxism extols the virtues of the proletariat and sees it as the ultimate victor in the competition to control society, classical elite theory applauds the elite and sees it as the legitimate ruler, in all societies and throughout history. However, while constructing a model of society that assumes the existence of two distinct major categories probably has certain benefits, such as simplicity, it can also have certain disadvantages, such as oversimplification.

Where do the new middle classes fit into the picture if we categorize society as elite and nonelite? For example, are modern managers to be perceived as part of the elite or of the nonelite? Only a handful of managers have reached the very top decision-making positions, yet most managers wield enough influence in their own sphere of activity to make their placement in the nonelite appear out of order. This decision confronts elite theory with a major problem, one that might be overcome by reference to circulation of the elite. The new middle classes, or at least elements among them, could be viewed as counterelites achieving power through newly found economic wealth and influence. Burnham (1941) adopts such a perspective in his *The Managerial Revolution*.

We have thus far portrayed elite theory and Marxism as being at log-gerheads—as they are in their classical forms—but there have also been important attempts to synthesize key Marxist and elitist concepts in interpreting the modern state. The main theme for such works was established by Burnham (1941). While following the elitist tradition in portraying politics as a struggle between governing elites and counterelites, Burnham also adopted the Marxist practice of estimating power in terms of the control of each group over the means of production. In modern societies, he argues, managers are gaining control of the means of production; thus they are the ones who make key decisions. Through the "managerial revolution," this new counterelite is replacing the old capitalist elite. The new managerial elite achieves power by gaining control of key decision-making posts and, gradually, the state itself, rather than through amassing private capital. As the state and the business world merge, and as the distinction between controllers of private and public corporations diminish, the managerial elite increases its control of the state. In societies where the amalgamation of state and business is more complete, such as in the Soviet Union, the power of the managerial elite is more complete.

It is important to note, however, that Burnham (1941) is moving away from the social psychologically based theory of elites developed by Pareto. While the latter assumed rule by the elite to be inevitable because of the superior personal abilities of its members and the organized nature of their group, the former cites macroeconomic and social factors as the only factors responsible for elite rule: "Far from being incapable of constituting a ruling class, the managers, by the very conditions of modern technology and contemporary institutional evolution, would have a hard time avoiding it" (Burnham 1941, p. 281).

Elite Theory and the Caste System

The traditional Hindu caste system appears to represent a social structure that contradicts the most fundamental propositions of elite theory. According to elite theory, in conditions where circulation of individuals between the elite and the nonelite is not permitted, counterelites will form to challenge, and eventually defeat, the elite. The traditional picture of the Hindu caste system has been that of

> . . . a society in which religious values and ideas were the sole deter-minants of attitudes toward and chances for social mobility; in which little if any such mobility actually occurred; in which there were no discrepancies or incongruities between an individual's position in the "caste" dimension and his position in other social dimensions; in which there was practically no social change and resultant conse-quences for the alteration of the position of individuals in society;

and in which, in sum, a state of near-perfect integration, stability, and individual immobility prevailed for endless centuries, even millennia. (Barber 1968, p. 18).

If this picture proved to be valid, it would mean that the elite could remain a closed group yet still survive—contradicting the predictions of elite theory.

Pareto's response to the criticism that elite theory is not capable of explaining the survival of the caste system was to reject the traditional picture that social scientists have painted of Hindu society. In a passage that is prophetic of research findings almost half a century later, Pareto (1935, III) states: "We must not confuse the state of law with the state of fact. . . . There are many examples of castes that are legally closed, but into which, in point of fact, newcomers make their way, and often in large numbers" (p. 1427). By the end of the 1960s a different picture of the caste system was emerging, one that identified certain strategies through which social mobility of individuals between castes was made possible in certain conditions (Mandelbaum 1970; Silverberg 1968; Scrinivas 1968). It seems to be the case that the elite group in the caste system is not altogether closed, and that social mobility does take place in the caste system over long periods of time. Social mobility in this context can take place in terms of both individuals and groups. Elite theory predicts that talented members of the nonelite castes will first try to move up individually, and form counterelites and try to mobilize entire castes only when they have found individual social mobility impossible to achieve.

Elites, Elite Theory, and Democratic Values

There is a persistent confusion about the ethics of conducting research designed to test elite theory. It is sometimes assumed that conducting such research is synonymous with supporting elite rule and being anti-democratic. This viewpoint is strengthened, implicitly at least, by certain researchers studying elite behavior. For example, Field and Higley (1980), who have made one of the rare attempts in recent times to further develop classical elite theory, state:

> . . . to advance elitist hypotheses today it is not enough to argue, as Pareto, Mosca and Michels could, that elites always or usually exist and that they are probably of decisive importance. In addition to this, it is now necessary to refute the widely held assumptions that values such as equality, liberty and freedom are universal and objective. Probably only by making this refutation can contemporary thought be brought to see the importance and the propriety of elitists' assumptions. (p. 3)

Unlike Field and Higley, we believe that "elitist assumptions" are fundamentally different, depending on which tradition of elite theory research one deals with, and it is essential that such traditions be distinguished.

Confusion about the supposedly contradictory nature of elite theory research and democratic values can be clarified by distinguishing between two traditions of research on the elite: the supportive and the critical. Those working in the supportive traditions, such as Pareto, have assumed not only that the elite does rule in all societies but also that it *should* rule in all societies. This approach is explicitly normative. Such researchers have constructed visions of the ideal society as one that is ruled by the elite having the particular personal qualities they most cherish—for Pareto, these qualities consist of superior personal talents, and the will to use force to retain power and maintain law and order. Thus, research in the supportive tradition has the explicit ideological aim of supporting elite rule.

Researchers following the critical tradition have studied elites with the intentions of demonstrating the inefficiencies and inadequacies of the present system, and of weakening rather than supporting elite rule. Writing in the foreword to Prewitt and Stone's *The Ruling Elites*, Lowi reflects the dominant mood of the critical tradition when he points out that ". . . you don't have to like elites to study them" (1973, p. x). He then goes on to describe the main concerns of what we have termed critical elite research:

> There should no longer be any question in anybody's mind that elites of the public and the private sphere, of government, business, religious, and university spheres—not even to mention the most obvious sphere, the military—have failed us. They have learned about communications media only to use them for mass exercises in duplicity and manipulation. They have learned about computers and used them mainly as leverage for market power or self-aggrandizement, or both. They have learned to profit by the excitation of false expectations, and they have learned how to use bureaucracies in order to evade responsibility as well as to gain higher efficiency. (1973, pp. x–xi)

Thus, research in the critical tradition has the intention, sometimes made explicit, ultimately to change the present system in fundamental ways and give nonelites more power. This endeavor would lead to a strengthening, rather than a weakening, of democratic values and practices.

CONCLUSION

The movement to enhance the importance of intergroup behavior as a topic of study for social psychology would be aided considerably by the incorporation of elite theory and research. The social psychological account of intergroup behavior offered by elite theory entails many constructive qualities and insights—it certainly deserves more attention from psychologists. While certain exponents of elite theory have explicitly aimed to support the elite cause, there also exists a tradition of critical research involving efforts to expose the inefficiencies and the unfairness of elite rule. The political connotations of elite theory have sometimes been wrongly interpreted to mean that elite research is necessarily anti-democratic. Once this fallacy is exposed, and once the problems of operationalizing elite theory concepts and designing experiments to test key postulates are tackled, the path is open to a fruitful, experimentally based social psychology of intergroup behavior based upon elite theory. In terms of both dynamism and scope, the behavioral model that emerges from the marriage of elite theory and the experimental methods of social psychology would be of great value.

SUGGESTED READINGS

Bottomore, T. B. 1966. *Elite and Society*. Harmondsworth, England: Penguin.
Dye, T. R., and L. H. Zeigler. 1970. *The Irony of Democracy: An Uncommon Introduction to American Politics*. Belmont, Cal.: Wadsworth.
Prewitt, K., and A. Stone. 1973. *The Ruling Elites: Elite Theory, Power, and American Democracy*. New York: Harper & Row.

8   A Five-Stage Model
of Intergroup Relations

Scope: The five-stage model deals with a broad range of relations between groups. The focus is largely on groups of unequal status, and on the individual or collective responses of disadvantaged, and to a lesser extent advantaged, groups.

Assumptions: The major assumptions are (1) that all intergroup relations pass through the same five developmental stages in the same sequential manner and (2) that upward social mobility will be initiated by members of a disadvantaged group in an individual manner prior to collective action being instigated.

Propositions: Five developmental stages of intergroup relations are proposed. At stage 1, group stratification is rigid and based on societal categories, such as race or sex. The concept that individual effort and ability determine group membership emerges at stage 2. During stage 3, individual upward mobility is attempted by talented members of the disadvantaged group. Where this attempt is unsuccessful, talented members of the disadvantaged group attempt ''consciousness raising,'' which can lead the disadvantaged group to collectively challenge the advantaged group (stage 4). At stage 5, the two groups are in a healthy state of competition as long as neither group consistently dominates the other. However, if relative equality is not established, the groups return to an earlier stage and begin the process anew.

The five-stage model of intergroup relations, developed by Taylor and McKirnan (1984), is the most recent of the theories examined in this volume and can be usefully viewed in the context of the move toward nonreductionist social psychological accounts of intergroup relations. Taylor and McKirnan have attempted to produce a model of intergroup relations that is broad in scope and has theoretical underpinnings that are well established in mainstream social psychology. As such, the five-stage model can be seen as attempting to incorporate both macro and micro processes in interpreting intergroup behavior, thus aiming for a truly social psychological perspective. Although Taylor and McKirnan cannot be said to have succeeded completely in this endeavor, their model does, at least, indicate the form that broadly based social psychological accounts of intergroup relations might usefully take.

In explaining the historical background to the five-stage model, it is relevant to point out that this model was developed at McGill, a Canadian university influenced by the academic traditions of both Europe and the United States. While most of Taylor and McKirnan's work is in the tradition of mainstream North American social research, their links with European researchers, especially Tajfel and his associates, have been particularly strong. These European and North American influences are reflected in the scope and concerns of the five-stage model. On the one hand, the model reflects the European concern with minority influence and responses to inequality; while on the other hand, the theoretical underpinnings of the model are central to North American social psychology.

An assumption inherent in the five-stage model is that rarely, if ever, is the relationship between two groups perfectly equal. Thus, the model attempts to explain relations between groups where one is advantaged and the other is disadvantaged. The use of the labels "advantaged" and "disadvantaged" by Taylor and McKirnan (1984) should not go unnoticed, since it hints at a possible a priori bias. Some theorists use such labels as "majority" and "minority," which are neutral but misleading because numbers may not be a true indication of power. Others, such as Tajfel and Turner (1979), use the labels "dominant" and "subordinate," or "high" and "low" status, implying, however subtly, that the groups themselves are somehow responsible for their position or status. Taylor and McKirnan's use of "advantaged" and "disadvantaged" seems to imply that external conditions, rather than the traits of groups, are responsible for inequality.

Another feature of the five-stage model is its focus upon both the advantaged group and the disadvantaged group in an unequal relationship. This focus on both groups is welcome, given the rather unbalanced perspective that has characterized intergroup relations thus far. This imbalance has tended to be to the detriment of disadvantaged groups, since it is generally in Europe that research has, at least to some extent, focused upon minority group behavior (Mugny 1984). Interestingly, the issue of the underdog and minority group behavior was a major concern of North American researchers, but only in the immediate postwar period. For example, this is clearly reflected in the research reviewed in Allport's classic study *The Nature of Prejudice* (1954) since the object of prejudice is generally a disadvantaged individual or group, a "minority" by definition (see Asch 1956). However, the issue of minority group behavior seems to have been set aside by North American psychologists since the early 1960s, and biases in favor of majority groups seem to have crept into all aspects of research (Sampson 1981). Thus, the issue of responses to inequality, which is necessarily a minority group concern, is a relatively neglected issue in contemporary social psychology.

As a social psychological model, the five-stage model is unusual both in its temporal expanse and in the scope of the factors it encompasses. The model deals with intergroup developmental processes that are assumed to be influenced by large-scale social changes, such as industrialization. Thus, it has a historical perspective. Moreover, the model deals with processes that can take more than the lifetime of any individual group member to complete. This implies that the processes underlying the five-stage model are in some ways more extensive than the psychology of any one generation of group members.

In the first part of this chapter, we shall review the main propositions of the five-stage model. This will be followed by an outline of a typical experiment designed to test major propositions of the model. In the final major section, we present a critical review of the theory, focusing on its strengths and weaknesses.

AN OUTLINE OF THE FIVE-STAGE MODEL

Taylor and McKirnan (1984) propose five distinct developmental stages to intergroup behavior; they are presented schematically in Figure 8.1. The stages include (1) clearly stratified intergroup relations, (2) individualistic ideology, (3) individual social mobility, (4) consciousness raising, (5) collective action. It is assumed that all intergroup relations involve this five-stage development in the same sequential order. In terms of time frame, the five stages can take centuries to be completed, or they may take a much shorter period. The time required for intergroup relations to move from one stage to the next is not specified, but is assumed to be variable and dependent upon historical, social, economic, political, and psychological factors.

An important feature of the model, one that remains constant throughout the five stages, is the assumption that there are high- and low-status groups in society. That is, the stratified and differential state of society is accepted as part of social reality.

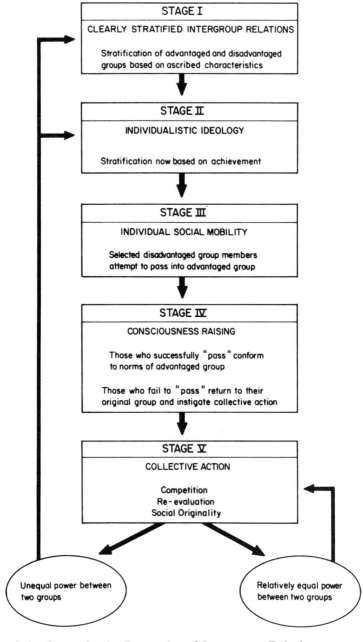

Figure 8.1   Stages in the Dynamics of Intergroup Relations

Finally, it is hypothesized that the key processes linking the sequence of stages are two mainstream social psychological concepts, causal attribution and social comparison. Beyond this, an important extension is made to both causal attribution and social comparison in order that they can be more effectively applied to an intergroup context. Specifically, two levels of causal attribution and social comparison are distinguished. In terms of causal attribution, the two levels are, individual attribution, where causes and explanations are sought for individual behavior, and group attribution, where the individual seeks an explanation for the behavior of his or her own or another group.

A similar distinction is made for social comparison. Individualistic social comparisons involve a person making social comparisons with other in-group members, whereas group comparisons involve the comparisons a person makes between his or her own group and some other relevant outgroup.

Stage I: Clearly Stratified Intergroup Relations

At stage I, groups are stratified on the basis of ascribed characteristics and there is an unbridged division between the advantaged group and the disadvantaged group. Examples of such societies are feudal and caste social structures, as well as what Van den Berghe (1967) has referred to as "paternalistic" societies. An example would be the relationship between slave owners and slaves in early U.S. history. A current example of this phenomenon might be the caste system in India. The basis for social stratification in such societies can be inherent, such as race and sex, or ascribed, such as religious belief and role. However, in all cases it is assumed that stratification takes place only on the basis of the selected criteria for group membership, and this division is not questioned by members of either group.

In such intergroup contexts, the pattern of social attributions and social comparisons is dictated by the power relations between the groups. Only individualistic or intragroup social comparisons are deemed legitimate, since the out-group, whether it is advantaged or disadvantaged, is seen as being so dissimilar to the in-group that social comparison with its members is judged to be illegitimate (Festinger 1954). Group membership covaries perfectly with an easily recognizable characteristic such as race or sex, and the intergroup status situation is completely rigid.

Paradoxically, disadvantaged group members attribute their disadvantaged position to themselves, on the assumption that it is their own race or sex, for example, that has led them to be disadvantaged. Such "own responsible" attributions are, naturally, propagated by the advantaged group; and disadvantaged group members have such limited power that they have little option but to share the advantaged group's views on social reality.

Stage II: Emerging Individualistic Social Ideology

During stage II, stratification is on the basis of achievement rather than ascribed characteristics. This stage of development is reached as an outcome of modernization and the growth of a middle class. The increased importance of occupational skill, role complexity, and the implication that individual ability and effort determine the occupational role and status of a person gradually leads to the ideology of individual social mobility. That is, although there are still two groups during stage II, one relatively advantaged and the other disadvantaged, group membership is now assumed to be based on individual achievement rather than ascribed group characteristics.

While in stage I perceptions of the basis of social stratification correspond to the actual basis, in stage II the actual basis of social stratification may be different from the perceived basis. Thus, while the perceived basis of membership in an advantaged group might be individual achievement, the actual basis could still be race, sex, or birth into a rich family.

The key psychological difference between stages I and II is that in stage I the groups are accurately perceived as being closed, but in stage II the groups are perceived as being open. Also, the social comparisons and social attributions made in stage II legitimize the perception that individual ability and effort determine status. Members of both advantaged and disadvantaged groups attribute their status to individual characteristics for which they are assumed to be responsible, such as ability and effort. From the perspective of the advantaged group, this "person blame" ideology is particularly important, since it exonerates them from responsibility for the disadvantaged position of the out-group members.

Since individuals are perceived as being responsible for group membership, social comparisons take place at the inter-individual level. In terms of equity theory (see Chapter 5), disadvantaged group members comparing themselves with members of the out-group downplay their own input until the ratio of inputs to outcomes is identical with that of the out-group. For example, working-class persons are socialized to believe that their inputs to society are less valuable than those of persons in professional positions. Through this process, they come to feel that they "get what they deserve," thereby justifying their disadvantaged position.

Stage III: Social Mobility

At stage III, individual members of the disadvantaged group attempt to move into the advantaged group. This social mobility will be in two forms. The first involves an attempt by a disadvantaged group member to completely change his or her characteristics so as to "pass" as a member of the advantaged group. The second form of social mobility is less extensive and involves an attempt by a disadvantaged group member to adopt enough of the advantaged group's characteristics to be accepted as a member of that group, yet retain enough features of the disadvantaged group to maintain his or her original identity.

The motivation for an attempt to move into the advantaged group is assumed to be a need for positive social identity. In this key respect, therefore, the five-stage model is similar to social identity theory (see Chapter 4), which perhaps reflects the influence of Tajfel and his associates on this model. By passing into an advantaged group, a disadvantaged group member necessarily rejects some of the features of the disadvantaged group.

The five-stage model goes some way toward identifying the characteristics of the individuals who are most likely to attempt upward social mobility. This move will be attempted only by a select few among the disadvantaged group, the most talented and the ones most likely to initiate interpersonal comparisons with individual members of the advantaged group. In terms of elite theory (Chapter 7), such individuals are members of the "potential elite" who must be allowed to move freely up into the elite group.

The social comparisons encouraged by the stage II ideology lead the most talented disadvantaged group members to initiate upward social mobility. The key feature of the social comparisons encouraged by the stage II ideology is that they are inter-individual. Moreover, they are not on the basis of ascribed characteristics, but of the criteria that are relevant to the requirements for entry into the advantaged group. Thus, when social comparisons are made on the basis of ability and effort, it is the most talented among the disadvantaged group who come closest to having the requirements for entry into the advantaged group.

The social attribution patterns of the stage II ideology also encourage attempts at upward social mobility by the most talented members of the disadvantaged group. Advantaged group members attribute the acquisition of their status to factors for which they are personally responsible, such as effort and ability. Disadvantaged group members who are closest to the advantaged group in terms of relevant characteristics, and who share the ideology of the advantaged group, are thus motivated to attempt upward social mobility, since they see themselves as good enough to succeed according to the rules of the system.

The key assumption made with respect to stage III is that individual attempts at upward social mobility are always the first strategy by which the most talented members of a disadvantaged group cope with inequality. According to the five-stage model, collective action occurs only after individual attempts at upward social mobility have failed. Historic examples of such behavior are the blacks in North America, and the French in Canada, both of whom first reacted to their unequal status by attempting to "pass" individually into the advantaged group. Only later did collective action predominate.

Stage IV: Consciousness Raising

The talented members of the disadvantaged group who attempt upward social mobility are not always successful. However, the few who do succeed play an important role in strengthening the social system. They do this in two main ways. First, their success reaffirms their belief in the ideology and justice of the system, and leads them to assimilate in the extreme into the advantaged group. According to the dominant ideology, it was hard work and talent that moved them up into the advantaged group, and they are justified in feeling proud about their success.

The disadvantaged group members who do succeed in moving up into the advantaged group serve as evidence that the system works, that it is just, and that anyone with the required abilities can "make it." Also, since these individuals are the potential leaders of the disadvantaged group, their upward social mobility serves to weaken the disadvantaged group and strengthen the advantaged group. We have already noted that in elite theory (Chapter 7) this process of the circulation of the elite is seen to be critical, since it is assumed that if the elite are not permitted to move freely from one group to another, then the system will be in danger of collapsing. However, elite theory deals with a two-way movement between advantaged and disadvantaged groups, whereas the five-stage model deals principally with a one-way movement from the disadvantaged to the advantaged group.

There will also be some disadvantaged group members who attempt upward social mobility but fail to gain entry into the advantaged group. They may, in accordance with the prevailing ideology, attribute their failure to their own personal characteristics. Thus, the notion "I am just not good enough" or "I should have tried harder" could be used to explain their failure to gain entrance into the advantaged group. However, Taylor and McKirnan (1984) argue that this is unlikely, since these individuals will probably be influenced by self-serving biases in attribution. Thus, they will look to external factors to explain their failure to move into the advantaged group. More specifically, they will see the actions of the advantaged group as having unjustly prevented their upward social mobility. Furthermore, they will switch from seeing their own personal characteristics as being the cause of their disadvantaged position to seeing the actions of the dominant group as being causally responsible. Thus, they will gradually see events in intergroup rather than in individualistic terms.

Those disadvantaged group members who fail in their attempt at upward social mobility will come to believe that their personal esteem is tied up with that of the entire disadvantaged group, rather than being based on their personal characteristics. That is, the only way in which the position of the self can be improved is by improving the position of the entire group. This transition in perspective involves a shift from interpersonal to intergroup social comparisons.

However, a move toward collective action by the disadvantaged group would require that a large number of disadvantaged group members come to believe that the ideology linking ability and effort to station in life is invalid. Specifically, they must come to believe that social status is not in fact determined by individual characteristics, but is unjustly determined on the basis of characteristics such as race or sex. Those disadvantaged group members who have failed to achieve upward social mobility play a key part in bringing about this awareness by embarking upon consciousness raising among the disadvantaged group members. Their mission is to convince all members of the disadvantaged group to share their view that membership in a disadvantaged group is not based upon such individual characteristics as ability and effort, but is unjustly determined on the basis of ascribed characteristics such as ethnicity and race.

Stage V: Competitive Intergroup Relations

Consciousness raising among the disadvantaged group members leads to collective attempts to improve the group's position vis-à-vis the advantaged group. The collective strategies envisaged in the five-stage model are those outlined by Tajfel and Turner (1979) in social identity theory (see Chapter 4). The first collective strategy is collective competition, which involves attempts to compete with the advantaged group along particular dimensions of competence or status in a given society. This would be competition according to the existing rules of the game. A second collective strategy involves redefinition. That is, characteristics of the group that were previously defined as negative are redefined as positive, and attempts are made to obtain acceptance for this reevaluation. A classic example would be the "Black is beautiful" movement among North American blacks. A third collective strategy is referred to as "social originality" and involves the creation of new dimensions for social comparison by the disadvantaged group. For example, a disadvantaged group might emphasize not the outcome of a performance but the environmental hardships that have to be overcome in order to achieve the outcome. By implication, those persons who are less advantaged in terms of environmental conditions are now seen as higher achievers, even if they do not do quite as well as advantaged persons who enjoy good environmental conditions.

At this stage, the disadvantaged group encourages intergroup comparisons, while the advantaged group attempts to show that only individualistic comparisons are legitimate. That is, the advantaged group will argue that there is free movement between groups, and anyone who has the necessary entry requirements will be able to achieve upward social mobility into the advantaged group. By contrast, the disadvantaged group will attempt to show that social categorization is on the basis of ascribed characteristics and movement between groups is not possible.

The pattern of attribution at this stage is particularly interesting. While disadvantaged group members attribute responsibility for past subordination to the advantaged group (external attribution), hope for the future is attributed to the disadvantaged group in the form of controllable internal characteristics of the disadvantaged group (internal attribution). This pattern of external attributions for past status and internal attributions for future status has been found, for example, among North American blacks (Rappaport 1977).

Once the stage of intergroup competitive relations (stage V) has been reached, three possible outcomes are hypothesized. The first and second of these lead the groups back to stage I or II, with the cycle beginning anew. That is, first the relative power between the advantaged and disadvantaged groups may remain unchanged, resulting in a return to stage II relations. Second, the previously disadvantaged group may emerge as dominant, resulting in a return to stage II relations with the status position of the groups now reversed. Third, the groups may become relatively, although never completely, equal in status and power. In this situation, constant intergroup social comparisons, with no clear-cut victor, will keep the intergroup situation in a healthy state of competition.

A TYPICAL EXPERIMENT STIMULATED BY THE FIVE-STAGE MODEL

The five-stage model is a relatively recent addition to the field of intergroup relations. Consequently, few studies have been undertaken to test its propositions. However, two experimental studies testing key aspects of the model have been completed (Taylor, Moghaddam, Gamble, Zellerer, in press). We shall briefly outline their method and findings.

The two experiments tested propositions based on the five-stage model that deal with the broadly based issue of how members of a group respond to being in a disadvantaged position. Specifically, the issues investigated were under what conditions group members will (a) apparently accept their negative status, (b) take some form of individual action, (c) instigate collective action. Especially important is the attempt to specify the precise conditions associated with collective action. According to the five-stage model, the perception of injustice is associated with members of the disadvantaged group initiating action designed to change the relative situation. Moreover, a distinction is made between distributive and procedural justice, the former being concerned with resource distribution among individuals and the latter involving the manner in which the distribution is conducted.

An important assumption entailed in the five-stage model is that questions of distributive justice involve individual differences, whereas procedural justice concerns the collectivity. This leads to the prediction that members of the disadvantaged group will engage in collective action when unjust procedures are perceived and will take individual action when the focus of perceived injustice is distributive.

The five-stage model also predicts that the first response to disadvantaged group membership is in the form of individualistic attempts at upward social mobility (stage III). Collective action is attempted only after such individualistic attempts have failed (stages IV and V). Also, only those disadvantaged group members who are closest to the advantaged group in terms of the necessary entry requirements will attempt upward social mobility (stage III).

It is hypothesized that those disadvantaged group members who are close to gaining entry but are refused on what they perceive to be unjust grounds will attempt collective action (stage V). However, if those who are close to entry fail in their attempt at upward social mobility on what they perceive to be just grounds, they will take individualistic action. Those who are not close to gaining entry into the advantaged group and perceive their position to be just will accept their disadvantaged position.

The experimental paradigm adopted was an attempt to reproduce in the laboratory certain features of the North American "meritocracy" ideology. Participants began the experiment as members of a disadvantaged group, in a situation where moving from a disadvantaged to an advantaged group was both desirable and possible on the basis of performance criteria. In both experiments, this criterion was performance of a decision-making task, which involved a stabbing incident. The motivations to perform well were (1) association with a high-status group, (2) the opportunity to join the advantaged group that made all decisions concerning movement from group to group, (3) greater monetary rewards available to the advantaged group in the form of a $100 lottery (compared with a $10 lottery for the disadvantaged group).

Experiment 1

Participants answered the test case questions, and their answers were ostensibly evaluated by members of the advantaged group. While participants waited for the advantaged group members to grade their performance, the two justice manipulations were introduced. Distributive justice was manipulated by providing participants with either an excellent model answer (distributive "just" condition) or a very poor model (distributive "unjust" condition) with which to compare their own performance. Procedural justice was manipulated by giving participants information that would lead them to believe that their performance had been evaluated on the basis of either purely objective criteria ("just" procedure condition) or subjective criteria, such as sex ("unjust" procedure condition).

For all conditions, participants were given a failing mark and informed that they must remain in the disadvantaged group. They were then asked to consider the following four behavioral options for the remainder of the experiment: (1) accept option—the respondent accepts the evaluation received and agrees to participate in the next part of the experiment as a member of the disadvantaged group; (2) individual retest option—the respondent is dissatisfied with the decision and requests a second attempt at answering questions; (3) individual protest option—the respondent is dissatisfied with the decision and requests the opportunity to send a message to the advantaged group asking them to reconsider their decision about the respondent's particular case; (4) collective action—the respondent is dissatisfied with the evaluation procedure and wishes to solicit the support of other members of the disadvantaged group, with the aim of inducing the advantaged group to change the evaluation procedure.

The results indicated that it is possible to specify some of the conditions associated with individual, as opposed to collective, action. Specifically, results showed that only when both the procedure and the distribution were unjust did participants endorse the collective action option. When the procedure was just but distribution was unjust, participants reacted equally strongly, but individualistically rather than collectively. Failure in a condition where both distribution and procedure were just led to passive acceptance, with little motivation even to retake the test. The results of Experiment 1 indicate that it may be possible to specify the conditions in which collective action will be the preferred response to inequality.

Experiment 2

The same experimental paradigm as in experiment 1 was used to test the hypothesis that (1) collective action would be advocated by those who were close to gaining entry into an advantaged group but are refused entry on unjust grounds, (2) individualistic action would be preferred by those who were close, but unsuccessful on legitimate grounds, and (3) those who are far from gaining entry on a legitimate basis would passively accept their situation.

Participants took part in the same decision-making task as in experiment 1 and received feedback on their performance, ostensibly from the advantaged group. Participants were informed that a grade of 85 percent was required for entry into the advantaged group. Closeness of entry was manipulated by informing the participants that they had received a grade of either 82 percent ("close" condition) or 50 percent ("far" condition). Justice was manipulated by informing participants that they had been evaluated either on objective criteria ("just" condition) or subjective criteria ("unjust" condition). As in experiment 1, respondents received feedback informing them that they must remain in the disadvantaged group. They were then presented the four behavioral options: accept, individual retest, individual protest, collective action.

The main hypothesis was confirmed. The participants who endorsed collective action were those in the close-unjust condition. Individualistic options were preferred by those whose evaluations were just. However, contrary to expectation, those who were in the far-unjust condition endorsed the no-action option. A possible explanation is that their low status robbed them of the confidence needed to try to control the outcome. An example of such behavior from the real world might be ethnic minorities who experience severe injustice, feel powerless, and thus remain passive toward their disadvantaged position.

In summary, these two experiments represent a modest attempt to test hypotheses derived from the five-stage model. That hypotheses derived from the model can be tested in the laboratory suggests the model could provide some direction and framework for laboratory research on intergroup behavior. With respect to the two studies described, it is encouraging to note that there seem to be concrete conditions that do discriminate between individual and collective action. If these can be researched in a more complete fashion, we may gain important insights into the puzzle associated with when members of a group might act collectively.

CRITICAL REVIEW OF THE FIVE-STAGE MODEL

The most important strength of the five-stage model is probably that it encompasses both macro- and micro-level processes. That is, Taylor and McKirnan (1974) have attempted to explain intergroup relations by referring to social processes that function at the intergroup level as well as to psychological processes that function at the intra- and interpersonal levels. For example, the transition they envisage from stratification based on ascribed characteristics (stage I) to stratification based on achievement (stage II) is assumed to involve, and partly derive from, large-scale processes of industrialization and the emergence of a middle class in society. At the same time, this transition is assumed to involve psychological changes related to social attribution and social comparison at the intra- and interpersonal levels. This incorporation of micro and macro processes is surely a feature toward which social psychological accounts of intergroup relations should strive.

Second, the five-stage model has the strength of being realistic, in that it presents a picture of unequal groups in situations of actual or potential competition for scarce resources. This model also seems to take an ideological stand, in that it focuses upon responses to inequality and minority group behavior. Despite the increase of interest in minority group behavior during the 1980s (see Moscovici et al. 1984; Mugny 1984), there is still little research on the behavior of disadvantaged groups, and this neglect is especially apparent in North America. The five-stage model should prove useful in redressing this imbalance.

Third, by outlining a historical development of intergroup relations, the five-stage model attempts to avoid working in a historical vacuum. By linking the five stages of intergroup development to evolutionary stages in social history, such as feudalism and industrialization, it goes some way to placing intergroup behavior in a historical context.

Fourth, although a broad-based theory, the five-stage model has generated specific hypotheses that can be tested through the methods of experimental social psychology. Thus, this model has an advantage over elite theory, which has not yet been developed in such a way that its main hypotheses can be experimentally tested, although field studies testing its propositions abound.

However, the five-stage model also seems to have a number of weaknesses, some of which will be reviewed in the following discussion. First, stages I and II represent two different social systems, the first based on ascribed characteristics and the second on achieved characteristics. However, only the second of these, the one based on achieved characteristics, is elaborated in stages III through V. That is, stages II through V all revolve around the validity of an ideology based on achieved characteristics. It might be expected that the "ascribed characteristics" ideology depicted in stage I could lead to a series of dynamic relations between groups. However, this possibility has not been explored by Taylor and McKirnan (1984).

Second, the five-stage model deals with collective action by a disadvantaged group led by talented members who have failed to achieve upward social mobility. However, it does not deal with what the historical evidence would suggest is an equally important phenomenon in terms of collective responses to inequality: collective action by a disadvantaged group led by disenchanted members of the advantaged group. Such revolutionary leaders as Mao, Gandhi, and Castro serve as possible examples of how disenchanted members of advantaged groups can desert their original social class and lead disadvantaged groups to rebellion. Thus, the five-stage model needs also to deal with movement from the advantaged group to the disadvantaged group, particularly in terms of individuals who reject the dominant ideology.

Similarly, the model would benefit from an extension that would allow it to explain advantaged group reactions to rebellion by disadvantaged groups or individuals. This omission in the model might be explained by claiming that it is designed to deal mainly with responses to inequality rather than with responses to superiority. However, the responses of disadvantaged groups must, to some extent at least, be influenced by reactions on the part of the advantaged group.

Third, the model does not adequately explain the processes that enable interstage transitions to take more time than the lifespan of an individual person. A central assumption in the model is that a transition from each to the next could take several centuries. However, it is also assumed that the social psychological processes of social comparison and social attribution are influential in these transitions. The assumption implicit in the model is that there can be a transfer of the necessary perceptions, values, and ideas from one generation to the next, so that the social and psychological links between one stage and the next remain intact across generations. This assumption needs to be elaborated and supported.

Finally, the five-stage model shares with equity theory the problem of being in some ways circular and nonfalsifiable. That is, just as inputs and outputs are almost impossible to pin down exactly in equity theory, the time frame for intergroup developments has not been specified in the five-stage model. Thus, predictions regarding transition from one stage to the next might be almost impossible to test in the real world, since the model does not specify any time limits for their development. However, as suggested by the experimental study conducted by Taylor et al. (in press), some of the major predictions of the model concerning responses to inequality are experimentally testable.

CONCLUSION

The five-stage model of intergroup relations attempts to sketch a heuristically useful model of relations between groups. There are several features of the model that are noteworthy, given the major themes that have recurred in this volume. First, an attempt is made to provide a descriptive framework in the form of five relatively discrete stages and a fixed sequence to these stages that can be applied to any intergroup situation. The aim is to provide a set of guidelines so that research can be integrated and cumulative. Second, it is hypothesized that a true understanding of intergroup relations requires appreciation of basic social psychological processes, with special concern for how they are influenced and modulated by the larger social, political, and economic contexts. It is proposed that causal attribution and social comparison are two basic processes that explain the maintenance of any particular stage, and the transition from one stage to another. Moreover, explicit account is taken of the need to consider causal attribution and social comparison at both the individual and the collective level. Although it is perhaps too early to determine the heuristic value of the model, it does represent an attempt to deal with some of the recurrent limitations we have noted on many current theories, and it does attempt to meet the demands of a truly social psychological theory of intergroup relations.

SUGGESTED READING

Taylor, D. M., and D. J. McKirnan. 1984. A five-stage model of intergroup relations. *British Journal of Social Psychology, 23,* 291–300.

9 Stereotypes, Attributions, and Attitudes

Scope: Stereotypes, attributions, and attitudes are fundamental cognitive processes that influence how we perceive ourselves and others, in both inter-individual and intergroup contexts.

Assumptions: In all three processes, it is assumed that they organize our perceptions about in-group and out-group members, and thereby help shape our behavior in the context of intergroup relations.

Propositions: Each process has had its own unique history of research and theory. In each case the argument presented here is that they do not in and of themselves constitute a major theoretical orientation to intergroup relations. Rather, they are processes central to all of social psychology, and hence should be relevant to any major theory dealing with groups.

We have now systematically reviewed six theoretical orientations to the social psychology of intergroup relations. Anyone at all familiar with the field of social psychology will be puzzled at the apparent omission of certain key concepts and processes that are usually associated with intergroup relations. As was noted in Chapter 1, mainstream social psychology texts tend to subsume the topic of intergroup relations under some more topical title, such as prejudice, racism, peace building, or aggression. Within such chapters, the key processes of stereotypes, attributions, and attitudes are generally discussed, but not in such a way that they constitute, singly or in combination, an integrated theoretical orientation to intergroup relations. The reasons why these concepts do not represent a unique perspective on intergroup relations that would qualify them as major chapters for the present volume need to be clarified.

Stereotypes, attributions, and attitudes are all basic social psychological processes that are applied to virtually every domain of social behavior. As such, they do not represent broadly based frameworks for thinking specifically about intergroup relations. This in no way diminishes the importance of their role as social psychological processes. Rather, it underscores that they are applied to all social behavior, not just intergroup behavior. Precisely because of this breadth of application, we would expect each of these concepts to emerge in any theory that claims to explain intergroup relations from a social psychological perspective.

Our analysis is supported by the fact that we can see evidence of all three processes in many of the six major theories of intergroup relations presented in this volume. The purpose of this chapter is to review each of these important processes and comment on its role in intergroup relations. Our aim is to clarify the extent to which mainstream social psychological concepts can usefully contribute to our understanding of intergroup relations.

STEREOTYPES

The stereotype, or ethnic stereotype, is a fundamental cognitive process in mainstream social psychology that, more than any other, is directly linked to intergroup relations. If any concept could have emerged as the basis for a broad framework for intergroup relations, it is the ethnic stereotype. A brief history of the development of the concept within mainstream social psychology may provide some explanation of why it remains an important and influential concept, but one that at present cannot form the basis of a theory of intergroup relations.

The definition of stereotype generally adopted by researchers reflects the strong link that this concept has had with ethnic groups (for major reviews of the stereotype literature see Brigham 1971; Campbell 1967; Cauthen, Robinson & Krauss, 1971; Fishman 1956; Gardner 1973; Hamilton 1981; A. G. Miller 1982; Tajfel 1969; Taylor 1981; Taylor & Lalonde (in press). Brigham's (1971) representative definition is that a stereotype involves ". . . a generalization made about an ethnic group, concerning a trait attribution, which is considered to be unjustified by an observer" (p. 29). Others have added further clarifications and, indeed, explicit moral judgments, by noting that stereotypes are rigid impressions conforming very little to the facts (Katz & Braly 1935), exaggerated beliefs (Allport 1954), and inaccurate and irrational overgeneralizations (Middlebrook 1974). In the same tradition, Baron and Byrne (1977) have argued that stereotypes are ". . . clusters of preconceived notions regarding various groups . . ." in which there are ". . . strong tendencies to overgeneralize about individuals solely on the basis of their membership in particular racial, ethnic, or religious groups" (p. 155).

There are two aspects to these definitions that particularly warrant comment in the present context. First, the stereotype, unlike attitudes, attributions, values, schemata, and other cognitive predispositions, refers directly to the perception of societal groups or at least to individuals as members of groups.

But there is also a second way in which the stereotype is a truly group or collective process, and this has gone virtually unrecognized. This is best exemplified by the manner in which stereotypes are operationalized, that is, in terms of the methods that have been developed to measure stereotypes. The basic procedure was introduced by Katz and Braly (1933), and while there have been several more recent innovations (Brigham 1971; Gardner, Wonnacott & Taylor, 1968; Triandis & Vassiliou 1967), the underlying rationale remains unchanged. Subjects are presented with an ethnic group label and are asked to check off or rate the extent to which each of a long list of trait adjectives best describes the ethnic group in question. Thus, the stereotype is operationally defined by those characteristics which are chosen or endorsed most frequently.

By definition, then, the stereotype is a collective process, since only when there is consensus among members of one group about the attributes of another can an attribute be included as part of the stereotype. In this sense the stereotype is very different from an attitude or an attribution. With attitudes, the aim is to assess an individual's evaluative response to a social object. The stereotype is concerned with group perceptions of a social object in such a way that it is theoretically impossible to determine the stereotype from the perceptions of one individual.

We might have expected this collective feature of stereotypes to be a major focus for theory and research. However, it has received little attention from researchers. For example, Gardner, Kirby and Finley (1973) and Lalonde (1985) are among the few even to explore the implications of the consensual aspect of stereotypes by examining how the shared features of stereotypes facilitate in-group communication.

Until very recently, the study of stereotypes has been largely a descriptive exercise, aimed at identifying the stereotype that one particular group has of another. The negative implications of the traits often identified by research on stereotyping is probably one of the reasons why the stereotype has been viewed as morally wrong. For example, we learned that college students from the United States stereotype Jewish people as intelligent, industrious, and shrewd; Turks as treacherous; Germans as industrious and scientifically minded; and blacks as musical, happy-go-lucky, and lazy (Karlins, Coffman & Walters, 1969). In Canada, English Canadians stereotype French Canadians as talkative, excitable, and proud (Gardner et al. 1968), and French Canadians describe English Canadians as educated, dominant, and ambitious (Aboud & Taylor 1971). Although a useful point of departure, this legacy of descriptive research has done little to thrust the concept of stereotype to center stage in social psychology. Nor has it advanced our understanding of the dynamics of intergroup relations.

Recently, however, two major developments have taken place within the field of stereotypes, the first no doubt paving the way for the second. First, there has been a change in the way stereotypes are conceptualized and defined. Traditionally, the stereotype was defined as an undesirable process because it was either an inferior cognitive process in the form of an overgeneralization or oversimplification, or a process that was morally wrong because it categorized people who had no desire to be so categorized.

More recently, the trend is to view stereotyping as a basic cognitive process that is neither desirable or undesirable in and of itself (see, for example, Berry 1970; Tajfel 1969; Triandis 1971). So, for example, Hamilton (1979, 1981) describes the stereotype as a schema about members of an identifiable group. Taylor (1981) has defined the stereotype as consensus among members of one group regarding the attributes of another, explicitly rejecting the view of the stereotype as an inferior process or morally wrong. The social psychology text by Deaux and Wrightsman (1984) underlines this point. They remark that ". . . although stereotypes may have certain negatively valued characteristics, most psychologists today would not consider them automatically bad things to have" (p. 90).

This change in evaluative judgment about the stereotype has had the effect of shifting attention away from the descriptive aspects of the stereotype and to understanding how it operates as a basic cognitive process. So, for example, Hamilton and his colleagues (Hamilton 1979; Hamilton & Gifford 1976) have focused on the illusory correlation arising in stereotypes whereby a group becomes associated with a particular characteristic, not as a function of explicit prejudice but out of a basic cognitive process. This process involves people perceiving a relation between events that are distinctive, even when the relation is not warranted on the basis of the actual frequency with which the event occurs. For example, when a newspaper reports that a minority group member committed a brutal murder, the illusory correlation process is set in motion. To be a member of a minority group and to commit murder are both unusual or very distinctive. Thus, an association is made between that minority group and the brutal behavior in the form of a stereotype, even if the frequency with which members of that minority commit such acts does not warrant such a generalization.

The current drama associated with international terrorism no doubt lends itself precisely to this process, and indeed may be responsible for the current wave of "Arab-bashing" in America. A representative *Newsweek* article (Newell, McKillop & Monroe, 1986) on the harassment experienced by Arab Americans notes that while youngsters cope with being labeled "camel jockey" and "rag head," and the Arab community is stereotyped as "terrorists," most are "themselves victims of terror: war-weary expatriates from the Middle East who hoped to find safety in America." Despite these implications for group perception, this focus on stereotypes as a basic and normal process represents an important new level of inquiry, but one that is still not sufficiently intergroup in its emphasis.

Some of the recent work in the cognitive tradition does begin to implicate relations between groups more directly. For example, Rothbart and his colleagues have been examining systematic differences between in-group and out-group stereotypes (Park & Rothbart 1982; Rothbart, Dawes & Park, 1984). One key hypothesis in this domain is that people perceive more variability in the charcteristics of their own group than in the characteristics of out-groups. This "out-group homogeneity" effect is captured in popular phrases such as "I can't tell one from the other" and "They all look the same to me." Of greater interest from an intergroup perspective will be the pinning down of explanations for this "out-group homogeneity" effect, with which subsequent research will probably deal in greater depth. Is this effect, as Wilder (1984) suggests, a desire to maintain individuality within the in-group while preserving or enhancing in-group favoritism by deindividualization of the out-group? Or is it strictly a question of familiarity such that the less familiar we are with a group, the more likely we are to have a uniform stereotype of that group?

Studies on the out-group homogeneity effect are representative of research that is designed to understand the stereotype as a proess having more direct implications for intergroup relations. But in order for stereotypes to become the basis for a theory of intergroup relations, the intergroup feature of stereotypes must serve as the research focus.

One such attempt has been made by Taylor (1981) and Taylor and Simard (1979). They began with the intergroup implications of the traditional view of the stereotype as an inferior and morally wrong process. This view implies that group stereotypes should be eliminated to the extent possible—for example, through educational programs and cooperative exposure to members of the other group. However, Taylor (1981) has argued that there are intergroup situations where stereotyping may in fact be desirable. Specifically, to the extent that a group wishes to maintain its distinctiveness, it would be proud to be stereotyped, as long as the stereotype attributed to it was accurate and was respected by members of another group. From this perspective, then, harmonious intergroup relations would arise when the pattern of stereotypes is consistent with that depicted in Figure 9.1.

The column classification represents the group (I or II) doing the stereotyping and the rows refer to the group being stereotyped. The capital letters in each case represent specific stereotype attributes, and the (+) sign is used to indicate a positive attitude toward the stereotype attribute. What is depicted in Figure 9.1, then, is a situation where each group stereotypes the other in a manner consistent with each group's stereotype of itself. Further, members of each group value their own attributes as well as those of the other group. Thus, we have a socially desirable intergroup situation where each group retains its own cultural distinctiveness but is respectful of the attributes that are distinctive of the other group.

Such a socially desirable configuration is, of course, difficult to achieve, and the peaceful coexistence among groups, idealized here, remains one of society's most pressing challenges. Nevertheless, certain examples come to mind as attempts to approximate such an ideal. Some subgroups of women take the stand that they bring to high-status professional positions certain characteristics (such as sophisticated interpersonal skills), in addition to their basic qualifications, that make them particularly valuable. Ethnic minority groups in the United States and Canada strongly endorse the concept of multiculturalism (Taylor & Lambert 1985), whereby groups maintain their heritage, language, and culture while participating fully in mainstream society.

These encouraging examples notwithstanding, there remain the vast majority of relations between groups that are less than desirable, in terms of the ideal depicted in Figure 9.1. These less desirable situations can be presented

| | Group doing stereotyping | |
	I	II
Group being stereotyped I	ABC +	ABC +
II	XYZ +	XYZ +

Figure 9.1 **Schematic Representation of Situation Where Stereotyping May Have Desirable Consequences**

schematically in the form of systematic departures from the ideal (see Figure 9.2.). For example, intergroup conflict would be represented by a situation where the intergroup perceptions contain minus (−) signs instead of the plus (+) signs (Figure 9.2A). An inferiority complex would involve a minus sign for a group's stereotype of itself (Figure 9.2B), and misunderstandings would arise when the letters depicting the attributes were inconsistent (Figure 9.2C).

A. INTERGROUP CONFLICT

Group doing stereotyping

		I	II
Group being stereotyped	I	ABC+	ABC−
	II	XYZ−	XYZ+

B. INFERIORITY COMPLEX

Group doing stereotyping

		I	II
Group being stereotyped	I	ABC+	ABC+
	II	XYZ−	XYZ−

C. STEREOTYPE MISATTRIBUTION

Group doing stereotyping

		I	II
Group being stereotyped	I	ABC	DEF
	II	UVW	XYZ

Figure 9.2 Schematic Representation of Less-Than-Desirable Patterns of Intergroup Stereotyping

This orientation begins with a concern for stereotyping as a social or intergroup process. Thus, it is the type of approach that might give rise to a theory of intergroup relations having the stereotype as its central concept. However, for the moment, stereotype retains the status of a very important concept in the discipline of social psychology, one that has special links to intergroup relations but does not by itself represent a broadly based theory of intergroup relations.

In terms of the theories reviewed in this volume, the stereotype has the status of an important outcome, result, or dependent variable related to the status of the relationship between two groups. The stereotype is not usually presented as the cause or independent variable in the context of relations between groups. Thus, for realistic conflict theory (Chapter 3) stereotypes develop as a result of group formation, they become particularly consensual and derogatory during the conflict stage, and they grow less prominent as a result of the introduction of superordinate goals.

Indeed, this same analysis can be applied to each of the six major theories reviewed, except for social identity theory (Chapter 4). The stereotype plays an especially significant role in social identity theory. The important motivation for group categorization is social identity. It is postulated that the need for social identity leads to a striving for group distinctiveness along positively valued dimensions. Group distinctiveness refers to those characteristics of a group that make it different from other groups—in other words, a stereotype. According to social identity theory, then, groups strive for a distinctive own-group stereotype that is valued positively by other groups. Thus, the creation and maintenance of a positively valued stereotype are postulated to be a fundamental human need. From this perspective, the view proposed by Taylor (1981) that intergroup stereotypes can be socially desirable is consistent with social identity theory.

In summary, the stereotype continues to play a central role in our understanding of intergroup relations. The current interest in stereotypes as a basic cognitive process is already providing new insights, and if this can be coupled with a perspective focusing more on intergroup processes, an integrated theory of intergroup relations may emerge.

ATTRIBUTIONS

Not since the emergence of cognitive dissonance theory in the 1950s (Festinger 1957) has an approach to social behavior had such a dramatic impact as that of causal attribution. The important influence of causal attribution is not limited to the field of social psychology, but has extended to the domain of developmental and clinical psychology, and the study of personality. Like other basic concepts in social psychology, attribution principles are applicable to virtually all aspects of social behavior. Theorists interested in group and intergroup processes, then, cannot reasonably ignore attribution processes, even though to date most of the research has been approached from an individualistic perspective.

Attribution processes are concerned with how we make judgments about people, ourselves as well as others. The popularity of attribution, we believe, arises because of the intuitive appeal of certain key assumptions that underlie attribution principles. First, there is the assumption that people seek to make sense of the world, and specifically that making sense of or understanding the world involves making a judgment about the cause or causes of behavior. Second, unlike more traditional approaches to person perception, it is assumed that the raw material from which judgments are made is the actual behavior of another, or one's own behavior. This is in contrast with earlier approaches that took as the starting point abstract traits rather than concrete behavior. Finally, it is assumed that the potential causes of any behavior can be classified, and that the particular classification of a cause that is selected as the explanation for behavior will have a profound impact on subsequent behavior.

The most basic classification for causes is internal and external, and it is assumed that this distinction has important implications. As a teacher, my reaction to a student who has failed an exmination will be quite different if I attribute the cause to a lack of studying (internal) rather than to an unexpected illness in the family (external). Or, to give an example from the intergroup context, the attribution for the low status of South African blacks in terms of the internal-external classification has profound implications. An internal attribution (such as lazy, unintelligent) provides the perfect justification for apartheid. An external attribution (such as exploitation) demands that there should be fundamental socio-political changes in South African society.

The foundations for various attribution principles were laid by Heider (1958) and elaborated in various ways by theorists such as Kelley (1973), Jones and Davis (1965), and Weiner, Frieze, Kukla, Reed, Rest & Rosenbaum (1972). The key question addressed by attribution theorists is how the individual comes to focus on one or more causes from among the many possible causes for an instance of social behavior.

Reviewing the principles that have been articulated to answer this question is beyond the scope of the present chapter. For our purposes, it is useful to consider two broad categories of principles: rational and emotional. The rational category involves the logical use of information that people employ to arrive at decisions about the cause of an instance of behavior. For example, to return to the student who has failed an examination, if he or she had consistently earned high marks in the past, the teacher might rationally be inclined to make an external attribution for the failure, believing that family illness was indeed the cause of the poor performance.

The emotional category involves ignoring information that might lead to a rational judgment and, instead, making attributions designed to meet the perceiver's needs. Foremost among these more "irrational" or emotional processes is the self-serving bias. Current controversies notwithstanding (see Bradley 1978; D. T. Miller 1978; Miller & Ross 1975; Weary 1979), there is a tendency for individuals to make attributions that protect or enhance their ego. That is, individuals have a tendency to take undue credit for success and to deny responsibility for failure.

As might be expected, attribution processes have been addressed from an individualistic perspective, focusing almost exclusively on how the individual arrives at causal explanations about the behavior of another individual. Thus, we would expect attribution processes to play an important role in any broadly based theory of intergroup relations, but we would not expect attribution by itself to be the framework for a theory of intergroup relations.

Attribution theory could play an even greater role in explaining behavior in intergroup contexts once attention begins to focus more directly on how attribution processes operate at the intergroup level. Fortunately, there are signs that interest in this area may be developing.

Pettigrew (1978, 1979) has made an important application of attribution processes to the intergroup context. His starting point was a basic attribution phenomenon labeled the "fundamental attribution error" by Ross (1977). The error involves an inherent bias to individuals' attributions; when attributing behavior, individuals tend to underestimate the impact of situation (external) and overestimate the importance of the actor's traits and attitudes (internal). Pettigrew (1978, 1979) suggests that this "fundamental attribution error" becomes the "ultimate attribution error" when applied to attributions made in an intergroup context. Like the self-serving bias, the error in this case operates in such a way that when members of an in-group make attributions about the socially desirable behavior of their own group, they focus on the positive traits (internal), but when attributing the same desirable behavior to an out-group, an external cause is the focus.

Conversely, for socially undesirable behavior, external causes are the focus for the in-group. However, when the undesirable behavior is performed by an out-group, the focus is an internal factor, such as the negative traits of the out-group. This "ultimate attribution error" builds on an initial experiment by Taylor and Jaggi (1974), which demonstrated this basic intergroup bias in group attribution, and has been elaborated by Hewstone and Ward (1985). This process can be further clarified by considering the context of a race riot. The authorities are likely to attribute the antisocial behavior to the irresponsible and wicked intentions of the rioters (internal), whereas the rioters might view their behavior as caused by the oppression they have experienced (external). In each case, the attributions made serve to justify the behavior of the group making the attributions and to condemn the opposing group. Or, to coin a phrase, "one group's terrorist is the other's freedom fighter."

Pettigrew's analysis involves taking a process that has been articulated at the individual level and extrapolating it to groups. Taylor and his colleagues (Taylor & Doria 1981; Taylor, Doria & Tyler, 1983) have taken the attribution process as it has been applied to groups one step further. They argue that when examining the usual internal-external distinction in a group context, it is necessary to expand this bipolar classification to include a third important possibility. Specifically, Taylor et al. (1983) posit three attribution categories: internal, the individual attributes group behavior to the self; external within group, the individual attributes group behavior to other members of his or her own group; external, the individual attributes group behavior to forces that lie not only outside the self but outside the group as well.

This tripartite distinction has important implications for group cohesion. For example, if, in order to protect the self, individual group members make an external attribution for group failure, cohesion is maintained. However, if instead an external within group attribution is made, group cohesion would be adversely affected. Conversely, avoiding external within group attributions for group failure, and focusing on external within group attributions for group success, should lead to increased cohesion in a group. This was precisely the attribution pattern found by Taylor et al. (1983) to predominate in the case of naturalistic groups who are extremely cohesive.

The context for this study was an athletic team that experienced an extremely poor season within its league. Despite consistent failure, team cohesion was extremely high. An attribution analysis indicated that individual team members took personal responsibility for team failures, and on those few instances of team success, shared responsibility with their teammates. This pattern was labeled "group serving bias" in attribution since, on the surface at least, group cohesion was being maintained at the expense of the individual.

In general, however, how processes of attribution operate in an intergroup context is still a relatively understudied topic. However, there would seem to be sufficient evidence to suggest that the processes of attribution that have been delineated at the individual level cannot always be applied directly to the group level.

Nevertheless, given the importance of attribution processes in modern social psychology, we would expect to see evidence of their operation in any major theory of intergroup relations. For example, attribution is explicitly described as one of the key processes for the five-stage model of intergroup relations (Chapter 8). Because attribution is so basic to that theory, and is so explicit, its role need not be elaborated here.

Another theory that is quite explicit about the importance of attribution is relative deprivation theory (Chaper 6). Our analysis of that theory revolved around a set of necessary and sufficient conditions for relative deprivation to be experienced (Crosby 1976). An important condition specified by Crosby was that the individual not feel responsible for not having, or having less of, a desired commodity. In fact, this is a fundamental attribution assertion. If the individual makes an internal attribution of the form "It is my fault," then no relative deprivation will be experienced. If, however, the cause is perceived to be external, "It is not my fault," then all of the negative emotions associated with relative deprivation will surface.

Equity theory (Chapter 5) involves important applications of attribution. For example, attribution is especially prominent when, in an inequitable relationship, advantaged or disadvantaged group members attempt the psychological restoration of equity. Under certain conditions advantaged group members will alter their perceptions of inputs and outcomes in order to propagate the belief that the outcomes of disadvantaged people are equitable. How can advantaged group members come to believe their position is justified? The answer is to develop the belief that disadvantaged persons make fewer inputs than advantaged persons, and so their disadvantaged position is just and fair—in short, "blame the victim." This term reflects the attribution implications—the cause of poor outcomes is internal; the disadvantaged group member is the cause of his or her situation. For example, when it is pointed out that women and blacks account for the greatest number of the unemployed, this might be justified by propagating the idea that this situation is a result of their own laziness and lack of training.

Attribution is also implicated in equity theory's explanation of why disadvantaged persons or groups may take no action in the face of inequity. It was noted that despite their motivation actually to restore equity, disadvantaged persons may lack the power or resources to do so. Thus, they may come to restore equity psychologically by perceiving the inputs and outcomes of their own group and the advantaged group in such a way that equity is restored. Again, such a judgment requires that the self or own group (internal) be perceived as the cause of poor outcomes rather than holding the advantaged group responsible. It is hard to take action against another group when one's own group is to blame for a poor situation—and such a conclusion requires a very specific attribution about the cause of unequal outcomes.

The remaining theories—realistic conflict theory (Chapter 3), social identity theory (Chapter 4), and elite theory (Chapter 7)—also allude to attribution processes, but only indirectly and in a way that shows the breadth of attribution as a process. These theories focus on the trait characteristics of low-status and high-status groups, and the terms "attitude" and "stereotype" are used in this context. However, an attribution approach would interpret the perception of a group in terms of a specific trait as merely the internal attribution for a specific behavior. So when, in terms of realistic conflict theory, one group judges the other to be "cheaters" or, in terms of social identity theory, group members define their identity in terms of being "technologically sophisticated," this involves an internal attribution. That is, the focus for the explanation of the group behavior is the personality of its members, not external circumstances.

In summary, attribution processes are fundamental to all social behavior, and as we have seen, they surface explicitly or implicitly in every major theory of intergroup relations. However, to date the tendency has been to extrapolate attribution principles at the interindividual level to the level of groups. The aspects of attribution that are unique to group contexts have only begun to be explored, and it is these unique features that are sure to play an even more central role in theories of intergroup relations.

ATTITUDES

The study of attitudes lies at the very heart of social psychology, and may even lay claim to being the most influential concept in the discipline (see McGuire 1969). An attitude involves the predisposition to respond positively or negatively to a social object. Often attitudes are analyzed in terms of three separate components: cognitive, affective, and behavioral intention, the so-called ABC's of attitudes. However, we share the view of Fishbein and Ajzen (1972), who suggest that "attitude" be used to refer to the evaluative dimension, to indicate like or dislike toward a social object. Most formal measures of attitude and most research on attitude are concerned with people's affective or evaluative reactions to other people, institutions, ideas, or aspects of the physical environment.

This focus on the evaluative aspect of attitude in no way diminishes its importance. Surely, there is no predisposition more pervasive and more socially important than our emotional or evaluative reaction to something: in the present case, our attitude to members of our own and other groups.

Our aim in this chapter is not to review the vast literature on attitudes but, rather, to show how this fundamental concept relates to intergroup relations. As we noted at the outset, attitude is a basic process that affects all of social behavior. However, it does not constitute a systematic orientation to intergroup relations. But we would expect such a basic process to be central to most theories of intergroup relations. As we shall see, attitudes are involved in most intergroup theories, but not in as central a manner as their historic importance might lead us to expect. The reason for the rather peripheral role of attitudes is the manner in which they are incorporated within most intergroup theories. They are described as an outcome of conflict or resolution rather than as a primary cause. In other terms, they are relegated to the status of dependent variables, not independent variables, in the causal sequence of explanation for intergroup behavior. This is a point that must be kept in mind when considering the role of attitudes in the intergroup literature.

This is best exemplified by the role of attitudes in realistic conflict theory (Chapter 3). In this theory, negative intergroup attitudes are viewed as the outcome of a competition for scarce resources. The cause of conflict is the reality of the competition rather than any person's or group's attitudes toward others. So, as an intergroup conflict becomes more intense, intergroup attitudes become more negative. Conversely, with the introduction of superordinate goals, intergroup attitudes become more positive. Even if the "bottom line" in terms of intergroup relations is the engineering of positive intergroup attitudes, theories of attitude organization and change are not viewed as the cause of intergroup harmony; it is the structure of the intergroup relationship that is central.

Attitudes have a similar role in equity theory (Chapter 5), although the focus is different. Once again intergroup attitudes are the result, not the cause. In terms of equity theory, causal factors are to be found in a person's analysis of the relationship between two groups. Inequity produces a negative attitude about the relationship, not the reverse. Equity theory does have a more fundamental link with attitude, in the sense that it exactly parallels the most influential of all attitude theories, dissonance. Dissonance theory (Festinger 1957) postulates a psychological distress that arises when two cognitions or an action and a cognition are dissonant for the individual. For equity theory, the hypothesis is that the same distress is felt when there is dissonance in terms of the ratio of inputs and outputs between people. Here we have one example of a case where attitude theory has had a profound effect on a theory of intergroup relations.

The last example not withstanding, the more general point about the conceptualization of attitude as a dependent variable is further reinforced by relative deprivation theory (Chapter 6). Here the causal mechanism is social comparison, and the outcome or result is a negative attitude.

The role of attitudes in intergroup relations can be further clarified by considering the example of racism among the working class in Europe. Several European countries, especially England, have experienced race riots since the mid-1970s. An integral part of the intergroup context is negative attitudes among some whites towards visible minority groups. Such attitudes are not considered to be causes of racial conflict but the results of other factors leading to racial conflicts. According to realistic conflict theory, for example, competition for scarce resources, such as jobs, and high unemployment have led to the development of negative intergroup attitudes. Thus, some working-class English people have negative attitudes toward visible minority groups because they think that these immigrants have taken jobs that rightly belong to "English" people.

There is one final conceptual aspect of attitudes that limits their applicability to intergroup relations. Attitudes are usually treated as an individual-difference variable. That is, we tend to focus on the individual's attitude and to speculate about why one person's attitude may be positive, another's negative, and a third person's indifferent. Rarely is the interest in terms of the shared attitudes that are so central to an intergroup context. Consequently, researchers interested in attitude theory have not addressed questions such as under what conditions a consensus in attitude will develop, or what function shared attitudes serve for solidarity, communication, and social behavior.

In summary, the topic of intergroup attitudes does not constitute an intergrated theory of intergroup relations, despite the importance of attitude to the domain of social psychology. Attitudes are fundamental to all social behavior, but it is unreasonable to believe that a theory of attitudes would or should by itself constitute a theory of intergroup relations. At the same time, however, advances in our understanding of attitudes must be accommodated by any theory of intergroup relations if it is to maintain any credibility.

CONCLUSION

In this chapter we have attempted to briefly describe three important concepts that are often associated with the topic of intergroup relations, but do not by themselves constitute a major theoretical orientation to intergroup relations. This is not to belittle the importance of these concepts. Their general importance in the field of social psychology virtually dictates that they will not evolve into a theory of intergroup relations on their own, since their application is indeed much wider, to all dimensions of social behavior. However, their importance for social behavior generally is one of the most compelling reasons for their conscious consideration by theorists who wish to understand intergroup behavior. These concepts may not constitute the structural framework for such a theory, but their influence and importance cannot be avoided.

SUGGESTED READINGS

Fishbein, M., and I. Ajzen 1975. *Belief, attitude, intention and behavior: An introduction to theory and research.* Reading, Mass.: Addison-Wesley.

Hamilton, D. L. (ed.) 1981. *Cognitive processes in stereoptyping and intergroup behavior.* Hillsdale, N.J.: Erlbaum.

Kelley, H. H. 1973. The processes of causal attribution. *American Psychologist, 28,* 107–128.

10   Toward an Integrated Theory of Intergroup Relations

In this volume we have reviewed six major theoretical approaches to the social psychology of intergroup relations, analyzed Freud's contribution to the field, and discussed three mainstream social psychological concepts that are likely to play a significant role in any theory of intergroup relations. Having reviewed these theories in some detail, it is important that we highlight their similarities and differences, with a view to providing a constructive framework for future theory and research. Of course, as each theory was presented, similarities to and contrasts with the other theories were discussed. The purpose here is to highlight these in terms of all six theories so that an overall perspective can be achieved.

In order to provide a framework for our review, we focus on important themes that were raised in Chapter 1 as recurrent issues or that emerged from our discussion of a particular theory. The major themes include level of analysis, time frame, "open" as opposed to "closed" groups, group structure, status relationship between groups, and social psychological processes.

We will discuss each of these themes in turn. Their status with respect to each of the six theories is presented in summary fashion in Table 10.1. Although simplistic, the table has the advantage of allowing quick reference to the status of each theory with respect to all the different themes.

LEVEL OF ANALYSIS

A theme that has predominated our discussion of the different theories is reductionism. From our initial analysis of mainstream social psychology as an individual-oriented discipline, we have underscored the need for an approach to intergroup relations that includes a focus on group processes while retaining the integrity of the fundamental unit of psychological analysis, the individual. The need is for theories that discuss the psychological processes affecting the individual but that simultaneously take into account the role of group structure and the role that the dynamics of group relations play in the psychology of the individual.

The simple summary presented in Table 10.1 indicates the dual nature of the challenge. For example, both realistic conflict theory and elite theory *do* address intergroup relations from a group perspective. However, they do not spell out the specific psychological processes that play a causal role in their structural analysis. That is, both theories offer a macro analysis, with psychological processes being introduced only as an outcome of these broad social processes. Freud's theory of group processes, equity theory, and relative deprivation theory are depicted as reductionist, as being limited to an individual level of analysis. While generally true, this overview represents somewhat of an overgeneralization, since relative deprivation theorists have addressed (Runciman 1966) and are explicitly addressing (Crosby 1982; Martin 1980) relative

Table 10.1 Status of Intergroup Theories in Terms of Major Themes

	REALISTIC CONFLICT THEORY	SOCIAL IDENTITY THEORY	EQUITY THEORY	RELATIVE DEPRIVATION THEORY	ELITE THEORY	FIVE-STAGE MODEL
LEVEL OF ANALYSIS	group	individual and group	individual	individual	group	individual and group
TIME FRAME	long and short term	long and short term	short term	short term	long and short term	long and short term
OPEN VS. CLOSED GROUPS	closed	open and closed	closed	closed	open and closed	open and closed
GROUPS STRUCTURE	homogeneous	homogeneous	homogeneous	homogeneous	individual differences	individual differences
STATUS OF GROUP FOCUSED UPON	equal status	disadvantaged	advantaged and disadvantaged	disadvantaged	advantaged and disadvantaged	disadvantaged
SOCIAL PSYCHOLOGICAL PROCESSES		categorization social identity psychological distinctiveness social comparison justice	justice social comparison dissonance	social comparison justice attribution		social comparison attribution justice

deprivation from a group perspective. We applaud this development and hope that this interest in collective processes will extend to such theories as equity, which has proved to have a wide application.

The two theories that do attempt an analysis at both the group and the individual level are social identity theory and the five-stage model of intergroup relations. Their attempts represent, we believe, the direction that future theories should take. This is not to suggest that the specific content and structure of these theories are more useful than those of the others, but only that in terms of unit of analysis, the social and individualistic dimensions should be integrated.

TIME FRAME

In the real world, relations between most groups have a history; they are often influenced by complex sociocultural factors that extend their influence over long periods of time. For example, to explain the present state of relations between blacks and whites in the United States, or the newly arrived immigrant groups and indigenous populations in Europe, or English and French Canadians, it is necessary to keep in mind the historical background to relations between each of these groups. The history of slavery in the United States is likely to be relevant to the present relations between blacks and whites in this country; the history of European colonialism is likely to be relevant to the present relations between newly arrived Third World immigrants and indigenous European populations; and the past history of English domination in Canada is likely to influence the present state of relations between English and French Canadians.

These historical examples suggest the presence of developmental processes in intergroup relations. Subsequently, in order to explain the present state of relations between two social groups, it is useful to keep in mind the past history of their relations. However, not all theories that have been applied to intergroup relations explicitly attempt to incorporate such a developmental perspective.

Elite theory and the five-stage model are probably the theories that explicitly and most directly incorporate a developmental perspective on intergroup relations. Both these theories have a cyclical view of the historical development of intergroup relations. Classical elite theory assumes that all elite groups eventually "dig their own graves" by preventing entrance to the elite, thus leading talented members of the lower classes to rebel and form counterelites to challenge for power. Eventually, through a process that might take centuries, the "closed" elite group will experience a loss of talent while challenging counterelites become increasingly talented and powerful. The outcome is a successful bid for power by a counterelite, which eventually takes over the role and functions of the elite.

Thus, according to elite theory, in order to appreciate the relationship between the elite, the nongoverning elite, and the nonelite, it is necessary to know their past history and what particular point in the cycle they have reached. However, it is important to note that according to elite theory, the speed of this cyclical development depends upon psychological factors, the most important of which are the psychological characteristics of the elite, the nongoverning elite, and the nonelite.

The five-stage model of intergroup relations also explicitly adopts a historical, developmental approach. Intergroup relations are assumed to pass through the same five developmental stages; the transition from one stage to another is assumed to take varying amounts of time, which can extend to several centuries. According to the five-stage model, in order to fully appreciate the state of relations between two groups, it is necessary to have information on the past history of the groups.

Realistic conflict theory has also, to some extent, given importance to the historical development of an intergroup relationship. This has evolved in both the theoretical writings of the researchers and the operationalization of concepts in research projects. For example, Sherif (1966) makes a specific point of using real groups with a history in his research involving boys at summer camp. Moreover, he conceptualized a developmental process for intergroup relations. The most important stages of this process that were incorporated in his research were (1) spontaneous intergroup friendship choices, (2) group formation, (3) intergroup conflict, and (4) intergroup cooperation. The same concern for the development of intergroup relations over time is shown by Deutsch (1973, 1985) when he discusses the cycles of constructive and destructive conflict.

Social identity theory makes some attempt to incorporate longer-term developmental processes into its elaboration of intergroup relations. In particular, the importance that it gives to the development of cognitive alternatives and the perceived legitimacy-illegitimacy of the system leads to an emphasis on what generally tend to be long-term processes. Historically, the perception of cognitive alternatives to a system has tended to evolve over long time periods and has been influenced by large-scale structural changes. For example, the women's liberation movement has involved a radical change in perspectives, in that many women now conceive of a society where women enjoy parity with men. That is, most women have evolved cognitive alternatives to the traditional male-dominated society. However, the evolution of this cognitive alternative has been influenced by large-scale structural changes that have taken place over the last few centuries, such as those giving women a key role in the labor force and the economy.

Equity theory and relative deprivation theory have given little importance to the developmental aspects of intergroup relations and the long-term historical factors that might be involved. The main reason for this is probably that these are basically individualistic theories that have not yet been adequately extended to account for behavior at the intergroup level. However, such an extension should involve considerable attention to developmental processes in intergroup relations. Not only would this provide a broader understanding of intergroup relations, but it might also lead both equity theory and relative deprivation theory to become much better predictors of collective action. For example, justice is a central concept to both these theories, and the perception of justice by both minority and majority groups is likely to be influenced by the past history of each group and its relations with other groups.

"OPEN" AND "CLOSED" GROUPS

Just as a comprehensive theory of intergroup relations should include the complete range of power relations between groups, so must such a theory deal with both "open" and "closed" groups. There are three theories that deal with both types of groups: social identity theory, elite theory, and the five-stage model of intergroup relations. All three have the same implications: open groups are associated with individual action in the form of mobility between groups of different status; closed groups lend themselves to the instigation of collective action. The distinction between individual and collective action is so socially important that it must be taken into account by any theory of intergroup relations that seeks to be comprehensive.

The three theories that limit their attention to closed groups are realistic conflict theory, equity theory, and relative deprivation theory. Realistic conflict theory deals explicitly with the collective behavior associated with closed groups. Equity and relative deprivation theories deal with closed groups, but more by default than by design. Thus, it should be possible to extend both theories to incorporate the distinction without seriously altering their basic principles.

GROUP STRUCTURE

Freud's analysis of group processes (Chapter 2) focused on two important categories of people within any group, the leader and followers. In this very fundamental way, Freud initiated a line of thought that we believe must be continued in order to achieve a broadly based theory of intergroup relations. It is based on the assumption that a group should not be viewed as a homogeneous collection of individuals of equal role and status.

In his classic experiment in the context of realistic conflict theory, Sherif unfortunately did not capitalize on individual differences that he recognized within a group. For example, in the "group formation" stage of his field experiments, he noted how each group developed its own structure of roles and leadership. However, he did not pursue these individual differences in order to elaborate upon the extent to which they might play a particular role in the escalation of group conflict or its resolution.

Relative deprivation and equity theories focus little attention on groups generally, and thus do not address the question of individual differences within groups. Social identity theory, despite explicitly dealing with groups, also makes no such distinction. Thus, individualistic and collective actions are hypothesized to arise among all or some members of a disadvantaged group under specified conditions.

By contrast, for elite theory and the five-stage model, individual differences within a group are crucial. In both theories it is a special subgroup of individuals within the disadvantaged group who play an especially significant role in the instigation of action. In both cases it is the talented members of the disadvantaged group who instigate social mobility or collective action, or engage in consciousness raising among other members. However, while elite theory deals with intragroup, interindividual differences within both the advantaged and the disadvantaged groups, the five-stage model deals with such differences only within the disadvantaged group. Similarly, while elite theory deals with differences between individuals in terms of movement to and from both the advantaged and the disadvantaged groups, the five-stage model deals only with movements from the disadvantaged group.

The individual differences alluded to by elite theory and the five-stage model are rudimentary at this stage. An integrated theory of intergroup relations will ultimately have to deal with the complexity of differences among individuals who make up any particular group.

STATUS RELATIONSHIP BETWEEN GROUPS

Intergroup relations encompass different types of relationships between societal groups, especially in regard to the very important dimension of power. Subsequently, relations between groups of equal power, and disadvantaged and advantaged groups in an unequal relationship, must be addressed by any comprehensive theory. From Table 10.1 it will be clear that this goal has not been met, which may well explain why the theories so often do not generate competing hypotheses, but hypotheses dealing with quite different intergroup situations.

Realistic conflict theory, perhaps the most influential theory to date, emphasizes equal status relations. However, in fairness we should note that certain key theorists in this tradition (such as Deutsch 1973, 1985) do take into consideration differential power relations between the groups. Social identity theory, relative deprivation theory, and the five-stage model focus on the disadvantaged group, thus offering a somewhat limited perspective. Equity theory and elite theory are listed in Table 10.1 as being equally concerned with both the advantaged and the disadvantaged group in a relationship. However, this perhaps gives these theoretical perspectives too much credit. Elite theory tends to emphasize the disadvantaged group, although it also considers how the advantaged group maintains status in response to instigations from disadvantaged group members. Equity theory certainly deals with both groups, but as Martin (1980) points out, it is ideologically biased in terms of the advantaged group.

Having criticized all six theories as being limited in their focus, it is clear that the various theories are broad enough to encompass the most important of the status relations that can exist between groups. That is, it would not be necessary for any of the theories reviewed in this volume to abandon their fundamental principles in order to achieve this aim. Rather, it would be necessary only to expand the range of principles offered so as to include the complete range of intergroup situations.

SOCIAL PSYCHOLOGICAL PROCESSES

An essential component of any social psychological theory of intergroup relations should be the fundamental psychological processes that are hypothesized to underlie relations between groups. The various theories addressed in this volume offer a range of important psychological processes that are broad enough to serve as building blocks for an integrated theory. Four psychological concepts form the basis of social identity theory: social categorization, social identity, social comparison, and psychological distinctiveness. Also, in terms of social identity theory, the norm of justice is central to the instigation of action. Equity theory, of course, focuses directly on the norms of justice and exchange, but includes the notions of social comparison and cognitive dissonance. Relative deprivation theory is fundamentally rooted in social comparison principles. However, the concepts of justice and attribution play a strong supporting role in relative deprivation theory.

The five-stage model deals explicitly with the concepts of social comparison and social attribution, with the notion of justice implicitly involved at crucial periods in the process of maintaining a stage or moving from one stage to another. Finally, in Chapter 9 we discussed how the processes of stereotypes, attributions, and attitudes are incorporated in theories of intergroup relations, although most often as outgrowths of the relationships between groups rather than as the explicit shaper or causal factor in the relationship itself.

The two concepts that arise most frequently are social comparison and justice. Does this mean that these are the most promising candidates for the focus of future theory and research on intergroup relations? Frequency may not be the only, or indeed the best, criterion for such a decision, but our critical review of the various theories discussed in this volume leads us to anticipate that justice and social comparison deserve more attention. The specific challenge will be to capitalize on the development of these concepts in mainstream social psychology, and to integrate this development with a truly intergroup perspective.

INTERGROUP RELATIONS: AN EMERGING FIELD

We began this volume by expressing optimism about the future development of intergroup relations as a major field of study. Having critically reviewed six major theoretical perspectives on intergroup relations, as well as describing typical examples of research studies stimulated by each theory, we are now in a better position to make a judgment on the future of this emerging field. The first point to emphasize is that social psychology *does* have an important and unique contribution to make to our understanding of intergroup relations. This contribution is already evident in the understanding provided by the major theories reviewed in this volume, as well as in the valuable insights provided by the research studies they have stimulated. While the structure of group relations and economic factors do have an important influence on behavior at the intergroup level, as suggested by realistic conflict theory, the central role of social psychological processes in determining the nature of such behavior has also become clear, as suggested by the theories and supporting evidence reviewed in this volume.

Two sets of factors are likely to increase the importance of intergroup relations as a field of study in the next few decades. First is the move toward a more "social" social psychology that is directly concerned with the relationship between human psychological behavior and macro-level social processes. It seems fair to claim that this movement has been spearheaded by European social psychology (see Tajfel 1984). In discussing the development of European social psychology since the mid-1960s, Tajfel et al. (1984) comment that "Social psychology in Europe is today much more *social* than it was twenty years ago" (p. 1). The general perspective of this "new" European social psychology can be said to be ". . . that social psychology can and must include in its theoretical and research preoccupations a direct concern with the relationship between human psychological functioning and the large-scale social processes and events which shape this functioning and are shaped by it" (Tajfel, Jaspers, and Fraser, 1984, p. 3). This move toward a more "social" social psychology inevitably involves a greater concern for processes at the intergroup level and a move away from reductionist explanations of intergroup behavior.

A second factor that is likely to increase the importance of intergroup relations as a field of study is the growing power of minorities in many societies, not only those in Europe and North America but those in the Third World as well. The women's liberation, gay rights, and black power movements probably represent the most visible examples of this phenomenon to date. However, ethnic minorities generally seem to be more vocal and increasingly concerned with improving their status. This trend appears to be reflected by the official acceptance of a multicultural policy in Canada and Australia, as well as by the "unofficial" prominence gained by minority cultures and languages in Europe and the United States. The cultural impact and growing political cohesion of South Asians in Britain, Algerians in France, Asian "guest workers" in West Germany, and the Hispanic minority in the United States bear witness to this trend. Finally, there are the ongoing struggles for freedom and distinctiveness that characterize Third World nations on the continents of Africa, Asia, and South America, as well as minorities within these nations. The influence of minorities seems to be gaining recognition, both in the larger society and in the more limited domain of social research (Doms, 1983; Mugny 1984), and this in turn is leading to a greater concern with intergroup relations.

The increased possibility of conflict, whether between terrorists and authorities or between the superpowers, represents the more frightening aspects of intergroup life in the contemporary world. In the past, a great deal of theory and experimental research have been concerned with peacemaking although the approaches used by researchers have been seriously flawed—by reductionism, for example—and the practical importance of this work has been rather limited. The challenge that remains is to achieve a truly intergroup perspective on problems of intergroup conflict, and thus contribute effectively to efforts for achieving peace, cooperation, and *justice* between groups. An integral part of this challenge is a commitment to fully appreciating the social psychological processes that involve both minority and majority groups, and relations between them.

Bibliography

Aboud, F. E., and D. M. Taylor. 1971. Ethnic and role stereotypes: Their relative importance in person perception. *Journal of Social Psychology, 85,* 17–27.

Adam, J. 1963. *The Republic of Plato.* 2 vols. Cambridge: Cambridge University Press.

Adams, J. S. 1965. Inequity in social exchange. In L. Berkowitz (ed.), *Advances in experimental social psychology.* Vol. 2, pp. 267–299. New York: Academic Press.

Adams, J. S., and W. B. Rosenbaum. 1962. The relationship of worker productivity to cognitive dissonance about wage inequities. *Journal of Applied Psychology, 46,* 161–164.

Adorno, T. W., E. Frenkel-Brunswik, D. J. Levinson, and R. W. Sanford. 1950. *The authoritarian personality.* New York: Harper & Row.

Allen, V. L., and D. A. Wilder. 1975. Categorization, belief similarity, and group discrimination. *Journal of Personality and Social Psychology, 32,* 971–977.

Allport, G. W. 1954. *The nature of prejudice.* Cambridge, Mass.: Addison-Wesley.

———. 1968. The historical background of modern social psychology. In G. Lindzey and E. Aronson (eds.), *The handbook of social psychology.* 2nd ed. Vol. 1, pp. 1–80. Reading, Mass.: Addison-Wesley.

Anderson, N. H. 1976. Equity judgments as information integration. *Journal of Personality and Social Psychology, 33,* 291–299.

Anderson, N. H., and A. J. Farkas. 1975. Integration theory applied to models of inequity. *Personality and Social Psychology Bulletin, 1,* 588–591.

Aronson, E. 1984. *The social animal.* New York: W. H. Freeman.

Aronson, E., C. Stephan, J. Sikes, N. Blaney, and M. Snapp. 1978. *The jigsaw classroom.* Beverly Hills, Cal.: Sage Publications.

Asch, S. E. 1956. Studies of independence and conformity: A minority of one against a unanimous majority. *Psychological Monographs, 70* (9, whole no. 416).

Ashby-Wills, T. 1983. Downward comparison principles in social psychology. *Psychological Bulletin, 90,* 245–271.

Austin, W. G. 1979. Justice, freedom and self interest in intergroup conflict. In W. G. Austin and S. Worchell (eds.), *The social psychology of intergroup relations,* pp. 121–143. Monterey; Cal.: Brooks/Cole.

Austin, W., and E. Walster, 1974. Reactions to confirmations and disconfirmations of expectations of equity and inequity. *Journal of Personality and Social Psychology, 30,* 208-216.

Austin, W. G., and S. Worchell (eds.). 1979. *The social psychology of intergroup relations.* Monterey, Cal.: Brooks/Cole.

Axelrod, R. 1984. *The evolution of cooperation.* New York: Basic Books.

Barber, B. 1968. Social mobility in Hindu India. In J. Silverberg (ed.), *Social mobility in the caste system in India,* pp. 18–35. The Hague: Mouton.

Baron, R. A., and D. Byrne. 1977. *Social psychology: Understanding human interaction.* Boston: Allyn & Bacon.

Bercovitch, J. 1984. *Social conflicts and third parties: Strategies of conflict resolution.* Boulder, Colo.: Westview.

Berkowitz, L. 1962. *Aggression: A social psychological analysis.* New York: McGraw-Hill.

Berlyne, D. E. 1968. American and European psychology. *American Psychologist, 23,* 447–452.

Bernard, J. 1950. Where is the modern sociology of conflict? *American Journal of Sociology, 56,* 11–16.

Bernstein, M., and F. Crosby. 1980. An empirical exmination of relative deprivation theory. *Journal of Experimental Social Psychology, 16,* 442–456.

Berry, J. 1970. A functional approach to the relationship between stereotypes and familiarity. *Australian Journal of Psychology, 22,* 29–33.

Berscheid, E., and E. Walster. 1967. When does a harmdoer compensate a victim? *Journal of Personality and Social Psychology, 6,* 435–441.

Bettelheim, B. 1943. Individual and mass behavior in extreme situations. *Journal of Abnormal and Social Psychology, 38,* 417–452.

Billig, M. G. 1972. Social categorization and intergroup relations. Ph.D. diss., University of Bristol.

———. 1973. Normative communication in a minimal intergroup situation. *European Journal of Social Psychology, 3,* 339–343.

———. 1976. *Social psychology and intergroup relations.* London: Academic Press.

———. 1978. *Fascists: A social psychological view of the National Front.* London: Academic Press.

———. 1982. *Ideology and social psychology.* Oxford: Basil Blackwell.

Billig, M. G., and H. Tajfel. 1973. Social categorization and similarity in intergroup behaviour. *European Journal of Social Psychology, 3*, 27–52.

Blake, R. R., and J. S. Mouton. 1962. The intergroup dynamics of win-loss conflict and problem-solving collaboration in union-management relations. In M. Sherif (ed.), *Intergroup relations and leadership*, pp. 94–141. New York: John Wiley.

Blake, R. R., H. A. Shepard, and J. S. Mouton. 1964. *Managing intergroup conflict in industry*. Houston: Gulf.

Blau, P. M. 1964. *Exchange and power in social life*. New York: John Wiley.

Bottomore, T. B. 1966. *Elite and society*. Harmondsworth, England: Penguin.

Bradley, G. W. 1978. Self-serving biases in the attribution process: A re-examination of the fact or fiction question. *Journal of Personality and Social Psychology, 36*, 56–71.

Brandt, L. W. 1970. American psychology. *American Psychologist, 25*, 1091–1093.

Brewer, M. B. 1979. The role of ethnocentrism in intergroup conflict. In W. G. Austin and J. Worchel (eds.), *The social psychology of intergroup relations,* pp. 71–84. Monterey, Cal.: Brooks/Cole.

Brewer, M. B., and D. T. Campbell. 1976. *Ethnocentrism and intergroup attitudes: East African evidence*. New York: Halsted.

Brigham, J. C. 1971. Ethnic stereotypes. *Psychological Bulletin, 76*, 15–38.

Brown, R. J. 1984. The role of similarity in intergroup relations. In H. Tajfel (ed.), *The social dimension*, vol. 2, pp. 603–623. Cambridge: Cambridge University Press.

Brown, R. J., G. Wade, A. Mathews, S. Condor, and J. Williams. 1983. *Group identification and intergroup differentiation*. Paper presented at the annual conference of the British Psychological Society (Social Psychology Section), Sheffield.

Brown, R. J., and J. A. Williams. 1983. *Group identification: The same thing to all people?* Unpublished manuscript, Social Psychology Research Unit, University of Kent.

Bruner, J. S., J. J. Goodman, and G. A. Austin. 1956. *A study in thinking*. New York: John Wiley.

Burnham, J. 1941. *The managerial revolution*. Bloomington: Indiana University Press.

Caddick, B. 1981. Equity theory, social identity, and intergroup relations. *Review of Personality and Social Psychology, 1*, 219–245.

Campbell, D. T. 1967. Stereotypes and the perception of group differences. *American Psychologist, 22*, 817–829.

Caplan, N., and S. D. Nelson. 1973. On being useful: The nature and consequences of psychological research on social problems. *American Psychologist, 28*, 199–211.

Carlyle, Thomas. 1841, repr. 1901. *Heroes, hero-worship and the heroic in history.* London: Chapman & Hall.

Cauthen, N. R., I. E. Robinson, and H. H. Krauss. 1971. Stereotypes: A review of the literature 1926–1968. *Journal of Social Psychology, 84*, 103–126.

Collins, B. E., and B. H. Raven. 1968. Group structure: Attraction, coalitions, communication, and power. In G. Lindzey and E. Aronson (eds.), *The handbook of social psychology*, vol. 4, pp. 102–204. Reading, Mass.: Addison-Wesley.

Commins, B., and J. Lockwood. 1979a. The effects of status differences, favoured treatment and equity on intergroup comparisons. *European Journal of Social Psychology, 9*, 281–289.

_____ . 1979b. Social comparison and social inequality: An experimental investigation of intergroup behaviour. *British Journal of Social and Clinical Psychology, 18*, 285–289.

Cook, T. D., F. Crosby, and K. M. Hennigan. 1977. The construct validity of relative deprivation. In J. M. Suls and R. L. Miller (eds.), *Social comparison processes: Theoretical and empirical perspectives*, pp. 307–333. Washington, D. C.: Halsted-Wiley.

Coser, L. 1956. *The functions of social conflict.* New York: Free Press.

Crosby, F. 1976. A model of egoistical relative deprivation. *Psychological Review, 83*, 85–113.

_____ . 1982. *Relative deprivation and working women.* New York: Oxford University Press.

Crosby F., and M. Bernstein. 1978. Relative deprivation: testing the models. Paper presented at the meeting of the American Psychological Association, Toronto.

Dahrendorf, R. 1964. The new Germanies. *Encounter, 22*, 50–58.

Davis, J. 1959. A formal interpretation of the theory of relative deprivation. *Sociometry, 22*, 280–296.

Deaux, K. and L. S. Wrightsman. 1984. *Social psychology in the 80's.* Monterey, California: Brooks/Cole.

deCarufel, A., and J. Schopler. 1979. Evaluation of outcome improvement resulting from threats and appeals. *Journal of Personality and Social Psychology, 37*, 662–673.

Deschamps, J. C., and R. J. Brown. n.d. Superordinate goals and intergroup conflict. Unpublished manuscript, University of Bristol.

Deutsch, M. 1962. Psychological alternatives to war. *Journal of Social Issues, 18* (2), 97–119.

――――. 1969a. Socially relevant science: Reflections on some studies of interpersonal conflict. *American Psychologist, 24*, 1076–1092.

――――. 1969b. Conflicts productive and destructive. *Journal of Social Issues, 15*, 7–14.

――――. 1973. *The resolution of conflict*. New Haven: Yale University Press.

――――. 1975. Equity, equality and need: What determines which value will be used as the basis of distributive justice? *Journal of Social Issues, 31*, 137–149.

――――. 1985. *Distributive justice: A social-psychological perspective*. New Haven: Yale University Press.

Deutsch, M. and R. M. Krauss. 1960. The effect of threat on interpersonal bargaining. *Journal of Abnormal and Social Psychology, 61*, 181–189.

――――. 1962. Studies of interpersonal bargaining. *Journal of Conflict Resolution, 6*, 52–76.

Doise, W. 1978. *Groups and individuals: Explanations in social psychology*. Cambridge: Cambridge University Press.

Doise, W., G. Csepeli, H. D. Dann, G. C. Gouge, K. Larsen, and A. Ostell. 1972. An experimental investigation into the formation of intergroup representations. *European Journal of Social Psychology, 2*, 202–204.

Dollard, J., L. Doob, N. Miller, O. Mowrer, and R. Sears. 1939. *Frustration and aggression*. New Haven: Yale University Press.

Doms, M. 1983. The minority influence effect: An alternative approach. In W. Doise and S. Moscovici (eds.), *Current issues in European social psychology*, vol. 1, pp. 1–32. Cambridge: Cambridge University Press.

Donnerstein, E., M. Donnerstein, S. Simon, and R. Ditrichs. 1972. Variables in interracial aggression: Anonymity, expected retaliation, and a riot. *Journal of Personality and Social Psychology, 22*, 236–245.

Dostoevsky, Feodor. 1972. Notes from the underground. In R. Fernandez (ed.), *Social psychology through literature;* pp. 416–429. New York: John Wiley.

Douglas, A. 1957. The peaceful settlement of individual and intergroup disputes. *Journal of Conflict Resolution, 1*(1), 69–81.

Durkheim, E. 1960. *The division of labour in society*. G. Simpson, trans. 4th ed. Glencoe, Ill.: Free Press. (Original work published 1923.)

Dye, T. R., and L. H. Zeigler. 1970. *The irony of democracy: An uncommon introduction to American politics.* Belmont, Cal.: Wadsworth.

Eiser, J. R., and K. K. Bhavnani. 1974. The effect of situational meaning on the behaviour of subjects in the Prisoner's Dilemma game. *European Journal of Social Psychology, 4,* 93–97.

Eiser, J. R., and A. J. Smith. 1972. Preference for accuracy and positivity in the description of oneself by another. *European Journal of Social Psychology, 22,* 199–201.

Eulau, H., and M. M. Czudnowski. 1976. *Elite recruitment in democratic politics.* New York: Sage

Festinger, L. 1954. A theory of social comparison processes. *Human Relations, 7,* 117–140.

———. 1957. *A theory of cognitive dissonance.* Stanford, Cal.: Stanford University Press.

———. 1964. *Conflict, decision and dissonance.* Stanford, Cal.: Stanford University Press.

Field, G. L. and J. Higley. 1980. *Elitism.* London: Routledge & Kegan Paul.

Fishbein, M., and I. Ajzen. 1972. Attitudes toward objects as predictive of single and multiple behavioral criteria. *Psychological Review, 81,* 59–74.

———. 1975. *Belief, attitude, intention and behavior: An introduction to theory and research.* Reading, Mass.: Addison-Wesley.

Fisher, R. J. 1983. Third party consultation as a method of intergroup conflict resolution. *Journal of Conflict Resolution, 27,* 301–334.

Fishman, J. A. 1956. An examination of the process and functioning of social stereotyping. *Journal of Social Psychology, 43,* 27–64.

Frank, J. D. 1967. *Sanity and survival: Psychological aspects of war and peace.* London: Barrie & Rockliff.

Freud, S. 1953–1964. *Standard edition of complete psychological works.* J. Strachey, ed. and trans. London: Hogarth Press.

———. 1915. *Thought for the times on war and death. Standard edition;* vol. 14.

———. 1920. *Beyond the pleasure principle. Standard edition;* vol. 18.

———. 1921. *Group psychology and the analysis of the ego. Standard edition;* vol. 18.

———. 1923. *The ego and the id. Standard edition;* vol. 19.

———. 1927. *The future of an illusion. Standard edition;* vol. 21.

———. 1930. *Civilization and its discontents. Standard edition;* vol. 21.

———. 1933. *Why war? Standard edition;* vol. 22.

Friedrich, C. J. 1942. *The new belief in the common man*. Boston: Little, Brown.

Gardner, R. C. 1973. Ethnic stereotypes: The traditional approach, a new look. *Canadian Psychologist, 14*, 133–148.

Gardner, R. C., and R. Kalin (eds.). 1981. *A Canadian social psychology of ethnic relations*. Toronto: Methuen.

Gardner, R. C., D. M. Kirby, and J. C. Finley. 1973. Ethnic stereotypes: The significance of consensus. *Canadian Journal of Behavioural Science, 5*, 4–12.

Gardner, R. C., E. J. Wonnacott, and D. M. Taylor. 1968. Ethnic stereotypes: A factor analytic investigation. *Canadian Journal of Psychology, 22*, 35–44.

Gibb, C. A. 1968. Leadership. In G. Lindzey and E. Aronson (eds.), *The handbook of social psychology*, vol. 4, pp. 205–282. Reading, Mass.: Addison-Wesley.

Goffman, E. 1963. *Stigma: Notes on the management of spoiled identity*. Englewood Cliffs, N. J.: Prentice-Hall.

Guimond, S., and L. Dubé-Simard. 1983. Relative deprivation theory and the Quebec nationalist movement: The cognition-emotion distinction and the person-group deprivation issue. *Journal of Personality and Social Psychology, 44*, 526–535.

Gurr, T. R. 1970. *Why men rebel*. Princeton: Princeton University Press.

Hamilton, D. L. 1979. A cognitive-attributional analysis of stereotyping. In L. Berkowitz (ed.), *Advances in experimental social psychology*, vol. 12, pp. 53–84. New York: Academic Press.

Hamilton, D. L. (ed.). 1981. *Cognitive processes in stereotyping and intergroup behavior*. Hillsdale, N. J.: Erlbaum.

Hamilton, D. L., and R. K. Gifford. 1976. Illusory correlation in interpersonal perception: a cognitive basis of stereotypic judgments. *Journal of Experimental Social Psychology, 12*, 392–407.

Hardin, G. 1968. The tragedy of the commons. *Science, 162*, 1243–1248.

Harding, J., H. Proshansky, B. Kutwer, and I. Chein. 1968. Prejudice and ethnic relations. In G. Lindzey and E. Aronson, (eds.), *The handbook of social psychology*, vol. 5, pp. 1–76. Reading, Mass.: Addison-Wesley.

Heider, F. 1946. Attitudes and cognitive organization. *Journal of Psychology, 21*, 107–112.

―――― . 1958. *The psychology of interpersonal relations*. New York: John Wiley.

Hewstone, M., and C. Ward. 1985. Ethnocentrism and causal attribution in Southeast Asia. *Journal of Personality and Social Psychology, 48*, 614–623.

Hirschman, A. O. 1970. *Exit, voice and loyalty: Responses to decline in firms, organizations and states*. Cambridge, Mass: Harvard University Press.

———— . 1974. Exit, voice and loyalty. *Social Science Information, 13* (1), 7-26.

Homans, G. C. 1961. *Social Behavior: Its elementary forms.* New York: Harcourt, Brace & World.

Hook, J. G., and T. D. Cook. 1979. Equity theory and the cognitive ability of children. *Psychological Bulletin, 86,* 429-445.

Horowitz, D. L. 1973. Direct, displaced and cumulative ethnic aggression. *Comparative Politics, 6,* 1-16.

Ittelson, W. H. 1973. *Environmental cognition.* Seminar Press.

Ittelson, W. H., H. M. Proshansky, L. G. Rivlin, and G. A. Winkel. 1974. *An introduction to environmental psychology,* ch. 5, pp. 102-125. New York: Holt, Rinehart & Winston.

Jaspers, J. 1986. Forum and focus: A personal view of European social psychology. *European Journal of Social Psychology, 16,* 3-15.

Jones, E. E., and K. E. Davis. 1965. From acts to dispositions: The attribution process in person perception. In L. Berkowitz (ed.), *Advances in experimental social psychology,* vol. 2, pp. 220-256. New York: Academic Press.

Kaltefleiter, W. 1976. The recruitment market of the German political elite. In H. Eulan and M. M. Czudnowski (eds.), *Elite recruitment in democratic politics,* pp. 239-262. New York: Sage.

Kaplan, A. 1964. *The conduct of inquiry: Methodology for behavioral science.* San Francisco: Chandler.

Karlins, M., T. L. Coffman, and G. Walters. 1969. On the fading of social stereotypes: Studies in three generations of college students. *Journal of Personality and Social Psychology, 13,* 1-6.

Katz, D., and K. Braly. 1933. Racial stereotypes of one hundred college students. *Journal of Abnormal and Social Psychology, 28,* 280-290.

———— . 1935. Racial prejudice and racial stereotypes. *Journal of Abnormal and Social Psychology, 30,* 175-193.

Kelley, H. H. 1973. The processes of causal attribution. *American Psychologist, 28,* 107-128.

Kelley, H. H., and J. W. Thibaut. 1968. Group problem solving. In G. Lindzey and E. Aronson (eds.), *The handbook of social psychology,* vol. 4, pp. 1-101. Reading, Mass.: Addison-Wesley.

Kennedy, S., J. Scheirer, and A. Rogers. 1984. The price of our success: Our monocultural science. *American Psychologist, 39,* 996-997.

Kidder, L. H., and V. M. Stewart. 1975. *The psychology of intergroup relations: Conflict and consciousness.* New York: John Wiley.

Kressel, K., and D. G. Pruitt. (eds.). 1985. The mediation of social conflict. *Journal of Social Issues, 4* (2).

Lalonde, R. N. 1985. Ethnic stereotype processing and organization as a function of group membership. Ph.D. diss., University of Western Ontario.

Lambert, W. E. 1956. The use of Pareto's residue-deviation classification as a method of content analysis. *Contributions à 1'Étude des Sciences de l'Homme, 3*, 183–191.

––––––. 1969. A social psychology of bilingualism. *Journal of Social Issues, 25*, 55–63.

Lambert, W. E., and D. M. Taylor. 1986. Cultural and racial diversity in the lives of urban Americans: The Hamtramck/Pontiac study. Unpublished monograph, McGill University.

Lasker, B. 1929. *Race attitudes in children.* New York: Holt.

Lasswell, H. D. 1936. *Politics: Who gets what, when, how.* New York: McGraw-Hill.

Lasswell, H. D., and A. Kaplan. 1950. *Power and society.* New Haven: Yale University Press.

Lasswell, H. D., D. Lerner, and C. E. Rothwell. 1952. *The comparative study of elites.* Stanford, Cal.: Stanford University Press.

Lawler, J. E. 1985. *Advances in group process,* vol. 2. Greenwich, Conn.: JAI Press.

Le Bon, G. 1897. *The crowd: A study of the popular mind.* London: T. Fisher Unwin.

Lemain, G., and J. Kastersztein. 1971–1972. Recherches sur l'originalité sociale et l'incomparabilité. *Bulletin de Psychologie, 25*, 673–693.

Lenin, V. I. 1973. *What is to be done? Burning questions of our movement.* Peking: Foreign Language Press. (Original work published 1902).

Lerner, M. J. 1971. Justified self-interest and the responsibility for suffering: A replication and extension. *Journal of Human Relations, 19*, 550–559.

––––––. 1977. The justice motive: Some hypotheses as to its origins and forms. *Journal of Personality, 45*, 1–52.

Lerner, M. J., and C. H. Simmons. 1971. Observer's reaction to the "innocent victim": Compassion or rejection? *Journal of Personality and Social Psychology, 20*, 127–135.

Leventhal, G. S. 1979. Effects of external conflict on resource allocation and fairness within groups and organizations. In W.G. Austin and S. Worchel (eds.), *The social psychology of intergroup relations*, pp. 237–252. Monterey; Cal.: Brooks/Cole.

Leventhal, G. S., and D. W. Lane. 1970. Sex, age, and equity behavior. *Journal of Personality and Social Psychology, 15*, 312–316.

LeVine, R. A., and D. T. Campbell. 1972. *Ethnocentrism: Theories of conflict, ethnic attitudes and group behavior*. New York: John Wiley.

Lindzey, G., and E. Aronson (eds.). 1968. *The handbook of social psychology*, vol. 5. 2nd ed. Reading, Mass.: Addison-Wesley.

Lorenz, K. 1966. *On aggression*, M. Wilson, trans. New York: Harcourt, Brace & World.

Lott, A. J., and B. E. Lott. 1965. Group cohesiveness as interpersonal attraction: A review of relationships with antecedent and consequent variables. *Psychological Bulletin, 64*, 259–309.

Lowi, T. J. 1973. Foreword. In K. Prewitt and A. Stone, *The ruling elites*. pp. vii–xii, New York: Harper & Row.

Mandelbaum, D. G. 1970. *Society in India*, Vol. 2, *Change and continuity*. Berkeley: University of California Press.

Manis, M. 1972. Social interaction and the self-concept. In D. R. Heise (ed.), *Personality and socialization*, pp. 136–152. Chicago: Rand McNally.

Maquet, J. J. 1961. *The promise of inequality in Ruanda: A study of political relations in a central African community*. London: Oxford University Press.

Martin, J. 1980. *Pay equality and the perception of injustice: a relative deprivation perspective*. Research Paper no.553. Stanford University.

Martin, J. 1986. The tolerance of injustice. In J. M. Olson, C. P. Herman, and M. P. Zanna (eds.), *Relative deprivation and social comparison: The Ontario symposium*, vol. 4, pp. 217–242. Hillsdale, N.J.: Erlbaum.

Martin, J., P. Brickman, and A. Murray. (In press). Moral outrage and pragmatism: Explanations for collective action. *Journal of Experimental Social Psychology*.

Martin, J. and A. Murray. 1983. Distributive injustice and unfair exchange. In D. M. Messick and K. S. Cook (eds.), *Equity theory: Psychological and sociological perspectives*, pp. 169–202. New York: Praeger.

Martin, J., R. Price, R. Bies, and M. Powers, 1979. *Relative deprivation among secretaries: The effects of the token female executive*. Paper presented at American Psychological Association meeting, New York: September 1979.

Marvick, D. 1976. Continuities in recruitment theory and research: Toward a new model. In H. Eulau and M.M. Czudnowski (Eds.), *Elite recruitment in democratic politics*, pp. 29–44. New York: Sage.

McDougall, W. 1920. *The group mind*. Cambridge: Cambridge University Press.

———. 1935. Pareto as a psychologist. *Journal of Social Philosophy, 1*, 36–52.

McGuire, W. J. 1969. The nature of attitudes and attitude change. In G.

Lindzey and E. Aronson (eds.), *The handbook of social psychology*, vol. 3, pp. 136–314. Reading, Mass.: Addison-Wesley.

McKirnan, D. J., and E. V. Hamayan. In press. Social norms and perceptions of ethnolinguistic diversity: Toward a conceptual and research framework. *European Journal of Social Psychology*.

Messick, D. M., and K. S. Cook (eds.). 1983. *Equity theory: Psychological and sociological perspectives*. New York: Praeger.

Middlebrook, P. N. 1974. *Social psychology and modern life*. New York: Alfred A. Knopf.

Middleton, J., and D. Tait. 1958. *Tribes without rulers: Studies in African segmentary systems*. London: Kegan Paul.

Miller, A. G. 1972. *The social psychology of psychological research*. New York: Free Press.

———. 1982. Historical and contemporary perspectives on stereotyping. In A. G. Miller (ed.), *In the eye of the beholder: Contemporary issues in stereotyping*, pp. 1–40. New York: Praeger.

Miller, D. T. 1978. What constitutes a self-serving attributional bias? A reply to Bradley. *Journal of Personality and Social Psychology, 36*, 1221–1223.

Miller, D. T., and M. Ross. 1975. Self-serving biases in the attribution of causality: Fact or fiction? *Psychological Bulletin, 82*, 213–225.

Miller, R. L. 1977. Preferences for social vs. non-social comparison as a means of self-evaluation. *Journal of Personality, 45*, 458–468.

Mills, C. W. 1956. *The power elite*. New York: Oxford University Press.

Milner, D. 1975. *Children and race*. Harmondsworth, England: Penguin Books.

Moghaddam, F. M., and P. Stringer. 1986. "Trivial" and "important" criteria for social categorization in the minimal group paradigm. *Journal of Social Psychology, 126*, 345–354.

Morley, I. E., and G. M. Stephenson. 1969. Interpersonal and interparty exchange: A laboratory simulation of an industrial dispute at the plant level. *British Journal of Psychology, 60*, 543–545.

———. 1970a. Strength of case, communication systems and outcomes of simulated negotiations: Some social psychological aspects of bargaining. *Industrial Relations Journal, 1*, 19–29.

———. 1970b. Formality in experimental negotiations: A validation study. *British Journal of Psychology, 61*, 383–384.

Mosca, G. 1939. *The ruling class*. New York: McGraw-Hill. (Translated from Italian edition of 1896.)

Moscovici, S. 1972. Society and theory in social psychology. In J. Israel and

H. Tajfel (eds.), *The context of social psychology*, pp. 17–68. London: Academic Press.

———. 1976. *Social influence and social change* London: Academic Press.

———. 1980. Towards a theory of conversion behaviour. In L. Berkowitz (ed.), *Advances in experimental social psychology*, pp. 209–242. New York: Academic Press.

Moscovici, S., G. Mugny, and E. Van Avermaet, (eds.). 1984. *Perspectives on minority influence*. Cambridge: Cambridge University Press.

Mugny, G. 1982. *The power of minorities*. London: Academic Press.

———. 1984. The influence of minorities: Ten years after. In H. Tajfel (ed.), *The social dimension*, vol. 2, pp. 498–517. Cambridge: Cambridge University Press.

Mulkay, M. J., and B. S. Turner. 1971. Over-production of personnel and innovation in three social settings. *Sociology, 5*, 47–61.

Neisser, V. 1967. *Cognitive psychology*. New York: Appleton-Century-Crofts.

Nemeth, C. 1972. A critical analysis of research utilizing the Prisoner's Dilemma paradigm for the study of bargaining. In L. Berkowitz (ed.), *Advances in experimental social psychology*, vol. 6, pp. 203–234. New York: Academic Press.

Newell, D., P. McKillop, and S. Monroe. 1986. Arab-bashing in America. *Newsweek*, January 20, p. 21.

Ng, S. H. 1980. *The social psychology of power*. New York: Academic Press.

———. 1982. Power and intergroup discrimination. In J. Tajfel (ed.), *Social identity and intergroup relations*, pp. 179–206. Cambridge: Cambridge University Press.

———. 1984. Social psychology and political economy. In J. Tajfel (ed.), *The social dimension*, vol. 2, pp. 624–645. Cambridge: Cambridge University Press.

Olson, J. M., C. P. Herman, and M. P. Zanna. 1986. *Relative deprivation and social comparison: The Ontario symposium*, vol. 4. Hillsdale, N.J.: Erlbaum.

Pannen, D. E. 1976. Anticipation of future interaction and the estimation of current rewards. Ph.D. diss., University of Minnesota.

Papastamou, S. 1983. Strategies of minority and majority influence. In W. Doise and S. Moscovici (eds.), *Current issues in European social psychology*, vol. 1, pp. 33–83. Cambridge: Cambridge University Press.

Pareto, V. 1935. *The mind and society: A treatise on general sociology*, 4 vols. New York: Dover.

———. 1971. *Manual of political economy*. New York: Augustus M. Kelley. (Translated from French edition of 1927.)

Park, B., and M. Rothbart. 1982. Perception of out-group homogeneity and levels of social categorization: Memory for the subordinate attributes of in-group and out-group members. *Journal of Personality and Social Psychology, 42*, 1051-1068.

Pettigrew, T. F. 1967. Social evaluation theory: Convergencies and applications. In D. Levine (ed.), *Nebraska symposium on motivation*, pp. 241-315. Omaha: University of Nebraska Press.

———. 1978. Three issues in ethnicity: Boundaries, deprivations, and perceptions. In J. M. Yinger and S. J. Cutler (eds.), *Major social issues: A multidisciplinary view*, pp. 25-49. New York: Free Press.

———. 1979. The ultimate attribution error: Extending Allport's cognitive analysis of prejudice. *Personality and Social Psychology Bulletin, 5*, 461-476.

Pettigrew, T. F., G. W. Allport, and E. O. Barnett. 1958. Binocular resolution and perception of race in South Africa. *British Journal of Psychology, 49*, 265-278.

Plon, M. 1974. On the meaning and notion of conflict and its study in social psychology. *European Journal of Social Psychology, 4*, 389-436.

Popper, K. R. 1959. *The logic of scientific discovery*. New York: Harper.

Prewitt, K. and A. Stone. 1973. *The ruling elites: Elite theory, power, and American democracy*. New York: Harper & Row.

Pruitt, D. G. 1971. Conclusions: Toward an understanding of choice shifts in group discussion. *Journal of Personality and Social Psychology, 20*, 495-510.

Pruitt, D. G., and J. Z. Rubin. 1986. *Social conflict: Escalations, stalemate, and settlement*. New York: Random House.

Rapaport, A., and A. M. Chammah. 1965. *Prisoner's dilemma: A study in conflict and cooperation*. Ann Arbor: University of Michigan Press.

Rappaport, J. 1977. *Community psychology*. New York: Holt, Rinehart & Winston.

Rosenberg, M. J. and L. P. Abelson. 1960. An analysis of cognitive balancing. In M. J. Rosenberg and C. I. Houland (eds.), *Attitude organization and change*, pp. 112-163. New Haven: Yale University Press.

Ross, L. 1977. The intuitive psychologist and his shortcomings: Distortions in the attribution process. In L. Berkowitz (ed.), *Advances in experimental social psychology*, vol. 10, pp. 174-220. New York: Academic Press.

Rothbart, M., R. Dawes, and B. Park. 1984. Stereotyping and sampling biases in intergroup perception. In J. R. Eiser (ed.), *Attitudinal judgment*, pp. 109-134. New York: Gringer-Verlag.

Rubin, J. Z. 1981. *Dynamics of third party intervention: Kissinger in the Middle East*. New Haven: Yale University Press.

Runciman, W. G. 1966. *Relative deprivation and social justice: A study of attitudes to social inequality in twentieth-century England.* Berkeley: University of California Press.

Ryan, W. 1976. *Blaming the victim.* New York: Random House.

Sachdev, I., and R. Y. Bourhis. 1984. Minimal majorities and minorities. *European Journal of Social Psychology, 14,* 35–52.

———. 1985. Social categorization and power differentials in group relations. *European Journal of Social Psychology, 15,* 415–434.

Sampson, E. E. 1975. On justice as equality. *Journal of Social Issues, 31,* 45–63.

———. 1976. *Social psychology and contemporary society.* New York: John Wiley.

———. 1977. Psychology and the American ideal. *Journal of Personality and Social Psychology, 35,* 767–782.

———. 1981. Cognitive psychology as ideology. *American Psychologist, 36* (7), 730–743.

Schelling, T. C. 1957. Bargaining, communications and limited war. *Journal of Conflict Resolution, 1* (1), 19–36.

Schmitt, D. R., and G. Marwell. 1972. Withdrawal and reward allocation as responses to inequity. *Journal of Experimental Social Psychology, 8,* 207–221.

Scrinivas, M. N. 1968. Mobility in the caste system. In M. Singer and B. S. Cohn (eds.), *Structure and change in Indian society,* pp. 189–200. Chicago: Aldine.

Sexton, V. S., and H. Misiak. 1984. American psychology and psychology abroad. *American Psychologist, 39,* 1026–1031.

Shaw, J. I., and P. Skolnick. 1973. An investigation of relative preference for consistency motivation. *European Journal of Social Psychology, 3,* 271–280.

Shaw, M. E. 1976. *Group dynamics: The psychology of small group behaviour.* 2nd ed. Teta: McGraw-Hill.

Shaw, M. E., and P. R. Costanzo. 1982. *Theories of social psychology.* New York: McGraw-Hill.

Sherif, M. 1951. A preliminary experimental study of inter-group relations. In J. H. Rohrer and M. Sherif (eds.), *Social psychology at the crossroads,* pp. 388–424. New York: Harper.

———. 1966. *Group conflict and cooperation: Their social psychology.* London: Routledge & Kegan Paul.

Sherif, M., O. J. Harvey, B. J. White, W. R. Hood, and M. Sherif. 1961. *Intergroup conflict and cooperation: The Robbers Cave experiment.* Norman: University of Oklahoma Book Exchange.

Sherif, M., and C. W. Sherif. 1953. *Groups in harmony and tension*. New York: Harper.

———. 1969. *Social psychology*. New York: Harper & Row.

Sherif, M., B. J. White, and O. J. Harvey. 1955. Status in experimentally produced groups. *American Journal of Sociology, 60*, 370–379.

Sighele, S. 1981. *La coppia criminale*. Turin: Bocca.

Silverberg, J. (ed.) 1968. *Social mobility in the caste system in India*. The Hague: Mouton.

Skevington, S. 1980. Intergroup relations and social change within a nursing context. *British Journal of Social and Clinical Psychology, 9*, 201–213.

Smith, P. 1985. *Language, the sexes and society*. Oxford: Basil Blackwell.

Steiner, I. D. 1974. Whatever happened to the group in social psychology? *Journal of Experimental Social Psychology, 10*, 94–108.

Stephenson, G. M., and C. J. Botherton. 1975. Social progression and polarization: A study of discussion and negotiation in groups of mining supervisors. *British Journal of Social and Clinical Psychology, 14*, 241–252.

Stephenson, G. M., and B. H. Kniveton, 1978. Interpersonal and interparty exchange: An experimental study of the effect of seating position on the outcome of negotiations between teams representing parties in dispute. *Human Relations, 31*, 555–565.

Stouffer, S. A., E. A. Suchman, L. C. DeVinney, S. A. Starr, and R. M. Williams. 1949. *The American soldier: adjustment during army life*, vol. 1. Princeton: Princeton University Press.

Suls, J. M., and R. L. Miller. 1977. *Social comparison processes: Theoretical and empirical perspectives*. New York: John Wiley.

Sumner, W. G. 1906. *Folkways*. Boston: Ginn.

Tajfel, H. 1957. Value and the perceptual judgement of magnitude. *Psychological Review, 64*, 192–204.

———. 1959. Quantitative judgement in social perception. *British Journal of Psychology, 50*, 16–29.

———. 1969. Cognitive aspects of prejudice. *Journal of Social Issues, 25*, 79–97.

———. 1970. Experiments in intergroup discrimination. *Scientific American, 223* (5), 96–102.

———. 1972a. Introduction. In J. Israel and H. Tajfel (eds.), *The context of social psychology*, pp. 1–13. London and New York: Academic Press.

———. 1972b. Experiments in a vacuum. In J. Israel and H. Tajfel (eds.), *The context of social psychology*, pp. 69–119. London: Academic Press.

————. 1974a. Social identity and intergroup behaviour. *Social Science Information, 13*, 65–93.

————. 1974b. *Intergroup behaviour, social comparison and social change.* Unpublished manuscript; Katz-Newcomb lectures, University of Michigan at Ann Arbor.

————. 1978a. Social categorization, social identity and social comparison. In H. Tajfel (ed.), *Differentiation between social groups*, pp. 61–76. London and New York: Academic Press.

————. 1978b. *Differentiation between social groups: Studies in the social psychology of intergroup relations.* London and New York: Academic Press.

————. 1978c. The achievement of group differentiation. In H. Tajfel (ed.), *Differentiation between social groups*, pp. 77–98. London and New York: Academic Press.

————. 1978d. Intergroup behaviour: II-Group perspectives. In H. Tajfel and C. Fraser (eds.), *Introducing social psychology*, pp. 423–441. Harmondsworth, England: Penguin.

————. 1979. Individuals and groups in social psychology: A reply to Taylor and Brown. *British Journal of Social and Clinical Psychology, 18*, 183–190.

————. 1982a. Social psychology of intergroup relations. *Annual Review of Psychology, 33*, 1–39.

————. (ed.). 1982b. *Social identity and intergroup relations.* Cambridge: Cambridge University Press.

————. (ed.). 1984. *The social dimension.* 2 vols. Cambridge: Cambridge University Press.

Tajfel, H., C. Flament, M. G. Billig, and R. F. Bundy. 1971. Social categorization and intergroup behaviour. *European Journal of Social Psychology, 1*, 149–177.

Tajfel, H., J. M. Jaspers, and C. Fraser. 1984. The social dimensions in European social psychology. In H. Tajfel (ed.), *The social dimension*, vol. 1, pp. 1–8. Cambridge: Cambridge University Press.

Tajfel, H., and J. C. Turner. 1979. An integrative theory of intergroup conflict. In W. G. Austin and S. Worchel (eds.), *The social psychology of intergroup relations*, pp. 33–47. Monterey, Cal.: Brooks/Cole.

Tajfel, H., and A. L. Wilkes. 1963. Classification and quantitative judgement. *British Journal of Psychology, 54*, 101–113.

Taylor, D. M. 1981. Stereotypes and intergroup relations. In R. C. Gardner and R. Kalin (eds.), *A Canadian social psychology of ethnic relations*, pp. 151–171. Toronto: Methuen.

Taylor, D. M., and R. J. Brown. 1979. Towards a more social social psychology? *British Journal of Social and Clinical Psychology, 18*, 173–180.

Taylor, D. M., and J. R. Doria. 1981. Self-serving and group-serving bias in attribution. *Journal of Social Psychology, 113*, 202-211.

Taylor, D. M., J. R. Doria, and K. Tyler. 1983. Group performance and cohesiveness: An attribution analysis. *Journal of Social Psychology, 119*, 187-198.

Taylor, D. M., and L. Dubé. 1986. Two faces of identity: The "I" and the "we." *Journal of Social Issues, 42*:81-98.

Taylor, D. M., and V. Jaggi. 1974. Ethnocentrism in a south Indian context. *Journal of Cross-Cultural Psychology, 5*, 162-172.

Taylor, D. M., and R. N. Lalonde. In press. Ethnic stereotypes: A psychological analysis. In L. Driedger (ed.), *Ethnic Canada: Identities and inequalities*. Toronto: Copp, Clarke, Pittman.

Taylor, D. M. and W. E. Lambert. 1985. Social significance of bilingualism for minorities in North America. Paper presented at the American Psychological Association meetings, Los Angeles.

Taylor, D. M., and D. J. McKirnan. 1984. A five-stage model of intergroup relations. *British Journal of Social Psychology, 23*, 291-300.

Taylor, D. M., F. M. Moghaddam, and J. Bellerose. 1987. Social comparison in a group context. Unpublished manuscript; McGill University.

Taylor, D. M., F. M. Moghaddam, I. Gamble, and E. Zellerer. In press. Disadvantaged group responses to perceived inequality: from passive acceptance to collective action. *Journal of Social Psychology*.

Taylor, D. M., and L. M. Simard. 1979. Ethnic identity and intergroup relations. In D. J. Lee (ed.), *Emerging ethnic boundaries*, pp. 155-171. Ottawa: University of Ottawa Press.

Taylor, D. M., D. Wong-Rieger, D. J. McKirnan, and J. Bercusson. 1982. Interpreting and coping with threat in the context of intergroup relations. *Journal of Social Psychology, 117*, 257-269.

Thibaut, J. W., and H. H. Kelley. 1959. *The social psychology of groups*. New York: John Wiley.

Triandis, H. C. 1971. *Attiude and attitude change*. New York: John Wiley.

――――. 1979. Commentary. In W. G. Austin and S. Worchel (eds.), *The social psychology of intergroup relations*; pp. 321-334. Monterey, Cal.: Brooks/Cole.

Triandis, H. C., and V. Vassiliou. 1969. Frequency of contact and stereotyping. *Journal of Personality and Social Psychology, 7*, 316-328.

Turner, J. C. 1975. Social comparison and social identity: Some prospects for intergroup behaviour. *European Journal of Social Psychology, 5*, 5-34.

_____ . 1978a. Social categorization and social discrimination in the minimal group paradigm. In H. Tajfel (ed.), *Differentiation between social groups;* pp. 101–140. London and New York: Academic Press.

_____ . 1978b. Social comparison, similarity and ingroup favouritism. In H. Tajfel (ed.), *Differentiation between social groups;* pp. 235–250. London and New York: Academic Press.

_____ . 1981. The experimental social psychology of intergroup behaviour. In J. C. Turner and H. Giles (eds.), *Intergroup Behaviour*, pp. 66–101. Oxford: Basil Blackwell.

Turner, J. C. and R. J. Brown. 1978. Social status, cognitive alternatives and intergroup relations. In H. Tajfel (ed.), *Differentiation between social groups;* pp. 201–234.

Turner, J. C. and R. J. Brown. 1981. Interpersonal and intergroup behaviour. In J. C. Turner & H. Giles (eds.), *Intergroup behaviour*, pp. 33–65. Oxford: Basil Blackwell.

Turner, J. C., R. J. Brown, and H. Tajfel. 1979. Social comparison and group interest in ingroup favouritism. *European Journal of Social Psychology, 9*, 187–204.

Turner, J. C., and H. Giles (eds.). 1981. *Intergroup behaviour.* Oxford: Basil Blackwell.

Valenzi, E. R., and I. R. Andrews. 1971. Effect of hourly overpay inequity when tested with a new induction procedure. *Journal of Applied Psychology, 55*, 22–27.

Van den Berghe, P. L. 1967. Race and racism in South Africa. In P. L. Van den Berghe, (ed.) *Race and racism: A comparative perspective*, pp. 96–111. New York: John Wiley.

Vanneman, R. D., and T. F. Pettigrew. 1972. Race and relative deprivation in the United States. *Race, 13*, 461–486.

Walker, I., and T. F. Pettigrew. 1984. Relative deprivation theory: An overview and conceptual critique. *British Journal of Social Psychology, 23*, 301–310.

Walster, E., E. Berscheid, and G. W. Walster. 1973. New directions in equity research. *Journal of Personality and Social Psychology, 25*, 151–176.

Walster, E., G. W. Walster, and E. Berscheid. 1978. *Equity: Theory and research.* Boston: Allyn & Bacon.

Watson, G. 1985. Social factors in justice evaluation. Ph.D. diss. Oxford University.

Weary, G. 1979. Self-serving attributional biases: Perceptual or response distortions? *Journal of Personality and Social Psychology, 37*: 1418–1420.

Weiner, B., I. Frieze, A. Kukla, L. Reed, S. Rest, and R. M. Rosenbaum. 1972. Perceiving the cause of success and failure. In E. E. Jones, D. E. Kanouse, H. H. Kelley, R. E. Nisbett, S. Valins, and B. Weiner (eds.), *Attribution: Perceiving the cause of behavior*, pp. 95–120. Morristown, N. J.: General Learning Press.

Wicker, A. W. 1969. Attitude versus actions: The relationship of verbal and overt behavioural responses to attitude objects. *Journal of Social Issues, 25*, 41–78.

Wilder, D. A. 1984. Prediction of belief homogeneity and similarity following social categorization. *British Journal of Social Psychology, 23*, 323–333.

————. 1986. Social categorization: Implications for creation and reduction of intergroup bias. In L. Berkowitz (ed.), *Advances in experimental social psychology*, vol. 19, pp. 291–355. New York: Academic Press.

Wilkinson, R. (ed.). 1969. *Governing elites: Studies in training and selection.* New York: Oxford University Press.

Wilson, W. 1970. *War Gaming.* Harmondsworth, England: Penguin Books.

Wilson, W., and M. Kayatani. 1968. Intergroup attitudes and strategies in games between opponents of the same or a different race. *Journal of Personality and Social Psychology, 9*, 24–30.

Wilson, W., and J. Wong. 1968. Intergroup attitudes towards cooperative vs. competitive opponents in a modified prisoner's dilemma game. *Perception and Motor Skills, 27*, 1059–1066.

Yeats, William Butler. 1968. "The great day." In A. M. Jeffares (ed.), *Collected Poems*; p. 190. London: Macmillan.

Zartman, I. W., and M. R. Berman. 1982. *The practical negotiator.* New Haven: Yale University Press.

Zartman, I. W., and S. Touval. 1985. International mediation: Conflict and power politics. *Journal of Social Issues, 41*(2), 27–45.

Ziller, R. C. 1965. Toward a theory of open and closed groups. *Psychological Bulletin, 11*, 86–93.

Subject Index

Author Index

About the Authors

Donald M. Taylor is Professor of Psychology at McGill University, Montreal, Canada. Professor Taylor's research interest is in intergroup relations, including such topics as ethnic stereotypes, intergroup communication, ethnic identity, and multicultural societies. His research has been conducted in diverse regions of the world, including the United States, Canada, Britain, South and South-East Asia. Professor Taylor has contributed numerous articles in Canadian, American, European and Asian journals and co-authored a major work on multiculturalism in Canada. He also serves on the editorial board of a number of scientific journals.

Fathali M. Moghaddam researches at the Psychology Department, McGill University, Montreal, Canada. He previously worked for the United Nations Development Programme (UNDP) and has taught at Tehran University. Dr. Moghaddam's primary research interests are intergroup relations, with particular focus on minority group perspectives, and indigenous psychology for the Third World. His concern for achieving an international perspective in psychology is reflected in his contributions to international, American and European journals.